Books by Ted Nicholas

The Complete Book of Corporate Forms

The Complete Guide to Business Agreements

The Complete Guide to Consulting Success (coauthor, Howard Shenson)

The Complete Guide to Nonprofit Corporations

The Complete Guide to "S" Corporations

The Executive's Business Letter Book

43 Proven Ways To Raise Capital for Your Small Business

The Golden Mailbox: How To Get Rich Direct Marketing Your Product

How To Form Your Own Corporation Without a Lawyer for under $75.00

How To Get a Top Job in Tough Times (coauthor, Bethany Waller)

How To Get Your Own Trademark

How to Publish a Book and Sell a Million Copies

*Secrets of Entrepreneurial Leadership: Building Top Performance
    Through Trust and Teamwork*

Contents

How To Get Your Own Trademark

NEWLY
REVISED

Complete with
Trademark
Application Forms

■

Request for
Trademark Search

■

Federal
Regulations
and Codes

■

Everything
You Need

Ted Nicholas

Enterprise • Dearborn
a division of Dearborn Publishing Group, Inc.

While a great deal of care has been taken to provide accurate and current information, the ideas, suggestions, general principles and conclusions presented in this text are subject to local, state and federal laws and regulations, court cases and any revisions of same. The reader is thus urged to consult legal counsel regarding any points of law—this publication should not be used as a substitute for competent legal advice.

Publisher: Kathleen A. Welton
Acquisitions Editor: Patrick J. Hogan
Associate Editor: Karen A. Christensen
Senior Project Editor: Jack L. Kiburz
Interior Design: Lucy Jenkins
Cover Design: Jay Bensen Studios

Published by Enterprise • Dearborn,
a division of Dearborn Publishing Group, Inc.

Printed in the United States of America

93 94 95 10 9 8 7 6 5 4 3 2 1

Library of Congress Cataloging-in-Publication Data

Nicholas, Ted, 1934-
    How to get your own trademark / Ted Nicholas.
        p. cm.
    Includes index.
    ISBN 0-79310-487-4
    1. Trademarks—United States—Popular works. I. Title.
KF3180.Z9N53 1993
346.7304′88—dc20
[347.306488]   92-42201
                                    CIP

Why Do *I* Need This Book?

If you are operating a business, the single most important asset of that enterprise is the good name attached to your products or services. The products you sell or the services you provide will develop a reputation of their own. If that reputation is good, customers or clients will seek out that product or service by name. Again, that name may be of immeasurable value should you ever decide to sell your business. In fact, when some businesses are sold, particularly service businesses, the single most important asset they possess may be their good name and the unique name of the service they offer— i.e., the company's goodwill.

The safest, most effective way to ensure that a name you have worked to make valuable is not usurped by strangers is to obtain federal trademark protection for your most important asset—your good name.

A trademark may be a word, symbol, design or combined word and design, a slogan or even a distinctive sound if such "marks" identify and distinguish the goods or services of one person from those of another. When used to identify a product, the mark is known as a trademark; when used to identify a service, the mark is termed a servicemark.

Once your name is embraced by trademark protection, it can remain yours forever. All you need to do is use it, protect it and renew it every 20 years to retain the exclusive right to that name in perpetuity.

Should anyone doubt the value of a name, consider this possibility: Turn the hands of time back several decades and imagine that you have just created a chemical, acetylsalicylic acid. You discover that this chemical can reduce fevers, alleviate headaches and reduce the pain of arthritis. When you consider selling this product in tablet form, you realize it needs a catchier name than acetylsalicylic acid, and you come up with the name "aspirin." Within a relatively short time aspirin captures a huge market; it has no competitors.

Others may develop an identical product, but if you've trademarked your product's name, *and* you protect that trademark, your competitors cannot sell "aspirin." They can sell headache powders, fever diminishers and arthritis pain-reducers, *but they cannot sell aspirin.* Only you can do that.

The trouble with the example we've described here is that Dr. Bayer, the creator of aspirin, *did* originally trademark his product and for a while commanded the market for it. But he failed to protect his mark, and today anyone can manufacture and sell a product called aspirin.

The purpose of this book will be to demonstrate

- why your business should obtain trademark protection;
- how easy and inexpensive it can be for you to obtain that protection yourself, without engaging costly legal and other professional assistance; and

- the simple straightforward steps you can take to ensure that once you obtain trademark protection, you do not lose it.

All of the forms you will need to obtain trademark registration are contained in this book. The procedures you should follow to keep that protection in force will be described. Also, the documents you can use to help you guard the value of a name you have worked to instill with value are set out on the pages that follow.

Why Your Company Should Protect Its Name, Product or Service

To the extent that you have invested your energy, time and money to create a business name that has a good reputation and favorable recognition value, you have created an asset. That asset has a real, measurable value. If your business is on the road to success, then it is being run imaginatively and, more importantly, prudently. As a prudent businessperson, you take careful measures to protect your assets: you probably have locks on the doors leading to company property, plus insurance coverage and an alarm system for theft protection.

Doesn't your company's good name, which, more often than not, is of greater financial value than your physical assets, warrant the same protection? But that good name is more susceptible to theft than your automobile. The thief does not have to break into your office to steal your valued name, the thief will not go to jail and, if he or she has used it and applied for trademark protection, *you* may be denied use of your own valued name as against someone who came along and copied it.

Many people believe they have obtained that protection when they incorporate. However, they are mistaken for two reasons. First, there can be no assurance that when the Secretary of State authorizes an applicant to use a corporate name, that the office has not erred—another corporation may be using that name, and if this is so, your business will eventually be denied the right to use that name. Even if you are the first in your state to use the name, that does not prevent other businesses in other states from picking up on your name and using it to incorporate in their home states. Then, if they follow that up by obtaining a trademark registration based on their use of your name, you will be out in the cold—not only will the thief have a right to use your name, but he or she will have the right to prevent you from using your name.

Second, the grant of corporate authority from the state only relates to your corporate name—it does not cover any special product or service names you may have developed. Again, without trademark registration, you have an unprotected name.

It is just such a situation that the Trademark Act of 1946, otherwise known as the Lanham Act, was designed to avoid. The Lanham Act is reprinted in its entirety in Chapter 8 of this book. The very purpose of the Lanham Act was to protect the name and goodwill of entrepreneurs—i.e., their business and brand names. The protection is very broad and potentially unlimited. Once you have obtained a registration, you need only use your name and preclude others from using it. Registration may be renewed every 20 years for as long as you are using and protecting your mark.

Why should you obtain a trademark and protect it? Consider the very real financial loss that has been suffered by the people who once owned the following names, all of which are now in the public domain:

Aspirin	Nylon	Lanolin
Cornflakes	Shredded Wheat	Mimeograph
Escalator	Cellophane	Raisin Bran
Kerosene	Dry Ice	Trampoline
Linoleum	High Octane	Yo-Yo

The last product, the Yo-Yo, was not included only to amuse. Consider the simple device that has become loved by generations of children. What value would that product have today if the person who created it had protected the name Yo-Yo? How much is the product—one among many—worth today without the exclusive right to that name?

How the Lanham Act Works

The Lanham Act was designed to protect the names a company can place on its products or use to designate its services. The name, after registration as a trademark, can then be placed on labels or advertising without fear that it will be lost to infringers.

The term *trademark* is defined by the Act to "include any word, name, symbol or device or combination thereof adopted and used by a manufacturer or merchant to identify his goods and distinguish them from those manufactured or sold by others." This definition obviously applies to products. Services, however, may also be protected with a *servicemark*, which is defined by the Act to be "a mark used in the sale or advertising of services to identify the services of one person and distinguish them from the services of others."

The two terms *trademark* and *servicemark* are, for the most part, interchangeable. In fact, the Lanham Act defines the word *mark* to include both trademarks and servicemarks. Throughout this book, when the word *mark* is used, it should be read to mean both trademarks and servicemarks.

When registered, marks may be placed on either the Principal Register or the Supplemental Register of the Patent and Trademark Office (PTO). The difference between the two types of registration pertains to the issue of the various forms of redress available to a registrant who believes his or her mark has been infringed upon.

THE TWO REGISTERS

The PTO maintains two registers: the Principal Register and the Supplemental Register. The Supplemental Register is used when a proposed mark has the potential to distinguish an applicant's mark but does not yet do so. Marks of this nature are usually descriptive or surnames. In order for a mark to be placed on the Supplemental Register, it must have been used by the applicant for at least one year and must be ineligible for registration on the Principal Register.

The difference between registration on the two registers concerns the benefits provided for the registrant. Benefits are far more limited when a mark is registered on the Supplemental Register. Of all of the benefits available to the holder of a registered trademark or servicemark, the only ones that pertain to a person whose mark is registered on the Supplemental Register are (1) the right to sue in federal courts and (2) the ability to use the registration as a basis for filing in some foreign countries.

Registration on the Principal Register offers a much broader range of benefits.

Your Company Name

The Lanham Act was designed to protect the names of products and services—it is *not* intended to protect the name of a business. However, if the words you have chosen to identify your goods and services also serve as your company's name, they can be protected as a trademark or servicemark. So, for example, Kodak as a trademark for cameras, film and photographic supplies is a protected trademark for those products and serves as the producing company's name.

As noted in Chapter 2, the mere fact that you operate your business as a corporation does not ensure that you will have exclusive right to the name you have created—when the state authorizes the use of a name, it does so for the business, not its products or services. That protection is available only through trademark registration.

What You Can Register

There are eight broad categories of marks:

1. Word marks
2. Design marks
3. Initials or numbers
4. Slogans
5. Labels
6. Container designs
7. Certification marks
8. Collective marks

Word marks   A *word mark* is just what the term implies—a word that is used by a seller of goods or services to describe the products or services in question. It need not be a word that is listed in the dictionary. In fact, it is entitled to even stronger protection if it is not a dictionary word. Coined words, for example, are generally accorded the strongest possible protection—i.e., protection against the use of the word on totally unrelated products or services.

Kodak is an example of a coined word; it is a combination of letters that, when created, had no meaning other than to describe a product. Should someone seek to use the word *kodak* on a food product, for example, it is likely that the Kodak Company could obtain an injunction to stop that use. Other examples of coined words include such well-known names as Exxon, Pyrex and Sunoco.

A second category of word marks includes suggestive words—i.e., words that do appear in the dictionary but that are used in a highly original way to suggest a feature of the product or service being offered. Ban, the skin deodorant, is a mark that uses a common dictionary word to suggest a feature of the product. Because they involve the use of creative thinking and originality in usage, suggestive words when used as marks do receive a relatively strong degree of protection.

A third category of word marks includes dictionary words that are arbitrarily chosen to identify a product. The Apple computer is one such example. The word itself does not have a dictionary connation that relates to computers. Today, however, when the word is used in connection with an automated process, virtually all consumers recognize it as the brand name of Apple Computer, Inc. Again, because of the originality involved in the selection of the name, arbitrary marks are generally entitled to a broad degree of protection.

Less apt to be accepted for trademark registration are descriptive and generic words. So, for example, the word *exquisite,* although a part of the name of a well-known brand of women's undergarments, cannot in and of itself be the subject of a registration. A fabric maker, for example, could not be denied the right to use that word in connection with its products. Descriptive words, if accepted for registration, are likely to receive only a very narrow degree of protection. When registered, it is usually on the Supplemental Register.

Generic words, i.e., the names of a class of products or services, will not be granted a mark registration. The term *pet food,* for example, is a generic term and would not be registered as a mark.

Of course, the fact that you may have a trademark on a product that also applies to your company name does not preclude you from obtaining additional trademarks covering subcategories of products or services. The Apple Company, for example, has a product line that includes the trademarked Macintosh computers.

Design marks   Design marks are pictorial representations used to identify a product, service or company. Examples of design marks include the golden arches of the McDonald's franchise corporation and the flying horse that is the Mobil Corporation's trademark. Once accepted for registration, these marks are given the highest degree of protection. One caution should be noted—the mere fact that another company is using a character as a design mark does not mean that the entire generic class of characters is denied to you if you wish to use a character of the same generic class. So, for example, if an existing company uses a horse as its trademark, you will not be prevented from using a horse, so long as your trademark cannot be confused with the mark of the first company.

Another design element capable of trademark registration is a unique color. In September 1991, a federal judge awarded $8,000 in damages to a firm that manufactures press pads for the dry cleaning industry. The firm alleged and proved that it used a unique yellow-green color for its pads, and its trademark registration included the color. The award was made against a competing company that used a virtually identical color on its press pads.

Initials or numbers   Initials and numbers can be registered as trademarks. So, for example, IBM, 3M and AT&T are protected by trademark registration. One caution to be observed is that initials or numbers will not be accepted for registration if they also serve as industry or government grading characters.

Slogans Slogans such as "It Hasn't Scratched Yet" used in connection with Bon Ami scouring powder can be registered as marks. One caution to be observed here involves slogans that are mere descriptive phrases stating that the product is of a high quality. Just as descriptive words will often not be granted a registration, descriptive slogans may run into the same problem. Slogans that have failed the test include those that start with "America's Best . . ." The key to developing a registrable slogan seems to be to focus on a favorable characteristic of the product or service rather than a description of superior quality or appearance.

Labels If you devise a uniquely distinctive design for your product's labels, that design may be registered on the Principal Register of the PTO. If your label is judged capable of distinguishing your product or service, but it is determined that it does not *yet* do so, it may be registered on the Supplemental Register.

Containers and building designs Certain container and building designs are so unique that they have become associated with a specific product in the mind of the public. So, for example, the unique pinch bottle used for Haig & Haig Scotch, or the famous Coca Cola bottle are trademarked container designs. Similarly, the Fotomat structures were unique to that company and were trademarked. One key to obtaining trademark protection for a unique container or building design is that the design must pertain only to the appearance; if the design is a part of the function of the piece, then it probably cannot receive trademark protection.

Certification and collective marks These marks, which are beyond the scope of this work, are granted to testing agencies, unions, trade associations, cooperatives and other organizations. They are used to indicate that the product meets certain quality standards (e.g., Underwriters Laboratories,) or were produced by certain individuals (e.g., union labels).

Grounds for Denying Registration

A trademark registration can be denied for any one of nine grounds. However, the denial may not be absolute. If the Patent and Trademark Office finds that one of the nine bases below is present, it will deny registration on the Principal Register. The mark, however, may be such that it can be registered on the Supplemental Register.

The nine bases upon which the PTO may deny registration on the Principal Register are as follows:

1. The mark does not serve to identify the goods and services as coming from a particular source. However, if registration is denied because the mark does not *now* distinguish the applicant's goods or services, but

the Examining Attorney finds that the mark is *capable* of distinguishing the applicant's goods or services (as time goes on and the mark gets used), it may be approved for the Supplemental Register.

2. The mark is immoral, deceptive or scandalous, in which event it will not be accepted for filing on either register.

3. The mark may disparage or falsely suggest a connection with persons, living or dead, institutions, beliefs or national symbols, or may bring them into disrepute. If the mark falls into this category, it cannot be accepted for filing on either register.

4. The mark consists of, comprises or simulates the flag, coat of arms or other insignia of the United States or a state or municipality or foreign nation. Such a mark may not be accepted for filing on either register.

5. The mark will not be accepted for filing on either the Principal or Supplemental Register if it is
    *   the name, portrait or signature of a living person who has not consented to such use.
    *   the name, signature or portrait of a deceased President of the United States, and that President's widow is alive and has not consented to the use of the former President's name, signature or portrait on the mark in question.

6. The mark so closely resembles a mark already registered with the PTO that if it is accepted for registration and used, there is a likelihood that it might deceive people as to the source of goods or services. When a mark is rejected for this reason, it cannot be accepted for filing on either register.

7. The mark is merely descriptive or deceptively misdescriptive of your goods or services. If the basis for rejecting the mark is that it is merely descriptive of your goods or services but does not appear to be capable of distinguishing (in the future) your goods and services from those of another, it may be accepted for filing on the Supplemental Register. If the mark is deceptively misdescriptive, it will not be accepted for filing on either register.

8. The mark is merely geographically descriptive or deceptively misdescriptive of your goods or services. Geographically descriptive marks can be accepted for registration on the Supplemental Register (see 7 above); deceptively misdescriptive geographic terms will not be accepted for filing on either register.

9. Marks that are primarily surnames may be accepted for filing on only the Supplemental Register.

The Benefits You Obtain Through Registration

First and foremost, trademark registration provides you with the exclusive right to use the name you have chosen for the types of goods and services you provide. Furthermore, if you coin your own name or create a unique design, that mark may provide you with an exclusive right to its use even if a third person wishes to use your mark on a totally unrelated product or service.

In theory, a mark need not be protected by trademark registration to be protected against infringers. Both state and federal courts will entertain lawsuits based on unfair competition—i.e., your competitor is vying unfairly for business by copying your mark. These suits, however, are invariably time-consuming and, more importantly, extremely expensive to prosecute. And, there is no assurance that you will win. You must be able to prove, among other things, that you were *first,* and that your mark has gained public acceptance.

Trademark registration provides a series of benefits that ensures protection for your trademark for a relatively nominal investment. Because the underlying purpose of the Lanham Act is to protect your goodwill (i.e., your identifying mark), it provides the tools you need to protect your mark against infringement. The benefits of registration include the following:

1. The right to sue in the federal courts for trademark infringement. Along with this right, you have the right to recover:
   - the infringer's profits. All you need to do is show the infringer's sales; the infringer must show its costs.
   - any damages you have suffered. The court, however, is not limited to awarding you only your actual damages. It may, in fact, award you up to *three times* the dollar amount of the actual damages.
   - litigation costs, and if the court considers it appropriate, it may also reward you reasonable attorney's fees.
   - an injunction barring an infringer from continuing to use your mark
2. The right to assert constructive notice. This means that if a person infringes upon your registered mark, he or she cannot claim such actions were done in good faith, i.e., they did not know they were copying someone else's mark. Registration is viewed as constructive notice to everyone that the word, combination of words or design in question is yours.
3. *Prima facie* evidence of the validity of
   - the registration itself
   - your ownership of the mark and
   - your exclusive right to use the mark in connection with the goods or services specified in the registration certificate.
   The importance of this factor lies in the fact that whether a challenge involves a claim before the PTO or your lawsuit against an infringer, the court or the PTO starts with the assumption that you own and have the right to use the mark in question. The other party has the burden of showing that you do *not* have the right.
4. The right to claim incontestable ownership of the mark. This means that your right to use the mark simply is not open to question or challenge, and any infringer has virtually no defense if he or she usurps your mark. You can obtain the benefit of incontestability by filing an affidavit of use between the fifth and sixth years following registration (or at any later date if you so choose). The affidavit, which is a simple, straightforward document, states that your mark has been in continuous use for five years since registration. Once you have filed your

affidavit of use, you will be deemed to have incontestable ownership of your mark.

5. If an infringer counterfeits your mark, you may be able to recover criminal penalties. So, for example, although a court cannot send a corporation to jail, it can impose criminal fines against it.

6. You will have the right to stop foreign producers from usurping your mark on goods they ship into this country. All you need to do is deposit your registration with the Customs Office, and they will refuse to permit goods with infringing marks to be imported into the country.

7. Should your business warrant expansion into other countries, trademark registration in the United States can serve as the basis for registration in other nations.

CONCLUSION

As already discussed, the PTO maintains two registers—the Principal Register and the Supplemental Register. Obviously, registration on the Principal Register is the desired goal. The onus is on the applicant to select a name that does distinguish his or her goods or services from those of others and accomplishes that end *now*. If, in fact, the name you have chosen qualifies only for registration on the Supplemental Register, you may want to rethink the matter and come up with a more distinctive name. Your rethinking here would not only be guided by the fact of trademark registration but also more importantly by the fact that the name you have chosen probably does not do the job you intended it to do.

Applying for Federal Registration: The Procedure

THE PROCESS

A trademark registration application is a relatively simple process. Essentially, the client must file a written application with the Patent and Trademark Office (PTO). The application is then reviewed by a trademark examiner to determine if

1. the appropriate written application form has been submitted,
2. there is an acceptable drawing of the mark,
3. the applicant has submitted three specimens showing the mark's use in connection with goods or services and
4. the applicant has tendered the appropriate filing fee.

If those four requirements are satisfied, the application is given a serial number and a filing date, and the applicant is sent a filing receipt. If the application package is in any way incomplete, the entire package, including the filing fee, is returned to the applicant.

THE APPLICATION

The application itself must be filled out on the official form supplied by the PTO (clip-out copies of the official forms are reproduced in Chapter 7 of this book). In past years, the PTO used separate and slightly different forms that were tailored to the nature of the applicant—i.e., different forms for individuals, partnerships and corporations. Recently, the PTO reviewed its forms and came up with a single application form that can be used by any applicant, whether an individual, partnership or corporate applicant.

The Trademark/Servicemark Application, Principal Register, with Declaration form is fairly straightforward and can be filled out by nonlawyers with ease. Here are step-by-step directions to filling out the blanks on your application form.

Step One: Mark

This entry appears at the very top of the form. You must fill in either the words or the letters that will constitute the mark. If you also seek a trademark for a design, then you should add the words *and design* after the words or letters that constitute the mark.

> **Example:** If your trademark application consists of the words "Buks Unlimited" and will include a drawing of a

book, then you should fill in the mark box with the words "Buks Unlimited and design."

Step Two: Class Number

This entry appears at the very top of the form alongside the box titled "Mark." The class number refers to the International Schedule of Classes of Goods and Services (a copy of the International Schedules is set out in Appendix A of this book). There are 34 classes of goods and 8 classes of services. Just review the International Schedule to find the appropriate class and enter that number in the box. If you are not confident that you have selected the appropriate class (some categories overlap), then you may leave this box blank and the PTO will determine the correct class for you.

Step Three: Applicant's Name

Fill in the name of the person who will be owner of the mark in this box. For example, if you are the president of a corporation and the corporation owns the mark, you must fill in the corporation's name as the applicant. If you use your name, then you will be the owner of the mark.

If you are filing on behalf of yourself as an individual, then you should fill in this box with your full name. If you do business under a trade name (e.g., John Smith dba [doing business as] Smith Groceries), then decide whether you want to file in just your name (John Smith) or in your trade name (John Smith dba Smith Groceries).

If the filing is to be made on behalf of a partnership, then fill in the full name of the partnership. If the filing is for a corporation, then fill in the corporation's full name.

Step Four: Applicant's Business Address

Simply fill in the current mailing address of the applicant listed in step three. Keep in mind that this will be the address listed on the trademark registration and, if you have a choice, select the address that is least likely to change.

Step Five: Applicant's Entity Type

If you are filing in your own individual capacity, then check the box to the left of the word *Individual.* Then fill in your country of citizenship.

If the filing is for a partnership, check the box to the left of that word. Next, identify the state in which the partnership was formed or, if it was formed in a foreign country, identify the country.

On the next line, fill in the names and countries of citizenship for each of the partnership's partners. If the filing is being made for a limited partnership, you only need supply this information for the general partners.

If the filing is being made for a corporation, check the box to the left of that word and fill in the name of the state in which it was incorporated. *Caution:* If your corporation was formed in one state and now operates and has its principal office in another state, enter the name of the state in which it was formed, not the state in which it operates.

If the filing is being made for a corporation created in a foreign country, follow the general directions set out above for domestic corporations with one change: Substitute the name of the country in which it was incorporated for the state of incorporation.

Step Six: Goods and Services

This portion of the form must be filled out with great care and attention. Your trademark protection will be limited to exactly those goods or services you list in this box, and you will not be permitted to amend the form at some later date to include additional goods or services. By the same token, the PTO will reject an application in which the goods and services are so broadly worded that they are virtually indefinite in meaning.

> **Example:** Assume you have developed a formula for a flavor you wish to use in a chocolate bar. If you list chocolate bars as the goods to be covered by the registration, your registration will not cover subsequent applications of your formula to hard candies or syrups and flavorings used in connection with milk, soft drinks or cereals. In this case, you would be better advised to use the wording "food products, namely candies, syrups, carbonated and noncarbonated drinks, snack foods and cereals."

The entry should pass two tests. First, it should be as short and succinct as possible. Second, it should be as specific as possible without limiting future use. Some applicants seek to satisfy the second test by using indefinite words to get the maximum protection. For example, they may state that the trademark will be used in conjunction with food products. The PTO will reject such broadly worded applications, unless the words *food products* are followed by an explanatory clause such as "food products, namely. . . ."

A common error made in this portion of the form is that applicants include the way in which the trademark will be used. For example, in addition to identifying food products, including candies and syrups, an applicant may include the following: ". . . *and broadcast and print advertisements and labels including the trademark.*" These words are inappropriate in this box and may cause the PTO to ask you to reapply. Keep in mind that the only information required in this box is the identity of the goods or services for which you are seeking trademark protection.

You will note that the text in the Goods and Services box asks you to submit a drawing of the mark. This requirement will be discussed under step ten.

Step Seven: Basis for Application

As you look at this section of the form, you will note that it is divided into four parts. You must check off at least one of the four boxes in the left column, but *you must not check off both the top box and the second box*—if you do, your application will be rejected. Those boxes are mutually exclusive: The top box assumes you are currently using the mark, and the second box assumes you are not yet using it but intend to use it.

The first step, therefore, is to determine which boxes you must check. The following guides should help:

- The top box: Use this box if you now use your trademark.
- The second box: Use this box if you have not yet used the mark in commerce but intend to use it commercially.
- The third and fourth boxes: These boxes are usually used by applicants from foreign countries who are filing in this country under an international agreement. Box three is used by individuals who have filed for foreign protection, and box four is for individuals who have filed and have had their application registered in a foreign country.

Using the top box If you've used your mark before filing your application, then check off the top box. The very first sentence of this question informs you that you must submit three specimens that show the mark as it is used in commerce. For directions on how to comply with this requirement, see step nine below.

You will then have to answer four questions. The first question asks you to provide the date when you first used the mark in commerce that the U.S. Congress may regulate. Congress can only regulate commerce that takes place between two or more states or between a person or entity in this country and a person or entity in another country. In order to determine the date needed to answer this question, review your records and obtain the earliest date on which you or your company sold, leased or otherwise made the goods or services in question available to an out-of-state or foreign person or entity. Then simply type that date at the end of the first question.

The second question asks you to fill in the type of commerce. If the date you supplied in response to the first question was based on a sale to an out-of-state customer, respond with the word "interstate." If it was based on a sale to a customer in a foreign country, fill in the words "United States and [name of foreign country]."

The third question asks you to supply the date the mark was first used anywhere. If before selling to an out-of-state or foreign customer, you sold your goods or services to a customer located in the same state in which you do business, then supply that earlier date in response to this question. If your out-of-state or foreign sale came first, then repeat the date you supplied in response to the first question.

The fourth question asks you to specify the manner or mode of use of the mark on or in connection with the goods or services you seek to protect.

Simply respond by stating how the mark will be used. If you will use it in connection with goods, your response may be "on containers," "on labels affixed to the goods" or "on containers [and/or labels] and in advertisements for the goods." If you are seeking trademark protection in connection with services you provide, then simply state "in advertisements for the services."

Using the second box If you have not sold your goods or services to a customer but intend to do so, then check off the second box. Remember, you cannot check off both the top and second box!

This box has only one question, and it is the same as the fourth question in the top box. See the instructions we've provided to that question. If you check off the second box, then within six months you will have to file either an Amendment to Allege Use (PTO Form 1579) or a Statement of Use (PTO Form 1580). Copies of those forms are reproduced in Chapter 7 of this book. Those forms follow the pattern described for the top box above, and those instructions will lead you through either form.

Step Eight: Declaration

The reverse side of the PTO's form contains a declaration you must date and sign. In addition, you must supply your telephone number. If the filing is for a partnership, then a partner must sign the form and indicate that he or she is a partner. If the filing is for a corporation, it must be signed by an officer of the corporation, not a shareholder or director, unless that person is also an officer.

Step Nine: Specimens

In step seven we noted that you must provide three specimens in connection with your application. The specimens must be supplied regardless of which of the four boxes you checked in response to the Basis for Application section of the form.

If the application is made for a trademark, as opposed to a servicemark, you are required to supply five examples of the way in which the mark has been used. You may submit labels, tags, containers or displays, but only if they can be presented as a flat sheet no larger than 81/2 inches by 13 inches. The PTO will not accept either three-dimensional or bulk specimens. In the event that your label or tag is affixed to a bulky item, you may provide five copies of a photograph (no larger than 81/2 inches by 13 inches) that clearly show the mark and how it is used on the goods in question.

If you are filing an application for a servicemark, then you must supply three examples of how the mark is used in your advertising or promotional materials. A copy of an advertisement, brochure, single-sheet handout or any other promotional tool you use is sufficient. In the event that your servicemark is not used in printed form—i.e., it involves sound—you may offer three audio cassettes in lieu of the three written specimens required for printed marks.

Step Ten: The Drawing

In step six we observed that the "Goods and/or Services" section of the form requires you to provide a drawing of your mark. Although none of the requirements regarding the drawing is difficult to satisfy, they are typical in many respects of federal administrative regulations: highly specific, almost picayune in nature.

Set out below is a step-by-step guide to the requirements for your drawing:

The paper You must use paper that is 8 1/2 inches wide and 11 inches long. The paper must be white, durable and nonshiny (don't use onion skin sheets or glossy stock). The ordinary white bond paper you use for correspondence should be satisfactory.

The margins The paper itself should be written upon so that an 8 1/2-inch side is the top of the sheet. There must be a margin of at least one inch on both the right and left sides of the sheet and a similar margin at the bottom of the page.

The heading Starting one inch below the top of the sheet, you should type in the heading of your drawing. It is strongly urged that you type the heading. The heading should set out the following information, each item on a separate line:

1. The applicant's name
2. The applicant's address
3. The date the mark was first used
4. The date the mark was first used in commerce
5. The goods or services for which the mark is being used

Each of these entries should be identical to the entries you made when filling out the corresponding lines of the form itself. (Caution: When typing these five entries, you should take care to see that they do not occupy more space than the top one-quarter of the sheet.)

The drawing You may opt to register either of two types of marks. One type would consist of words or numbers, without any special design or typeface. The other type would use either a special typeface and/or design or artwork.

If you seek registration for words, letters and/or numbers without any design elements, your mark should be typed in capital letters and should be centered between the two side margins. (*Caution:* You should ensure that you leave at least one inch between the bottom of the last heading entry and the top of the words you have typed in as your "drawing.")

If you are registering a mark that contains design elements such as a pictorial symbol or a specific typeface, you must supply an actual drawing of the mark. The drawing should be placed on the paper so that the top of the drawing is at least one inch below the last entry of the heading. The drawing itself must not be more than four inches wide, nor may it be more than four inches long. Even if the amount of detail in your mark's drawing precludes the possibility of showing that detail within the four-by-four-inch limits, you may not go beyond that size. Instead, you will be asked to supply a written description of the detail work.

The drawing must be done in black ink. You may prepare your drawing by hand, but if you do, you should use either india ink or an ink that will provide sharp reproductions. Every line must be done in black ink. Since you must be using the mark in order to seek registration, the likelihood is that you have a photolithograph, printer's proof or camera-ready copy of your mark. These are all acceptable as drawings, as is a photocopy (but only if it provides a *very clear,* sharp black-and-white rendering). The following are *not acceptable* as drawings:

1. Half-tones
2. Gray lines
3. Photographs
4. Colors
5. Drawings upon which a white pigment has been used to cover one or more lines

If a feature of your design includes the use of one or more colors, your drawing must still be presented in a black-and-white rendering. Your colors are shown by a variety of line patterns that you place in appropriate portions of the drawing. A copy of the PTO's chart for these color patterns appears in Figure 4.1.

Figure 4.1 PTO Color-Pattern Chart

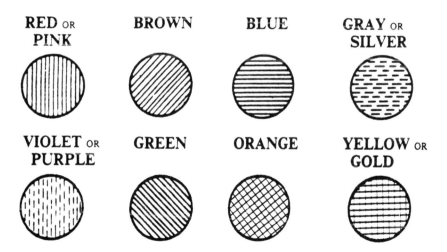

FILING FEES

Your application must be accompanied by a filing fee. Payable by personal or business checks, the fee is $200 for each class of goods and services as set forth on the International Schedule of Goods and Services (see Appendix A).

For most applicants, the total fee will not exceed $200 since they most often use their mark in connection with only one class of goods or services. Keep in mind that even if your mark is used on several products, it is very likely that they all are within the same class.

> **Example:** ABC Baking Company seeks to register a trademark it will use on its breads, cakes, pastries and biscuits. Although it has four different products, all are within the same class of goods—Class 30—according to the International Schedule of Goods and Services. If ABC also uses its mark on cooked fruits, however, it would have to pay an additional $200 in filing fees since jellies are a different class—Class 29.

The PTO's Registration Process

AFTER FILING

Once your application is filed, the PTO assigns your application to a Trademark Examining Attorney. After reviewing your form to ensure that you have satisfied the technical requirements described in the previous chapter, the examiner then makes a determination as to whether there are grounds to deny the application based on the mark itself (e.g., it is a generic name). If the mark passes the test, the examiner then engages in a search to determine whether the mark you have selected too closely resembles a mark that is already registered.

The search is the single most critical aspect of the review process. If the examiner finds a mark he or she believes closely resembles yours, he or she will notify you and refuse to register your mark. Aside from the fact that you will have lost your filing fee, you will know that you have effectively lost a mark that you have spent a great deal of time and money to promote. In other words, you will have lost what may be your most precious asset—the good business name you have been striving to build.

Virtually every experienced trademark professional urges entrepreneurs to run a mark search before expending time, money and energy on a name or design for which they expect to obtain a mark. By running the search before using your proposed mark, you can determine whether it will continue to be available once you make it well known.

If the examiner does object to your mark, he or she will generally do so within three months of the date you filed your application. You must respond to the objections within six months of the time the examiner makes them known, or your application will be treated as if you have abandoned it.

Should the examiner refuse to register your mark after you respond to the objections, you may appeal to the Trademark Trial and Appeal Board. If you lose at this level, you may file an appeal with the federal courts.

If the examiner finds that your mark does not conflict with an existing mark, it will be published in the *Trademark Official Gazette,* a weekly publication of the PTO. The purpose of the publication is to alert anyone who might object to your mark that the PTO is prepared to register it. Outsiders then have 30 days to object to registration. If an objection is filed, the Trademark Trial and Appeal Board hears the matter. Appeals to federal court are available from these hearings.

If no opposition is filed, the mark is registered 12 weeks after the date it was published in the *Gazette.* At this point you're entitled to use the symbol ® or the phrase "Registered in U.S. Patent and Trademark Office" or "Reg. U.S. Pat. & Trademark Office." According to the PTO, on average, a mark will be registered within 13 months of the date the application for registration is filed.

THE SEARCH—THE SINGLE MOST IMPORTANT STEP YOU CAN TAKE

Unless you belong to the school of thought that believes in locking the barn door only after your horse has been stolen, it should be clear that it does not make sense to invest time, money and energy in a brand name, let alone to file an application for a mark, unless you have reasonable assurance that your efforts will not be in vain.

Assuming your mark satisfies the statutory grounds for registration (i.e., it is not a generic name and is not misdescriptive, deceptive or immoral as discussed in Chapter 3), the only basis for the examiner to refuse registration would be that your name conflicts with someone else's registered mark. You can anticipate and avoid this possibility by running a search of existing marks before using the name you have selected.

The PTO maintains a search library that is open to the public. You can visit that library and run your own search to determine whether your name conflicts with an existing mark. The search library is located on the second floor of Crystal Plaza 2, 2011 Jefferson Davis Highway, Arlington, VA 22022. The library is open weekdays from 8:00 a.m. to 5:30 p.m., and there is no charge to use its facilities.

There are several drawbacks to relying on a limited search of just the PTO's search library. First, if you do not live in the Washington, D.C. area, the cost of travel, room and board can be somewhat costly. Second, many entrepreneurs value their time, and taking two or three days off to run a mark search is simply not feasible.

The most important drawback relates to the fact that the PTO's library is not complete. You will not pick up names that may have been registered at the state level, nor will it reveal marks that have never been registered but which are nevertheless used (called a common law mark).

Although neither state nor common law marks can take precedence over a federally registered mark, the possibility that their owners will object to your registration is quite strong. If you can do a search that identifies these owners, you will have the opportunity to find out whether (1) they are using their mark (if not, then you can go ahead with yours); (2) their mark applies to a completely different kind of product or service; and (3) they will object to your registration (very often there is no conflict and the parties can work out an accommodation).

As noted above, virtually every trademark professional urges applicants to run a search before investing in their proposed mark, and those same professionals urge potential applicants to use a trademark search organization to determine the status of their proposed mark. There are several reasons for using a search organization. First, it can run a far more extensive search than you can, and it can do so more quickly then you can. Second, it is significantly less costly to use a competent search organization than it is to do it yourself (consider the cost of running a search in all 50 states). Third, and most importantly, if a challenge to your mark ever arises from someone who claims priority, the fact that you have had a professional search company run your search will stand in your favor when the question of good faith arises. Furthermore, the more thorough your search, (i.e., requesting the search company to search federal, state and common law databases), the better your position when a challenge arises.

One qualified provider of these services is the Federal Trademark Services Company. It offers three search plans:

1. *A basic trademark search.* This search includes marks that have been registered in each of the 50 states and Puerto Rico (over 300,000 registered marks). The cost of this search is $75.
2. *Patent and Trademark Office search.* This search covers the federal database of 900,000 trademarks and includes both active and inactive names. The cost of this search is $95.
3. *A comprehensive search.* This includes both searches described above as well as a common law search and a history of mark owners. The cost of the comprehensive search is $195.

Clearly, an individual would have neither the time nor the resources to run a search such as the comprehensive search described above. Furthermore, the cost of the search would be prohibitive for an individual.

You may contact the Federal Trademark Services Company, c/o The Company Corporation, 3 Christina Centre, 201 N. Walnut Street, Wilmington, DE 19801, or call 800-542-2677.

Protecting Your Mark

BEFORE REGISTRATION

You do not have to wait until registration of your mark before taking measures to protect it. Assuming you have ordered a search and feel confident that your mark does not conflict with others, you will want to begin to use it—remember, your mark will not be registered unless you can show that it is being used by you. You can protect your mark by using the symbol™ (for goods) or ˢᴹ (for services). These legends indicate your claim of ownership of the mark, and if someone begins to use the same mark after your search is completed, the legend can be offered as proof of first usage. You do not have to file your trademark application before using the ™ or ˢᴹ legends.

AFTER REGISTRATION

Statutory Procedures

After your mark has been registered, the Lanham Act requires the registrant to file an affidavit of continuing use between the fifth and sixth years after the date of registration. If you have used the mark continuously since registration, you may be able to obtain an incontestable right to use the mark (see Chapter 3). An incontestable right to use the mark will be created if you can show five consecutive years of use and no outstanding challenges to that use.

If circumstances prevented you from using your mark continuously, but you intend to continue using it, you should file an affidavit of nonuse, which explains why the mark was not used continuously.

If you do not file either form of affidavit, your registration will be deemed forfeited.

Guarding Against Infringers

If you truly value your mark, you should be vigilant at all times to prevent any unauthorized use—the failure to do so can lead to the loss of your mark. Consider this example: When Dr. Bayer began to market aspirin he had a trademark for the word *Aspirin*. However, the popularity of the product was such that comparable products were referred to as aspirin. The Bayer Company did nothing to prevent this. The courts decided that the word became a generic word and was no longer entitled to protection as a mark.

Aspirin is not the only product to have suffered such a fate. Cornflakes, shredded wheat, thermos, linoleum and scores of other products were once highly valued trademarks. However, all were insufficiently protected and were lost.

How then do you protect your mark? First, by constantly monitoring the use of your mark. Second, by constantly monitoring other companies' activities. Third, by taking action whenever your mark is improperly used.

Most trademark owners are pleased when they see their mark come into popular usage—they consider it free advertising. In fact, nothing worthwhile is ever free. In this case, free advertising may well lead to a loss of protection, since a court may one day conclude that your word mark is now a generic word.

> **Example:**   Assume you operate a bakery and you have a trademark for the word *Rounders*—a circular doughnut. As your product gains popularity in the community, others begin to manufacture imitations, but they cannot call them Rounders, since you have the exclusive right to that name. As a goodwill gesture, one of your competitors, Infringer Bakery, provides a free supply of their product to the volunteer fire department for use in a fund drive. The local newspaper reports this by stating that "The Volunteer Fire Department's fund-raiser got off to a good start when Infringer Bakery contributed 12 dozen assorted Rounders."

> **Result:**   The newspaper article has started the ball rolling in the direction of a generic name.

How do you protect your mark when this happens? Write a letter to the newspaper advising them that Rounders is a trademarked name for your product, and that neither they nor your competitor can use that word to refer to any product other than the Rounder baked by your company.

This letter will serve two purposes. First, it will ensure that the newspaper will not make the same mistake again. Second, by showing that you always act whenever your trademark is improperly used, you demonstrate that you are not permitting it to fall into the public domain. Should anyone ever seek to challenge your right to use the mark on the grounds that it is a generic word, your active efforts to protect your mark will carry great weight.

If this procedure is considered worthwhile by large companies, then it should certainly be worth your while if you believe your mark has value. Consider the efforts of the Xerox Corporation. The word *Xerox* is a trademark belonging to the company. Many people erroneously use the word as a verb—e.g., "Please xerox two copies of this letter." In order to guard against the word falling into the public domain, the Xerox Corporation regularly advertises the fact that the word defines its machinery and services, and that it is trademarked. It uses the ®symbol at all times, and the corporation writes letters to publishers who misuse the word. Why? To protect its most precious asset, in which hundreds of millions of dollars have been invested, from suffering the fate that befell the mimeograph, the escalator and kerosene, as well as aspirin.

Next, you must be on the alert to monitor the activities of other companies. One easy way to do this is by running regular checks of new trademark applications. By ordering a comprehensive search once a year, you can determine whether anyone has been using a mark that may conflict with yours.

Other steps you can take include monitoring trade publications and listings, checking telephone books whenever you or anyone in your company travels out of town, and reviewing advertising in any publication you receive.

Should your search efforts reveal any unauthorized use of your mark, then you must act promptly. Usually, a strong letter to the infringer will bring about the desired result. (See Appendix C for a sample letter to an infringer.)

Again, these precautions serve two purposes. First, they demonstrate that you make a good faith effort to protect your mark. Second, by catching an improper use early on, you make it easier to reach an accommodation agreement with an infringer. If the infringer has acted in good faith, and you catch him or her before he or she has made a substantial investment in the mark, the likelihood is that he or she will give in without a fight—particularly if you offer the infringer time to bring about an orderly change of his or her brand name.

Trademark Application Forms

This section contains the four most commonly used forms in connection with trademark applications:

1. *PTO Form 1478.* This is the application form for registration on the Principal Register. Two completed samples of this form also have been included for the reader's convenience. One sample assumes the trademark has been used; the other assumes the applicant has not used the mark but intends to use it.

2. *PTO Form 1579.* This form should be used to allege use of a trademark. It is used when an applicant has filed Form 1478 and alleges only that he or she intends to use the mark. The mark, however, must be used in commerce before a registration will be issued. Form 1579 is used to allege such use and is generally filed before approval of the mark has been received.

3. *PTO Form 1580.* This form should be used to state the mark has actually been used after the PTO has issued a Notice of Allowance for the registration.

4. *PTO Form 1581.* An applicant must file Form 1580 within six months after receiving a Notice of Allowance from the PTO. In the event that the applicant has not yet put the mark to use, he or she can request a six-month extension of the time to file the statement of use. Form 1581 should be used to request the extension.

Editor's note: As you review each of the forms set out in this chapter, you will note (see the lower left-hand corner of each form) that all four forms state an expiration date of June 1992. As of August 1992, the author was informed that the PTO has not revised the forms and does not expect to revise them unless there is a change in the trademark laws. Therefore, the PTO acknowledges that these official forms are current and were in force when this book went to press.

Sample Application Based on Use in Commerce (Individual)

TRADEMARK/SERVICE MARK APPLICATION, PRINCIPAL REGISTER, WITH DECLARATION	MARK (Word(s) and/or Design) ADMARK SERVICES	CLASS NO. (If known) 35

TO THE ASSISTANT SECRETARY AND COMMISSIONER OF PATENTS AND TRADEMARKS:

APPLICANT'S NAME: Jane A. Doe

APPLICANT'S BUSINESS ADDRESS: 123 Main Street, Anytown, Kansas 67890
(Display address exactly as
it should appear on registration)

APPLICANT'S ENTITY TYPE: (**Check one** and supply requested information)

X	Individual - Citizen of (Country): United States
	Partnership - State where organized (Country, if appropriate): _____ Names and Citizenship (Country) of General Partners: _____
	Corporation - State (Country, if appropriate) of Incorporation:
	Other (Specify Nature of Entity and Domicile):

GOODS AND/OR SERVICES:

Applicant requests registration of the trademark/service mark shown in the accompanying drawing in the United States Patent and Trademark Office on the Principal Register established by the Act of July 5, 1946 (15 U.S.C. 1051 et. seq., as amended) for the following goods/services (**SPECIFIC GOODS AND/OR SERVICES MUST BE INSERTED HERE**):
the services of an advertising firm

BASIS FOR APPLICATION: (Check boxes which apply, **but never both the first AND second boxes,** and supply requested information related to each box checked.)

XX	Applicant is using the mark in commerce on or in connection with the above identified goods/services. (15 U.S.C. 1051(a), as amended.) Three specimens showing the mark as used in commerce are submitted with this application. •Date of first use of the mark in commerce which the U.S. Congress may regulate (for example, interstate or between the U.S. and a foreign country): 6/1/92 •Specify the type of commerce: interstate (for example, interstate or between the U.S. and a specified foreign country) •Date of first use anywhere (the same as or before use in commerce date): 4/1/92 •Specify manner or mode of use of mark on or in connection with the goods/services: in promotional brochures and letterheads advertising the services (for example, trademark is applied to labels, service mark is used in advertisements)
[ ]	Applicant has a bona fide intention to use the mark in commerce on or in connection with the above identified goods/services. (15 U.S.C. 1051(b), as amended.) •Specify intended manner or mode of use of mark on or in connection with the goods/services: _____ (for example, trademark will be applied to labels, service mark will be used in advertisements)
[ ]	Applicant has a bona fide intention to use the mark in commerce on or in connection with the above identified goods/services, and asserts a claim of priority based upon a foreign application in accordance with 15 U.S.C. 1126(d), as amended. • Country of foreign filing: _____ • Date of foreign filing: _____
[ ]	Applicant has a bona fide intention to use the mark in commerce on or in connection with the above identified goods/services and, accompanying this application, submits a certification or certified copy of a foreign registration in accordance with 15 U.S.C. 1126(e), as amended. • Country of registration: _____ • Registration number: _____

NOTE: Declaration, on Reverse Side, MUST be Signed

DECLARATION

The undersigned being hereby warned that willful false statements and the like so made are punishable by fine or imprisonment, or both, under 18 U.S.C. 1001, and that such willful false statements may jeopardize the validity of the application or any resulting registration, declares that he/she is properly authorized to execute this application on behalf of the applicant; he/she believes the applicant to be the owner of the trademark/service mark sought to be registered, or, if the application is being filed under 15 U.S.C. 1051(b), he/she believes applicant to be entitled to use such mark in commerce; to the best of his/her knowledge and belief no other person, firm, corporation, or association has the right to use the above identified mark in commerce, either in the identical form thereof or in such near resemblance thereto as to be likely, when used on or in connection with the goods/services of such other person, to cause confusion, or to cause mistake, or to deceive; and that all statements made of his/her own knowledge are true and that all statements made on information and belief are believed to be true.

June 21, 1992
DATE

Jane A. Doe
SIGNATURE

(999) 123-5678
TELEPHONE NUMBER

Jane A. Doe
PRINT OR TYPE NAME AND POSITION

INSTRUCTIONS AND INFORMATION FOR APPLICANT

TO RECEIVE A FILING DATE, THE APPLICATION <u>MUST</u> BE COMPLETED AND SIGNED BY THE APPLICANT AND SUBMITTED ALONG WITH:

1. The prescribed **FEE ($200.00)** for each class of goods/services listed in the application;
2. A **DRAWING PAGE** displaying the mark in conformance with 37 CFR 2.52;
3. If the application is based on use of the mark in commerce, **THREE (3) SPECIMENS** (evidence) of the mark as used in commerce for each class of goods/services listed in the application. All three specimens may be in the nature of: (a) labels showing the mark which are placed on the goods; (b) photographs of the mark as it appears on the goods, (c) brochures or advertisements showing the mark as used in connection with the services.
4. An **APPLICATION WITH DECLARATION** (this form) - The application must be signed in order for the application to receive a filing date. Only the following person may sign the declaration, depending on the applicant's legal entity: (a) the individual applicant; (b) an officer of the corporate applicant; (c) one general partner of a partnership applicant; (d) all joint applicants.

SEND APPLICATION FORM, DRAWING PAGE, FEE, AND SPECIMENS (IF APPROPRIATE) TO:

U.S. DEPARTMENT OF COMMERCE
Patent and Trademark Office, Box TRADEMARK
Washington, D.C. 20231

Additional information concerning the requirements for filing an application is available in a booklet entitled **Basic Facts About Trademarks**, which may be obtained by writing to the above address or by calling: (703) 305-HELP.

This form is estimated to take 15 minutes to complete. Time will vary depending upon the needs of the individual case. Any comments on the amount of time you require to complete this form should be sent to the Office of Management and Organization, U.S. Patent and Trademark Office, U.S. Department of Commerce, Washington D.C., 20231, and to the Office of Information and Regulatory Affairs, Office of Management and Budget, Washington, D.C. 20503.

Sample Application Based on Intent to Use (Corporation)

TRADEMARK/SERVICE MARK APPLICATION, PRINCIPAL REGISTER, WITH DECLARATION	MARK (Word(s) and/or Design) BRITE BITE TOOTHPASTE	CLASS NO. (If known) 3

TO THE ASSISTANT SECRETARY AND COMMISSIONER OF PATENTS AND TRADEMARKS:

APPLICANT'S NAME: Clean Cut Cosmetics Corporation

APPLICANT'S BUSINESS ADDRESS: 123 Main Street, Anytown, Delaware, 19000
(Display address exactly as
it should appear on registration)

APPLICANT'S ENTITY TYPE: (**Check one** and supply requested information)

	Individual - Citizen of (Country):
	Partnership - State where organized (Country, if appropriate): _____ Names and Citizenship (Country) of General Partners: _____
X	Corporation - State (Country, if appropriate) of Incorporation: Delaware
	Other (Specify Nature of Entity and Domicile):

GOODS AND/OR SERVICES:

Applicant requests registration of the trademark/service mark shown in the accompanying drawing in the United States Patent and Trademark Office on the Principal Register established by the Act of July 5, 1946 (15 U.S.C. 1051 et. seq., as amended) for the following goods/services (**SPECIFIC GOODS AND/OR SERVICES MUST BE INSERTED HERE**):
packaging for toothpaste, tooth powder and mouthwashes

BASIS FOR APPLICATION: (Check boxes which apply, **but never both the first AND second boxes**, and supply requested information related to each box checked.)

[ ]	Applicant is using the mark in commerce on or in connection with the above identified goods/services. (15 U.S.C. 1051(a), as amended.) Three specimens showing the mark as used in commerce are submitted with this application. •Date of first use of the mark in commerce which the U.S. Congress may regulate (for example, interstate or between the U.S. and a foreign country): _____ •Specify the type of commerce: _____ (for example, interstate or between the U.S. and a specified foreign country) •Date of first use anywhere (the same as or before use in commerce date): _____ •Specify manner or mode of use of mark on or in connection with the goods/services: _____ (for example, trademark is applied to labels, service mark is used in advertisements)
XX	Applicant has a bona fide intention to use the mark in commerce on or in connection with the above identified goods/services. (15 U.S.C. 1051(b), as amended.) •Specify intended manner or mode of use of mark on or in connection with the goods/services: packaging for toothpaste, tooth powder and mouthwashes and advertisements for the products (for example, trademark will be applied to labels, service mark will be used in advertisements)
[ ]	Applicant has a bona fide intention to use the mark in commerce on or in connection with the above identified goods/services, and asserts a claim of priority based upon a foreign application in accordance with 15 U.S.C. 1126(d), as amended. • Country of foreign filing: _____ • Date of foreign filing: _____
[ ]	Applicant has a bona fide intention to use the mark in commerce on or in connection with the above identified goods/services and, accompanying this application, submits a certification or certified copy of a foreign registration in accordance with 15 U.S.C. 1126(e), as amended. • Country of registration: _____ • Registration number: _____

NOTE: Declaration, on Reverse Side, MUST be Signed

PTO Form 1478 (REV. 5/91)
OMB No. 06510009 (Exp. 6/92)

U.S. DEPARTMENT OF COMMERCE/Patent and Trademark Office

DECLARATION

The undersigned being hereby warned that willful false statements and the like so made are punishable by fine or imprisonment, or both, under 18 U.S.C. 1001, and that such willful false statements may jeopardize the validity of the application or any resulting registration, declares that he/she is properly authorized to execute this application on behalf of the applicant; he/she believes the applicant to be the owner of the trademark/service mark sought to be registered, or, if the application is being filed under 15 U.S.C. 1051(b), he/she believes applicant to be entitled to use such mark in commerce; to the best of his/her knowledge and belief no other person, firm, corporation, or association has the right to use the above identified mark in commerce, either in the identical form thereof or in such near resemblance thereto as to be likely, when used on or in connection with the goods/services of such other person, to cause confusion, or to cause mistake, or to deceive; and that all statements made of his/her own knowledge are true and that all statements made on information and belief are believed to be true.

June 15, 1992	*John A. Doe*
DATE	SIGNATURE
(321) 987-6543	John A. Doe, President
TELEPHONE NUMBER	PRINT OR TYPE NAME AND POSITION

INSTRUCTIONS AND INFORMATION FOR APPLICANT

TO RECEIVE A FILING DATE, THE APPLICATION MUST BE COMPLETED AND SIGNED BY THE APPLICANT AND SUBMITTED ALONG WITH:

1. The prescribed **FEE ($200.00)** for each class of goods/services listed in the application;
2. A **DRAWING PAGE** displaying the mark in conformance with 37 CFR 2.52;
3. If the application is based on use of the mark in commerce, **THREE (3) SPECIMENS** (evidence) of the mark as used in commerce for each class of goods/services listed in the application. All three specimens may be in the nature of: (a) labels showing the mark which are placed on the goods; (b) photographs of the mark as it appears on the goods, (c) brochures or advertisements showing the mark as used in connection with the services.
4. An **APPLICATION WITH DECLARATION** (this form) - The application must be signed in order for the application to receive a filing date. Only the following person may sign the declaration, depending on the applicant's legal entity: (a) the individual applicant; (b) an officer of the corporate applicant; (c) one general partner of a partnership applicant; (d) all joint applicants.

SEND APPLICATION FORM, DRAWING PAGE, FEE, AND SPECIMENS (IF APPROPRIATE) TO:

U.S. DEPARTMENT OF COMMERCE
Patent and Trademark Office, Box TRADEMARK
Washington, D.C. 20231

Additional information concerning the requirements for filing an application is available in a booklet entitled **Basic Facts About Trademarks**, which may be obtained by writing to the above address or by calling: (703) 305-HELP.

This form is estimated to take 15 minutes to complete. Time will vary depending upon the needs of the individual case. Any comments on the amount of time you require to complete this form should be sent to the Office of Management and Organization, U.S. Patent and Trademark Office, U.S. Department of Commerce, Washington D.C., 20231, and to the Office of Information and Regulatory Affairs, Office of Management and Budget, Washington, D.C. 20503.

TRADEMARK/SERVICE MARK APPLICATION, PRINCIPAL REGISTER, WITH DECLARATION	MARK (Word(s) and/or Design)	CLASS NO. (If known)

TO THE ASSISTANT SECRETARY AND COMMISSIONER OF PATENTS AND TRADEMARKS:

APPLICANT'S NAME:

APPLICANT'S BUSINESS ADDRESS: _____
(Display address exactly as
it should appear on registration) _____

APPLICANT'S ENTITY TYPE: (Check one and supply requested information)

	Individual - Citizen of (Country):
	Partnership - State where organized (Country, if appropriate): _____ Names and Citizenship (Country) of General Partners: _____
	Corporation - State (Country, if appropriate) of Incorporation:
	Other (Specify Nature of Entity and Domicile):

GOODS AND/OR SERVICES:

Applicant requests registration of the trademark/service mark shown in the accompanying drawing in the United States Patent and Trademark Office on the Principal Register established by the Act of July 5, 1946 (15 U.S.C. 1051 et. seq., as amended) for the following goods/services (SPECIFIC GOODS AND/OR SERVICES MUST BE INSERTED HERE):

_____
_____
_____
_____
_____

BASIS FOR APPLICATION: (Check boxes which apply, but never both the first AND second boxes, and supply requested information related to each box checked.)

[ ]	Applicant is using the mark in commerce on or in connection with the above identified goods/services. (15 U.S.C. 1051(a), as amended.) Three specimens showing the mark as used in commerce are submitted with this application. •Date of first use of the mark in commerce which the U.S. Congress may regulate (for example, interstate or between the U.S. and a foreign country): _____ •Specify the type of commerce: _____ (for example, interstate or between the U.S. and a specified foreign country) •Date of first use anywhere (the same as or before use in commerce date): _____ •Specify manner or mode of use of mark on or in connection with the goods/services: _____ (for example, trademark is applied to labels, service mark is used in advertisements)
[ ]	Applicant has a bona fide intention to use the mark in commerce on or in connection with the above identified goods/services. (15 U.S.C. 1051(b), as amended.) •Specify intended manner or mode of use of mark on or in connection with the goods/services: _____ (for example, trademark will be applied to labels, service mark will be used in advertisements)
[ ]	Applicant has a bona fide intention to use the mark in commerce on or in connection with the above identified goods/services, and asserts a claim of priority based upon a foreign application in accordance with 15 U.S.C. 1126(d), as amended. • Country of foreign filing: _____ • Date of foreign filing: _____
[ ]	Applicant has a bona fide intention to use the mark in commerce on or in connection with the above identified goods/services and, accompanying this application, submits a certification or certified copy of a foreign registration in accordance with 15 U.S.C. 1126(e), as amended. • Country of registration: _____ • Registration number: _____

NOTE: Declaration, on Reverse Side, MUST be Signed

DECLARATION

The undersigned being hereby warned that willful false statements and the like so made are punishable by fine or imprisonment, or both, under 18 U.S.C. 1001, and that such willful false statements may jeopardize the validity of the application or any resulting registration, declares that he/she is properly authorized to execute this application on behalf of the applicant; he/she believes the applicant to be the owner of the trademark/service mark sought to be registered, or, if the application is being filed under 15 U.S.C. 1051(b), he/she believes applicant to be entitled to use such mark in commerce; to the best of his/her knowledge and belief no other person, firm, corporation, or association has the right to use the above identified mark in commerce, either in the identical form thereof or in such near resemblance thereto as to be likely, when used on or in connection with the goods/services of such other person, to cause confusion, or to cause mistake, or to deceive; and that all statements made of his/her own knowledge are true and that all statements made on information and belief are believed to be true.

_____   _____
DATE   SIGNATURE

_____   _____
TELEPHONE NUMBER   PRINT OR TYPE NAME AND POSITION

INSTRUCTIONS AND INFORMATION FOR APPLICANT

TO RECEIVE A FILING DATE, THE APPLICATION <u>MUST</u> BE COMPLETED AND SIGNED BY THE APPLICANT AND SUBMITTED ALONG WITH:

1. The prescribed **FEE ($200.00)** for each class of goods/services listed in the application;
2. A **DRAWING PAGE** displaying the mark in conformance with 37 CFR 2.52;
3. If the application is based on use of the mark in commerce, **THREE (3) SPECIMENS** (evidence) of the mark as used in commerce for each class of goods/services listed in the application. All three specimens may be in the nature of: (a) labels showing the mark which are placed on the goods; (b) photographs of the mark as it appears on the goods, (c) brochures or advertisements showing the mark as used in connection with the services.
4. An **APPLICATION WITH DECLARATION** (this form) - The application must be signed in order for the application to receive a filing date. Only the following person may sign the declaration, depending on the applicant's legal entity: (a) the individual applicant; (b) an officer of the corporate applicant; (c) one general partner of a partnership applicant; (d) all joint applicants.

SEND APPLICATION FORM, DRAWING PAGE, FEE, AND SPECIMENS (IF APPROPRIATE) TO:

U.S. DEPARTMENT OF COMMERCE
Patent and Trademark Office, Box TRADEMARK
Washington, D.C. 20231

Additional information concerning the requirements for filing an application is available in a booklet entitled **Basic Facts About Trademarks**, which may be obtained by writing to the above address or by calling: (703) 305-HELP.

This form is estimated to take 15 minutes to complete. Time will vary depending upon the needs of the individual case. Any comments on the amount of time you require to complete this form should be sent to the Office of Management and Organization, U.S. Patent and Trademark Office, U.S. Department of Commerce, Washington D.C., 20231, and to the Office of Information and Regulatory Affairs, Office of Management and Budget, Washington, D.C. 20503.

<table>
<tr>
<td rowspan="2">

AMENDMENT TO ALLEGE USE UNDER 37 CFR 2.76, WITH DECLARATION

</td>
<td>MARK (Identify the mark)</td>
</tr>
<tr>
<td>SERIAL NO</td>
</tr>
</table>

TO THE ASSISTANT SECRETARY AND COMMISSIONER OF PATENTS AND TRADEMARKS:

APPLICANT NAME:

Applicant requests registration of the above-identified trademark/service mark in the United States Patent and Trademark Office on the Principal Register established by the Act of July 5, 1946 (15 U.S.C. 1051 et. seq., as amended). Three specimens showing the mark as used in commerce are submitted with this amendment.

☐   Check here if Request to Divide under 37 CFR 2.87 is being submitted with this amendment.

Applicant is using the mark in commerce on or in connection with the following goods/services:

_____

_____

(NOTE: Goods/services listed above may not be broader than the goods/services identified in the application as filed)

Date of first use of mark anywhere: _____

Date of first use of mark in commerce
which the U.S. Congress may regulate: _____

Specify type of commerce: (e.g., interstate, between the U.S. and a specified foreign country) _____

_____

Specify manner or mode of use of mark on or in connection with the goods/services: (e.g., trademark is applied to labels, service mark is used in advertisements) _____

_____

The undersigned being hereby warned that willful false statements and the like so made are punishable by fine or imprisonment, or both, under 18 U.S.C. 1001, and that such willful false statements may jeopardize the validity of the application or any resulting registration, declares that he/she is properly authorized to execute this Amendment to Allege Use on behalf of the applicant; he/she believes the applicant to be the owner of the trademark/service mark sought to be registered; the trademark/ service mark is now in use in commerce; and all statements made of his/her own knowledge are true and all statements made on information and belief are believed to be true.

_____   _____
Date   Signature

_____   _____
Telephone Number   Print or Type Name and Position

INSTRUCTIONS AND INFORMATION FOR APPLICANT

In an application based upon a bona fide intention to use a mark in commerce, applicant must use its mark in commerce before a registration will be issued. After use begins, the applicant must submit, along with evidence of use (specimens) and the prescribed fee(s), **either**:

> (1) an Amendment to Allege Use under 37 CFR 2.76, or
> (2) a Statement of Use under 37 CFR 2.88.

The difference between these two filings is the timing of the filing. Applicant may file an Amendment to Allege Use before approval of the mark for publication for opposition in the **Official Gazette**, or, if a final refusal has been issued, prior to the expiration of the six month response period. Otherwise, applicant must file a Statement of Use after the Office issues a Notice of Allowance. The Notice of Allowance will issue after the opposition period is completed if no successful opposition is filed. Neither Amendment to Allege Use or Statement of Use papers will be accepted by the Office during the period of time between approval of the mark for publication for opposition in the **Official Gazette** and the issuance of the Notice of Allowance.

Applicant may call (703) 557-5249 to determine whether the mark has been approved for publication for opposition in the **Official Gazette.**

Before filing an Amendment to Allege Use or a Statement of Use, applicant must use the mark in commerce on or in connection with **all** of the goods/services for which applicant will seek registration, **unless** applicant submits with the papers, a request to divide out from the application the goods or services to which the Amendment to Allege Use or Statement of Use pertains. (See: 37 CFR 2.87, Dividing an application)

Applicant **must** submit with an Amendment to Allege Use or a Statement of Use:

> (1) the appropriate fee of $100 per class of goods/services listed in the Amendment to Allege Use or the Statement of Use, and

> (2) three (3) specimens or facsimiles of the mark as used in commerce for each class of goods/services asserted (e.g., photograph of mark as it appears on goods, label containing mark which is placed on goods, or brochure or advertisement showing mark as used in connection with services).

Cautions/Notes concerning completion of this Amendment to Allege Use form:

> (1) The goods/services identified in the Amendment to Allege Use must be within the scope of the goods/services identified in the application as filed. Applicant may delete goods/services. Deleted goods/services may not be reinstated in the application at a later time.

> (2) Applicant may list dates of use for only one item in each class of goods/services identified in the Amendment to Allege Use. However, applicant must have used the mark in commerce on all the goods/services in the class. Applicant must identify the particular item to which the dates apply.

> (3) Only the following person may sign the verification of the Amendment to Allege Use, depending on the applicant's legal entity: (a) the individual applicant; (b) an officer of corporate applicant; (c) one general partner of partnership applicant; (d) all joint applicants.

<table>
<tr>
<td colspan="2">STATEMENT OF USE
UNDER 37 CFR 2.88, WITH
DECLARATION</td>
<td>MARK (Identify the mark)</td>
</tr>
<tr>
<td colspan="2"></td>
<td>SERIAL NO.</td>
</tr>
</table>

TO THE ASSISTANT SECRETARY AND COMMISSIONER OF PATENTS AND TRADEMARKS:

APPLICANT NAME:

NOTICE OF ALLOWANCE ISSUE DATE:

Applicant requests registration of the above-identified trademark/service mark in the United States Patent and Trademark Office on the Principal Register established by the Act of July 5, 1946 (15 U.S.C. 1051 et. seq., as amended). Three (3) specimens showing the mark as used in commerce are submitted with this statement.

☐   Check here only if a Request to Divide under 37 CFR 2.87 is being submitted with this Statement.

Applicant is using the mark in commerce on or in connection with the following goods/services: (Check One)

☐   Those goods/services identified in the Notice of Allowance in this application.

☐   Those goods/services identified in the Notice of Allowance in this application except: (Identify goods/services to be deleted from application) _____

_____

_____

Date of first use of mark anywhere: _____

Date of first use of mark in commerce
which the U.S. Congress may regulate: _____

Specify type of commerce: (e.g., interstate, between the U.S. and a specified foreign country) _____

_____

Specify manner or mode of use of mark on or in connection with the goods/services: (e.g., trademark is applied to labels, service mark is used in advertisements) _____

_____

The undersigned being hereby warned that willful false statements and the like so made are punishable by fine or imprisonment, or both, under 18 U.S.C. 1001, and that such willful false statements may jeopardize the validity of the application or any resulting registration, declares that he/she is properly authorized to execute this Statement of Use on behalf of the applicant; he/she believes the applicant to be the owner of the trademark/service mark sought to be registered; the trademark/service mark is now in use in commerce; and all statements made of his/her own knowledge are true and all statements made on information and belief are believed to be true.

_____   _____
Date   Signature

_____   _____
Telephone Number   Print or Type Name and Position

PTO Form 1580 (REV. 9/89)
OMB No. 06510023
Exp. 6-30-92

U.S. DEPARTMENT OF COMMERCE/Patent and Trademark Office

INSTRUCTIONS AND INFORMATION FOR APPLICANT

In an application based upon a bona fide intention to use a mark in commerce, applicant must use its mark in commerce before a registration will be issued. After use begins, the applicant must submit, along with evidence of use (specimens) and the prescribed fee(s), **either:**

(1) an Amendment to Allege Use under 37 CFR 2.76, or
(2) a Statement of Use under 37 CFR 2.88.

The difference between these two filings is the timing of the filing. Applicant may file an Amendment to Allege Use before approval of the mark for publication for opposition in the **Official Gazette**, or, if a final refusal has been issued, prior to the expiration of the six month response period. Otherwise, applicant must file a Statement of Use after the Office issues a Notice of Allowance. The Notice of Allowance will issue after the opposition period is completed if no successful opposition is filed. Neither Amendment to Allege Use or Statement of Use papers will be accepted by the Office during the period of time between approval of the mark for publication for opposition in the **Official Gazette** and the issuance of the Notice of Allowance.

Applicant may call (703) 557-5249 to determine whether the mark has been approved for publication for opposition in the **Official Gazette.**

Before filing an Amendment to Allege Use or a Statement of Use, applicant must use the mark in commerce on or in connection with **all** of the goods/services for which applicant will **seek registration, unless** applicant submits with the papers, a request to divide out from the application the goods or services to which the Amendment to Allege Use or Statement of Use pertains. (See: 37 CFR 2.87, Dividing an application)

Applicant **must** submit with an Amendment to Allege Use or a Statement of Use:

(1) the appropriate fee of $100 per class of goods/services listed in the Amendment to Allege Use or the Statement of Use, and

(2) three (3) specimens or facsimiles of the mark as used in commerce for each class of goods/services asserted (e.g., photograph of mark as it appears on goods, label containing mark which is placed on goods, or brochure or advertisement showing mark as used in connection with services).

Cautions/Notes concerning completion of this Statement of Use form:

(1) The goods/services identified in the Statement of Use must be identical to the goods/services identified in the Notice of Allowance. Applicant may delete goods/services. Deleted goods/services may not be reinstated in the application at a later time.

(2) Applicant may list dates of use for only one item in each class of goods/services identified in the Statement of Use. However, applicant must have used the mark in commerce on all the goods/services in the class. Applicant must identify the particular item to which the dates apply.

(3) Only the following person may sign the verification of the Statement of Use, depending on the applicant's legal entity: (a) the individual applicant; (b) an officer of corporate applicant; (c) one general partner of partnership applicant; (d) all joint applicants.

<table>
<tr>
<td>REQUEST FOR EXTENSION OF TIME
UNDER 37 CFR 2.89 TO FILE A STATEMENT
OF USE, WITH DECLARATION</td>
<td>MARK (Identify the mark)

SERIAL NO</td>
</tr>
</table>

TO THE ASSISTANT SECRETARY AND COMMISSIONER OF PATENTS AND TRADEMARKS:

APPLICANT NAME:

NOTICE OF ALLOWANCE MAILING DATE:

Applicant requests a six-month extension of time to file the Statement of Use under 37 CFR 2.88 in this application.

☐ Check here if a Request to Divide under 37 CFR 2.87 is being submitted with this request.

Applicant has a continued bona fide intention to use the mark in commerce in connection with the following goods/services: (Check one below)

☐ Those goods/services identified in the Notice of Allowance in this application.

☐ Those goods/services identified in the Notice of Allowance in this application except: (Identify goods/services to be **deleted** from application) _____

_____

This is the _____ request for an Extension of Time following mailing of the Notice of Allowance.
(Specify first - fifth)

If this is not the first request for an Extension of Time, check one box below. If the first box is checked, explain the circumstance(s) of the non-use in the space provided:

☐ Applicant has not used the mark in commerce yet on all goods/services specified in the Notice of Allowance; however, applicant has made the following ongoing efforts to use the mark in commerce on or in connection with each of the goods/services specified above:

_____

If additional space is needed, please attach a separate sheet to this form

☐ Applicant believes that it has made valid use of the mark in commerce, as evidenced by the Statement of Use submitted with this request; however, if the Statement of Use is found by the Patent and Trademark Office to be fatally defective, applicant will need additional time in which to file a new statement.

The undersigned being hereby warned that willful false statements and the like so made are punishable by fine or imprisonment, or both, under 18 U.S.C. 1001, and that such willful false statements may jeopardize the validity of the application or any resulting registration, declares that he/she is properly authorized to execute this Request for Extension of Time to File a Statement of Use on behalf of the applicant; he/she believes the applicant to be the owner of the trademark/service mark sought to be registered; and all statements made of his/her own knowledge are true and all statements made on information and belief are believed to be true.

Date	Signature
Telephone Number	Print or Type Name and Position

PTO Form 1581 (REV. 9/89)
OMB No. 06510023
Exp. 6-30-92

U.S. DEPARTMENT OF COMMERCE/Patent and Trademark Office

INSTRUCTIONS AND INFORMATION FOR APPLICANT

Applicant must file a Statement of Use within six months after the mailing of the Notice of Allowance in an application based upon a bona fide intention to use a mark in commerce, UNLESS, within that same period, applicant submits a request for a six-month extension of time to file the Statement of Use. The request **must**:

    (1) be in writing,
    (2) include applicant's verified statement of continued bona fide intention to use the mark
    in commerce,
    (3) specify the goods/services to which the request pertains as they are identified in the
    Notice of Allowance, and
    (4) include a fee of $100 for each class of goods/services.

Applicant may request four further six-month extensions of time. No extension may extend beyond 36 months from the issue date of the Notice of Allowance. Each request must be filed within the previously granted six-month extension period and must include, in addition to the above requirements, a showing of **GOOD CAUSE**. This good cause showing must include:

    (1) applicant's statement that the mark has not been used in commerce yet on all the goods
    or services specified in the Notice of Allowance with which applicant has a continued bona
    fide intention to use the mark in commerce, **and**

    (2) applicant's statement of ongoing efforts to make such use, which may include the
    following: (a) product or service research or development, (b) market research,
    (c) promotional activities, (d) steps to acquire distributors, (e) steps to obtain required
    governmental approval, or (f) similar specified activity .

Applicant may submit one additional six-month extension request during the existing period in which applicant files the Statement of Use, unless the granting of this request would extend beyond 36 months from the issue date of the Notice of Allowance. As a showing of good cause, applicant should state its belief that applicant has made valid use of the mark in commerce, as evidenced by the submitted Statement of Use, but that if the Statement is found by the PTO to be defective, applicant will need additional time in which to file a new statement of use.

 Only the following person may sign the verification of the Request for Extentsion of Time, depending on the applicant's legal entity: (a) the individual applicant; (b) an officer of corporate applicant; (c) one general partner of partnership applicant; (d) all joint applicants.

This form is estimated to take 15 minutes to complete. Time will vary depending upon the needs of the individual case. Any comments on the amount of time you require to complete this form should be sent to the Office of Management and Organization, U.S. Patent and Trademark Office, U.S. Department of Commerce, Washington D.C., 20231, and to the Office of Information and Regulatory Affairs, Office of Management and Budget, Washington, D.C. 20503.

*U.S. Government Printing Office: 1992 — 313-161/62616

The Lanham Act

United States Code
Title 15, Chapter 22—Trademarks

Subchapter I—Principal Register

*§ 1051   Registration; application; payment of fees; designation of resident for service of process and notice [Section 1]

The owner of a trademark used in commerce may register his trademark under this chapter on the principal register established:

(a) By filing in the Patent and Trademark Office —

   (1) a written application, in such form as may be prescribed by the Commissioner, verified by the applicant, or by a member of the firm or an officer of the corporation or association applying specifying applicant's domicile and citizenship, the date of applicant's first use of the mark, the date of applicant's first use of the mark in commerce, the goods in connection with which the mark is used and the mode or manner in which the mark is used in connection with such goods, and including a statement to the effect that the person making the verification believes himself, or the firm, corporation, or association in whose behalf he makes the verification, to be the owner of the mark sought to be registered, that the mark is in use in commerce, and that no other person, firm, corporation, or association, to the best of his knowledge and belief, has the right to use such mark in commerce either in the identical form thereof or in such near resemblance thereto as to be likely, when applied to the goods of such other person, to cause confusion, or to cause mistake, or to deceive: *Provided,* That in the case of every application claiming concurrent use the applicant shall state exceptions to his claim of exclusive use, in which he shall specify, to the extent of his knowledge, any concurrent use by others, the goods in connection with which and the areas in which each concurrent use exists, the periods of each use, and the goods and area for which the applicant desires registration;

*[Ed. Note: Following each official section cite and caption, in brackets, is a reference to the unofficial, but often referred to, section citation. Thus, for example, 15 U.S.C. 1125(a) is also section 43(a) of the Trademark (Lanham) Act of 1946, as amended.]

(2) a drawing of the mark; and

(3) such number of specimens or facsimiles of the mark as actually used as may be required by the Commissioner.

(b) By paying into the Patent and Trademark Office the filing fee.

(c) By complying with such rules or regulations, not inconsistent with law, as may be prescribed by the Commissioner.

(d) If the applicant is not domiciled in the United States he shall designate by a written document filed in the Patent and Trademark Office the name and address of some person resident in the United States on whom may be served notices or process in proceedings affecting the mark. Such notices or process may be served upon the person so designated by leaving with him or mailing to him a copy thereof at the address specified in the last designation so filed. If the person so designated cannot be found at the address given in the last designation, such notice or process may be served upon the Commissioner. (July 5, 1946, c. 540, Title I, sec. 1, 60 Stat. 427; October 9, 1962, Public Law 87-772, sec. 1, 76 Stat. 769; January 2, 1975, Public Law 93-596, sec. 1, 88 Stat. 1949.)

§ 1052. Trademarks registrable on principal register; concurrent registration [Section 2]

No trademark by which the goods of the applicant may be distinguished from the goods of others shall be refused registration on the principal register on account of its nature unless it—

(a) Consists of or comprises immoral, deceptive, or scandalous matter; or matter which may disparage or falsely suggest a connection with persons, living or dead, institutions, beliefs, or national symbols, or bring them into contempt, or disrepute.

(b) Consists of or comprises the flag or coat of arms or other insignia of the United States, or of any State or municipality, or of any foreign nation, or any simulation thereof.

(c) Consists of or comprises a name, portrait, or signature identifying a particular living individual except by his written consent, or the name, signature, or portrait of a deceased President of the United States during the life of his widow, if any, except by the written consent of the widow.

(d) Consists of or comprises a mark which so resembles a mark registered in the Patent and Trademark Office or a mark or trade name previously used in the United States by another and not abandoned, as to be likely, when applied to the goods of the applicant, to cause confusion, or to cause mistake, or to deceive: *Provided,* That when the Commissioner determines that confusion, mistake, or deception is not likely to result from the continued use by more than one person of the same or similar marks under conditions and limitations as to the mode or place of use of the marks or the goods in connection with which such marks are used, concurrent registrations may be issued to such persons when they have become entitled to use such marks as a result of their concurrent lawful use in commerce prior to (i) the earliest of the filing dates of the applications pending or of any registration issued under this chapter; or (ii) July 5, 1947, in the case of registrations previously issued under the Act of March 3, 1881, or February 20, 1905, and continuing in full force and effect on that date; or (iii) July 5, 1947, in the case of applications filed under the Act of February 20, 1905, and registered after July 5, 1947. Concurrent registrations may also be issued by the Commissioner when a court of competent jurisdiction has finally determined that more than one person is entitled to use the same or similar marks in commerce. In issuing concurrent registrations, the Commissioner shall prescribe conditions and limitations as to the mode or place of use of the mark or the goods in connection with which such mark is registered to the respective persons.

(e) Consists of a mark which, (1) when applied to the goods of the applicant is merely descriptive or deceptively misdescriptive of them, or (2) when applied to the goods of the applicant is primarily geographically descriptive or deceptively misdescriptive of them, except as indications of regional origin may be registrable under section 1054 of this title, or (3) is primarily merely a surname.

(f) Except as expressly excluded in paragraphs (a)-(d) of this section, nothing in this chapter shall prevent the registration of a mark used by the applicant which has become distinctive of the applicant's goods in commerce. The Commissioner may accept as prima facie evidence that the mark has become distinctive, as applied to the applicant's goods in commerce, proof of substantially exclusive and continuous use thereof as a mark by the applicant in commerce for the five years next preceding the date of the filing of the application for its registration. (July 5, 1946, c. 540, Title I, sec. 2, 60 Stat. 428; October 9, 1962, Public Law 87-772, sec. 2, 76 Stat. 769; January 2, 1975, Public Law 93-596, sec. 1, 88 Stat. 1949.)

§ 1053. Service marks registrable [Section 3]

Subject to the provisions relating to the registration of trademarks, so far as they are applicable, service marks used in commerce shall be registrable, in the same manner and with the same effect as are trademarks, and when registered they shall be entitled to the protection provided in this chapter in the case of trademarks, except when used so as to represent falsely that the owner thereof makes or sells the goods on which such mark is used. The Commissioner may establish a separate register for such service marks. Applications and procedure under this section shall conform as nearly as practicable to those prescribed for the registration of trademarks. (July 5, 1946, c. 540, Title I, sec. 3, 60 Stat. 429.)

§ 1054. Collective marks and certification marks registrable [Section 4]

Subject to the provisions relating to the registration of trademarks, so far as they are applicable, collective and certification marks, including indications of regional origin used in commerce, shall be registrable under this chapter, in the same manner and with the same effect as are trademarks, by persons, and nations, States, municipalities, and the like, exercising legitimate control over the use of the marks sought to be registered, even though not possessing an industrial or commercial establishment, and when registered they shall be entitled to the protection provided in this chapter in the case of trademarks, except when used so as to represent falsely that the owner or a user thereof makes or sells the goods or performs the services on or in connection with which such mark is used. The Commissioner may establish a separate register for such collective marks and certification marks. Applications and procedure under this section shall conform as nearly as practicable to those prescribed for the registration of trademarks. (July 5, 1946, c. 540, Title I, sec. 4, 60 Stat. 429.)

§ 1055. Use by related companies affecting validity and registration [Section 5]

Where a registered mark or a mark sought to be registered is or may be used legitimately by related companies, such use shall inure to the benefit of the registrant or applicant for registration, and such use shall not affect the validity of such mark or of its registration, provided such mark is not used in such manner as to deceive the public. (July 5, 1946, c. 540, Title I, sec. 5, 60 Stat. 429.)

§ 1056. Disclaimer of unregistrable matter [Section 6]

(a) The Commissioner may require the applicant to disclaim an unregistrable component of a mark otherwise registrable. An applicant may voluntarily disclaim a component of a mark sought to be registered.

(b) No disclaimer, including those made under paragraph (d) of section 1057 of this title shall prejudice or affect the applicant's or registrant's rights then existing or thereafter arising in the disclaimed matter, or his right of registration on another application if the disclaimed matter be or shall have become distinctive of his goods or services. (July 5, 1946, c. 540, Title I, sec. 6, 60 Stat. 429; October 9, 1962, Public Law 87-772, sec. 3, 76 Stat. 769.)

§ 1057. Certificates of registration [Section 7]

Issuance and form

(a) Certificates of registration of marks registered upon the principal register shall be issued in the name of the United States of America, under the seal of the Patent and Trademark Office, and shall be signed by the Commissioner or have his signature placed thereon, and a record thereof shall be kept in the Patent and Trademark Office. The registration shall reproduce the mark, and state that the mark is registered on the principal register under this chapter, the date of the first use of the mark, the date of the first use of the mark in commerce, the particular goods or services for which it is registered, the number and date of the registration, the term thereof, the date on which the application for registration was received in the Patent and Trademark Office, and any conditions and limitations that may be imposed in the registration.

Certificate as prima facie evidence

(b) A certificate of registration of a mark upon the principal register provided by this chapter shall be prima facie evidence of the validity of the registration, registrant's ownership of the mark, and of registrant's exclusive right to use the mark in commerce in connection with the goods or services specified in the certificate, subject to any conditions and limitations stated therein.

Issuance to assignee

(c) A certificate of registration of a mark may be issued to the assignee of the applicant, but the assignment must first be recorded in the Patent and Trademark Office. In case of change of ownership the Commissioner shall, at the request of the owner and upon a proper showing and the payment of the fee provided in this chapter, issue to such assignee a new certificate of registration of the said mark in the name of such assignee, and for the unexpired part of the original period.

Surrender, cancellation, or amendment by registrant

(d) Upon application of the registant the Commissioner may permit any registration to be surrendered for cancellation, and upon cancellation appropriate entry shall be made in the records of the Patent and Trademark Office. Upon application of the registrant and payment of the prescribed fee, the Commissioner for good cause may permit any registration to be amended or to be disclaimed in part: *Provided,* That the amendment or disclaimer does not alter materially the character of the mark. Appropriate entry shall be made in the records of the Patent and Trademark Office and upon the certificate of registration or, if said certificate is lost or destroyed, upon a certified copy thereof.

Copies of Patent and Trademark Office records as evidence

(e) Copies of any records, books, papers, or drawings belonging to the Patent and Trademark Office relating to marks, and copies of registrations, when authenticated by the seal of the Patent and Trademark Office and certified by the Commissioner, or in his name by an employee of the Office duly designated by the Commissioner, shall be evidence in all cases wherein the originals would be evidence; and any person making application therefor and paying the fee required by law shall have such copies.

Correction of Patent and Trademark Office mistake

(f) Whenever a material mistake in a registration, incurred through the fault of the Patent and Trademark Office is clearly disclosed by the records of the Office a certificate stating the fact and nature of such mistake, shall be issued without charge and recorded and a printed copy thereof shall be attached to each printed copy of the registration and such corrected registration shall thereafter have the same effect as if the same had been originally issued in such corrected form, or in the discretion of the Commissioner a new certificate of registration may be issued without charge. All certificates of correction heretofore issued in accordance with the rules of the Patent and Trademark Office and the registrations to which they are attached shall have the same force and effect as if such certificates and their issue had been specifically authorized by statute.

Correction of applicant's mistake

(g) Whenever a mistake has been made in a registration and a showing has been made that such mistake occurred in good faith through the fault of the applicant, the Commissioner is authorized to issue a certificate of correction or, in his discretion, a new certificate upon the payment of the required fee: *Provided,* That the correction does not involve such changes in the registration as to require republication of the mark. (July 5, 1946, c. 540, Title I, sec. 7, 60 Stat. 430; August 17, 1950, c. 733, 64 Stat. 459; October 9, 1962, Public Law 87-772, sec. 4, 76 Stat. 769.)

§1058. Duration of registration; cancellation; affidavit of continued use; notice of Commissioner's action [Section 8]

(a) Each certificate of registration shall remain in force for twenty years: *Provided,* That the registration of any mark under the provisions of this chapter shall be canceled by the Commissioner at the end of six years following its date, unless within one year next preceding the expiration of such six years the registrant shall file in the Patent and Trademark Office an affidavit showing that said mark is in use in commerce or showing that its nonuse is due to special circumstances which excuse such nonuse and is not due to any intention to abandon the mark. Special notice of the requirement for such affidavit shall be attached to each certificate of registration.

(b) Any registration published under the provisions of subsection (c) of section 1062 of this title shall be canceled by the Commissioner at the end of six years after the date of such publication unless within one year next preceding the expiration of such six years the registrant shall file in the Patent and Trademark Office an affidavit showing that said mark is in use in commerce or showing that its nonuse is due to special circumstances which excuse such nonuse and is not due to any intention to abandon the mark.

(c) The Commissioner shall notify any registrant who files either of the above-prescribed affidavits of his acceptance or refusal thereof and, if a refusal, the reasons therefor. (As amended January 2, 1975, Public Law 93-596, sec. 1, 88 Stat. 1949; August 27, 1982, Public Law 97-247, sec. 8, 96 Stat. 320.)

§ 1059. Renewal of registration [Section 9]

(a) Each registration may be renewed for periods of twenty years from the end of the expiring period upon payment of the prescribed fee and the filing of a verified application therefor, setting forth those goods or services recited in the registration on or in connection with which the mark is still in use in commerce and having attached thereto a specimen or facsimile showing current use of the mark, or showing that any nonuse is due to special circumstances which excuse such nonuse and it is not due to any intention to abandon the mark. Such application may be made at any time within six months before the expiration of the period for which the registration was issued or renewed, or it may be made within three months after such expiration on payment of the additional fee herein prescribed.

(b) If the Commissioner refuses to renew the registration, he shall notify the registrant of his refusal and the reasons therefor.

(c) An applicant for renewal not domiciled in the United States shall be subject to and comply with the provisions of section 1051(d) of this title. (July 5, 1946, c. 540, Title I, sec. 9, 60 Stat. 431; October 9, 1962, Public Law 87-772, sec. 5, 76 Stat. 770.)

§ 1060. Assignment of mark; execution; recording; purchaser without notice [Section 10]

A registered mark or a mark for which application to register has been filed shall be assignable with the goodwill of the business in which the mark is used, or with that part of the goodwill of the business connected with the use of and symbolized by the mark, and in any such assignment it shall not be necessary to include the goodwill of the business connected with the use of and symbolized by any other mark used in the business or by the name or style under which the business is conducted. Assignments shall be by instruments in writing duly executed. Acknowledgment shall be prima facie evidence of the execution of an assignment and when recorded in the Patent and Trademark Office the record shall be prima facie evidence of execution. An assignment shall be void as against any subsequent purchaser for a valuable consideration without notice, unless it is recorded in the Patent and Trademark Office within three months after the date thereof or prior to such subsequent purchase. A separate record of assignments submitted for recording hereunder shall be maintained in the Patent and Trademark Office.

An assignee not domiciled in the United States shall be subject to and comply with the provisions of section 1051(d) of this title. (As amended January 2, 1975, Public Law 93-596, sec. 1, 88 Stat. 1949.)

§ 1061. Execution of acknowledgments and verifications [Section 11]

Acknowledgments and verifications required under this chapter may be made before any person within the United States authorized by law to administer oaths, or, when made in a foreign country, before any diplomatic or consular officer of the United States or before any official authorized to administer oaths in the foreign country concerned whose authority is proved by a certificate of a diplomatic or consular officer of the United States, or apostille of an official designated by a foreign country which, by treaty or convention, accords like effect to apostilles of designated officials in the United States, and shall be valid if they comply with the laws of the state or country where made. (July 5, 1946, c. 540, Title I, sec. 11, 60 Stat. 432. Amended August 27, 1982, Public Law 97-247, sec. 14(c), 96 Stat. 321.)

§ 1062. Publication; proceedings on refusal of registration; republication of marks registered under prior acts [Section 12]

(a) Upon the filing of an application for registration and payment of the fee provided in this chapter, the Commissioner shall refer the application to the examiner in charge of the registration of marks, who shall cause an examination to be made and, if on such examination it shall appear that the applicant is entitled to registration, the Commissioner shall cause the mark to be published in the Official Gazette of the Patent and Trademark Office: *Provided,* That in the case of an applicant claiming concurrent use, or in the case of an application to be placed in an interference as provided for in section 1066 of this title, the mark, if otherwise registrable, may be published subject to the determination of the rights of the parties to such proceedings.

(b) If the applicant is found not entitled to registration, the examiner shall advise the applicant thereof and of the reasons therefor. The applicant shall have a period of six months in which to reply or amend his application, which shall then be re-examined. This procedure may be repeated until (1) the examiner finally refuses registration of the mark or (2) the applicant fails for a period of six months to reply or amend or appeal, whereupon the application shall be deemed to have been abandoned, unless it can be shown to the satisfaction of the Commissioner that the delay in responding was unavoidable, whereupon such time may be extended.

(c) A registrant of a mark registered under the provisions of the Act of March 3, 1881, or the Act of February 20, 1905, may, at any time prior to the expiration of the registration thereof, upon the payment of the prescribed fee file with the Commissioner an affidavit setting forth those goods stated in the registration on which said mark is in use in commerce and that the registrant claims the benefits of this chapter for said mark. The Commissioner shall publish notice thereof with a reproduction of said mark in the Official Gazette, and notify the registrant of such publication and of the requirement for the affidavit of use or nonuse as provided for in subsection (b) of section 1058 of this title. Marks published under this subsection shall not be subject to the provisions of section 1063 of this title. (July 5, 1946, c. 540, Title I, sec. 12, 60 Stat. 432; October 9, 1962, Public Law 87-772, sec. 7, 76 Stat. 770.)

§ 1063. Opposition to registration [Section 13]

Any person who believes that he would be damaged by the registration of a mark upon the principal register may, upon payment of the required fee, file an opposition in the Patent and Trademark Office, stating the grounds therefore, within thirty days after the publication under subsection (a) of section 1062 of this title of the mark sought to be registered. Upon written request prior to the expiration of the thirty-day period, the time for filing opposition shall be extended for an additional thirty days, and further extensions of time for filing opposition may be granted by the Commissioner for good cause when requested prior to the expiration of an extension. The Commissioner shall notify the applicant of each extension of the time for filing opposition. An opposition may be amended under such conditions as may be prescribed by the Commissioner. (As amended January 2, 1975, Public Law 93-596, sec. 1, 88 Stat. 1949; January 2, 1975, Public Law 93-600, sec. 1, 88 Stat. 1955; August 27, 1982, Public Law 97-247, sec. 9(a), 96 Stat. 320.)

§ 1064. Cancellation of registration [Section 14]

A petition to cancel a registration of a mark, stating the grounds relied upon, may, upon payment of the prescribed fee, be filed by any person who believes that he is or will be damaged by the registration of a mark on the principal register established by this chapter, or under the Act of March 3, 1881, or the Act of February 20, 1905 —

(a) within five years from the date of the registration of the mark under this chapter; or

(b) within five years from the date of publication under section 1062(c) of this title of a mark registered under the Act of March 3, 1881, or the Act of February 20, 1905; or

(c) at any time if the registered mark becomes the common descriptive name of an article or substance, or has been abandoned, or its registration was obtained fraudulently or contrary to the provisions of section 1054 of this title or of subsections (a), (b), or (c) of section 1052 of this title for a registration hereunder, or contrary to similar prohibitory provisions of said prior Acts for a registration thereunder, or if the registered mark is being used by, or with the permission of, the registrant so as to misrepresent the source of the goods or services in connection with which the mark is used. A registered mark shall not be deemed to be the common descriptive name of goods or services solely because such mark is also used as a name of or to identify a unique product or service. The primary significance of the registered mark to the relevant public rather than purchaser motivation shall be the test for determining whether the registered mark has become the common descriptive name of goods or services in connection with which it has been used; or

(d) at any time if the mark is registered under the Act of March 3, 1881, or the Act of February 20, 1905, and has not been published under the provisions of subsection (c) of section 1062 of this title; or

(e) at any time in the case of a certification mark on the ground that the registrant (1) does not control, or is not able legitimately to exercise control over, the use of such mark, or (2) engages in the production or marketing of any goods or services to which the certification mark is applied, or (3) permits the use of the certification mark for purposes other than to certify, or (4) discriminately refuses to certify or to continue to certify the goods or services of any person who maintains the standards or conditions which such mark certifies: *Provided,* That the Federal Trade Commission may apply to cancel on the grounds specified in subsections (c) and (e) of this section any mark registered on the principal register established by this chapter, and the prescribed fee shall not be required. (July 5, 1946, c. 540, Title I, sec. 14, 60 Stat, 433; October 9, 1962, Public Law 87-772, sec. 9, 76 Stat. 771; August 27, 1982, Public Law 97-247, sec. 9(b), 96 Stat. 320, November 8, 1984; Public Law 98-620; sec. 102, 98 Stat. 3335.)

§ 1065.   Incontestability of right to use mark under certain conditions [Section 15]

Except on a ground for which application to cancel may be filed at any time under subsections (c) and (e) of section 1064 of this title, and except to the extent, if any, to which the use of a mark registered on the principal register infringes a valid right acquired under the law of any State or Territory by use of a mark or trade name continuing from a date prior to the date of registration under this chapter of such registered mark, the right of the registrant to use such registered mark in commerce for the goods or services on or in connection with which such registered mark has been in continuous use for five consecutive years subsequent to the date of such registration and is still in use in commerce, shall be incontestable: *Provided,* That —

(1)   there has been no final decision adverse to registrant's claim of ownership of such mark for such goods or services, or to registrant's right to register the same or to keep the same on the register; and

(2)   there is no proceeding involving said rights pending in the Patent and Trademark Office or in a court and not finally disposed of; and

(3)   an affidavit is filed with the Commissioner within one year after the expiration of any such five-year period setting forth those goods or services stated in the registration on or in connection with which such mark has been in continuous use for such five consecutive years and is still in use in commerce, and the other matters specified in subsections (1) and (2) of this section; and

(4)   no incontestable right shall be acquired in a mark which is the common descriptive name of any article or substance, patented or otherwise.

Subject to the conditions above specified in this section, the incontestable right with reference to a mark registered under this chapter shall apply to a mark registered under the Act of March 3, 1881, or the Act of February 20, 1905, upon the filing of the required affidavit with the Commissioner within one year after the expiration of any period of five consecutive years after the date of publication of a mark under the provisions of subsection (c) of section 1062 of this title.

The Commissioner shall notify any registrant who files the above-prescribed affidavit of the filing thereof. (As amended January 2, 1975, Public Law 93-596, sec. 1, 88 Stat. 1949; August 27, 1982, Public Law 97-247, sec. 10, 96 Stat. 320.)

§ 1066.   Interference; declaration by Commissioner [Section 16]

Upon petition showing extraordinary circumstances, the Commissioner may declare that an interference exists when application is made for the registration of a mark which so resembles a mark previously registered by another, or for the registration of which another has previously made application, as to be likely when applied to the goods or when used in connection with the services of the applicant to cause confusion or mistake or to deceive. No interference shall be declared between an application and the registration of a mark the right to the use of which has become incontestable. (July 5, 1946, c. 540, Title I, sec. 16, 60 Stat. 434; October 9, 1962, Public Law 87-772, sec. 11, 76 Stat. 771; August 27, 1982, Public Law 97-247, sec. 11, 96 Stat. 321.)

§ 1067. Interference, opposition, and proceedings for concurrent use registration or for cancellation; notice; Trademark Trial and Appeal Board [Section 17]

In every case of interference, opposition to registration, application to register as a lawful concurrent user, or application to cancel the registration of a mark, the Commissioner shall give notice to all parties and shall direct a Trademark Trial and Appeal Board to determine and decide the respective rights of registration.

The Trademark Trial and Appeal Board shall include the Commissioner, the Deputy Commissioner, the Assistant Commissioners, and members appointed by the Commissioner. Employees of the Patent and Trademark Office and other persons, all of whom shall be competent in trademark law, shall be eligible for appointment as members. Each case shall be heard by at least three members of the Board, the members hearing such case to be designated by the Commissioner. (As amended January 2, 1975, Public Law 93-596, sec. 1, 88 Stat. 1949; October 15, 1980, Public Law 96-455, sec. 1, 94 Stat. 2024.)

§ 1068. Same; action of Commissioner [Section 18]

In such proceedings the Commissioner may refuse to register the opposed mark, may cancel or restrict the registration of a registered mark, or may refuse to register any or all of several interfering marks, or may register the mark or marks for the person or persons entitled thereto, as the rights of the parties under this chapter may be established in the proceedings: *Provided,* That in the case of the registration of any mark based on concurrent use, the Commissioner shall determine and fix the conditions and limitations provided for in subsection (d) of section 1052 of this title. (July 5, 1946, c. 540, Title I, sec. 18, 60 Stat. 435.)

§ 1069. Application of equitable principles in inter partes proceedings [Section 19]

In all inter partes proceedings equitable principles of laches, estoppel, and acquiescence, where applicable may be considered and applied. The provisions of this section shall also govern proceedings heretofore begun in the Patent and Trademark Office and not finally determined. (As amended January 2, 1975, Public Law 93-596, sec. 1, 88 Stat. 1949.)

§ 1070. Appeals to Trademark Trial and Appeal Board from decisions of examiners [Section 20]

An appeal may be taken to the Trademark Trial and Appeal Board from any final decision of the examiner in charge of the registration of marks upon the payment of the prescribed fee. (July 5, 1946, c. 540, Title I, sec. 20, 60 Stat. 435; August 8, 1958, Public Law 85-609, sec. 1(b), 72 Stat. 540.)

§ 1071. Appeal to courts [Section 21]

(a) (1) An applicant for registration of a mark, party to an interference proceeding, party to an opposition proceeding, party to an application to register as a lawful concurrent user, party to a cancellation proceeding, a registrant who has filed an affidavit as provided in section 1058 of this title, or an applicant for renewal, who is dissatisfied with the decision of the Commissioner or Trademark Trial and Appeal Board, may appeal to the United States Court of Appeals for the Federal Circuit thereby waiving his right to proceed under subsection (b) of this section; *Provided,* That such appeal shall be dismissed if any adverse party to the proceeding, other than the Commissioner, shall, within twenty days after the appellant has filed notice of appeal according to subsection (a)(2) of this section, files notice with the Commissioner that he elects to have all further proceedings conducted as provided in subsection (b) of this section. Thereupon the appellant shall have thirty days thereafter within which to file a civil action under said subsection (b) of this section, in default of which the decision appealed from shall govern the further proceedings in the case.

(2) When an appeal is taken to the United States Court of Appeals for the Federal Circuit, the appellant shall file in the Patent and Trademark Office a written notice of appeal directed to the Commissioner, within such time after the date of the decision from which the appeal is taken as the Commissioner prescribes, but in no case less than 60 days after that date. (Amended November 8, 1984, Public Law 98-620, sec. 414(b), 98 Stat. 3363.)

(3) The Commissioner shall transmit to the United States Court of Appeals for the Federal Circuit a certified list of the documents comprising the record in the Patent and Trademark Office. The court may request that the Commissioner forward the original or certified copies of such documents during pendency of the appeal. In an ex parte case, the Commissioner shall submit to that court a brief explaining the grounds for the decision of the Patent and Trademark Office, addressing all the issues involved in the appeal. The court shall, before hearing an appeal, give notice of the time and place of the hearing to the Commissioner and the parties in the appeal. (Amended November 8, 1984, Public Law 98-620, sec. 414(b), 98 Stat. 3363.)

(4) The United States Court of Appeals for the Federal Circuit shall review the decision from which the appeal is taken on the record before the Patent and Trademark Office. Upon its determination the court shall issue its mandate and opinion to the Commissioner, which shall be entered of record in the Patent and Trademark Office and shall govern the further proceedings in the case. (Amended November 8, 1984, Public Law 98-620, sec. 414(b), 98 Stat. 3363.)

(b) (1) Whenever a person authorized by subsection (a) of this section to appeal to the United States Court of Appeals for the Federal Circuit is dissatisfied with the decision of the Commissioner or Trademark Trial and Appeal Board, said person may, unless appeal has been taken to said Court of Appeals for the Federal Circuit, have remedy by a civil action if commenced within such time after such decision, not less than sixty days, as the Commissioner appoints or as provided in subsection (a) of this section. The court may adjudge that an applicant is entitled to a registration upon the application involved, that a registration involved should be canceled, or such other matter as the issues in the proceeding require, as the facts in the case may appear. Such adjudication shall authorize the Commissioner to take any necessary action, upon compliance with the requirements of law.

(2) The Commissioner shall not be made a party to an inter partes proceeding under this subsection, but he shall be notified of the filing of the complaint by the clerk of the court in which it is filed and shall have the right to intervene in the action.

(3) In all cases where there is no adverse party, a copy of the complaint shall be served on the Commissioner; and all the expenses of the proceedings shall be paid by the party bringing them, whether the final decision is in his favor or not. In suits brought hereunder, the record in the Patent and Trademark Office shall be admitted on motion of any party, upon such terms and conditions as to costs, expenses, and the further cross-examination of the witnesses as the court imposes, without prejudice to the right of any part to take further testimony. The testimony and exhibits of the record in the Patent and Trademark Office, when admitted, shall have the same effect as if originally taken and produced in the suit.

(4) Where there is an adverse party, such suit may be instituted against the party in interest as shown by the records of the Patent and Trademark Office at the time of the decision complained of, but any party in interest may become a party to the action. If there be adverse parties residing in a plurality of districts not embraced within the same State, or an adverse party residing in a foreign country, the United States District Court for the District of Columbia shall have jurisdiction and may issue summons against the adverse parties directed to the marshal of any district in which any adverse party resides. Summons against adverse parties residing in foreign countries may be served by publication or otherwise as

the court directs. (As amended January 2, 1975, Public Law 93-596, sec. 1, 88 Stat. 1949; January 2, 1975, Public Law 93-600, sec. 2, 88 Stat. 1955; April 2, 1982, Public Law 97-164, sec. 162, 96 Stat. 49.)

§ 1072.   Registration as constructive notice of claim of ownership [Section 22]

Registration of a mark on the principal register provided by this chapter or under the Act of March 3, 1881, or the Act of February 20, 1905, shall be constructive notice of the registrant's claim of ownership thereof. (July 5, 1946, c. 540, Title I, sec. 22, 60 Stat. 435.)

Subchapter II—The Supplemental Register

Sec.

§ 1091.   Marks registrable on supplemental register; application and proceedings for registration; nature of mark; mark used in foreign commerce [Section 23]

In addition to the principal register, the Commissioner shall keep a continuation of the register provided in paragraph (b) of section 1 of the Act of March 19, 1920, entitled "An Act to give effect to certain provisions of the convention for the protection of trademarks and commercial names, made and signed in the city of Buenos Aires, in the Argentine Republic, August 20, 1910, and for other purposes," to be called the supplemental register. All marks capable of distinguishing applicant's goods or services and not registrable on the principal register provided in this chapter, except those declared to be unregistrable under paragraphs (a)-(d) of section 1052 of this title, which have been in lawful use in commerce by the proprietor thereof, upon or in connection with any goods or services for the year preceding the filing of the application may be registered on the supplemental register upon the payment of the prescribed fee and compliance with the provisions of section 1051 of this title so far as they are applicable.

Upon the filing of an application for registration on the supplemental register and payment of the fee herein provided the Commissioner shall refer the application to the examiner in charge of the registration of marks, who shall cause an examination to be made and if on such examination it shall appear that the applicant is entitled to registration, the registration shall be granted. If the applicant is found not entitled to registration the provisions of subsection (b) of section 1062 of this title shall apply.

For the purposes of registration on the supplemental register, a mark may consist of any trade-mark, symbol, label, package, configuration of goods, name, word, slogan, phrase, surname, geographical name, numeral, or device or any combination of any of the foregoing, but such mark must be capable of distinguishing the applicant's goods or services.

Upon a proper showing by the applicant that he requires domestic registration as a basis for foreign protection of his mark, the Commissioner may waive the requirement of a full year's use and may grant registration forthwith. (July 5, 1946, c. 540, Title II, sec. 23, 60 Stat. 435; October 9, 1962, Public Law 87-772, sec. 13, 76 Stat. 773.)

§ 1092.   Publication; not subject to opposition; cancellation [Section 24]

Marks for the supplemental register shall not be published for or be subject to opposition, but shall be published on registration in the Official Gazette of the Patent and Trademark Office. Whenever any person believes that he is or will be damaged by the registration of a mark on this register he may at any time, upon payment of the prescribed fee and the filing of a verified petition stating the ground therefor, apply to the Commissioner to cancel such registration. The Commissioner shall refer such application to the Trademark Trial and Appeal Board which shall give notice thereof to the registrant. If it is found after a hearing before the Board that the registrant was not entitled to register the mark at the time of his application for the registration thereof, or that the mark is not used by the registrant or has been abandoned, the registration shall be canceled by the Commissioner. (As amended January 2, 1975, Public Law 93-596, sec. 1, 88 Stat. 1949.)

§ 1093. Registration certificates for marks on principal and supplemental registers to be different [Section 25]

The certificates of registration for marks registered on the supplemental register shall be conspicuously different from certificates issued for marks registered on the principal register. (July 5, 1946, c. 540, Title II, sec. 25, 60 Stat. 436.)

§ 1094. Provisions of chapter applicable to registrations on supplemental register [Section 26]

The provisions of this chapter shall govern so far as applicable applications for registration and registrations on the supplemental register as well as those on the principal register, but applications for and registrations on the supplemental register shall not be subject to or receive the advantages of sections 1052(e), 1052(f), 1057(b), 1062(a), 1063 to 1068, inclusive, 1072, 1115 and 1124 of this title. (July 5, 1946, c. 540, Title II, sec. 26, 60 Stat. 436.)

§ 1095. Registration on principal register not precluded [Section 27]

Registration of a mark on the supplemental register, or under the Act of March 19, 1920, shall not preclude registration by the registrant on the principal register established by this chapter. (July 5, 1946, c. 540, Title II, sec. 27, 60 Stat. 436.)

§ 1096. Registration on supplemental register not used to stop importations [Section 28]

Registration on the supplemental register or under the Act of March 19, 1920, shall not be filed in the Department of the Treasury or be used to stop importations. (July 5, 1946, c. 540, Title II, sec. 28, 60 Stat. 436.)

§ 1096. Registration on supplemental register not used to stop importations [Section 28]

Registration on the supplemental register or under the Act of March 19, 1920, shall not be filed in the Department of the Treasury or be used to stop importations. (July 5, 1946, c. 540, Title II, sec. 28, 60 Stat. 436.)

Subchapter III—General Provisions

Sec.

§ 1111. Notice of registration; display with mark; recovery of profits and damages in infringement suit [Section 29]

Notwithstanding the provisions of section 1072 of this title, a registrant of a mark registered in the Patent and Trademark Office may give notice that his mark is registered by displaying with the mark as used the words "Registered in U.S. Patent and Trademark Office" or "Reg. U.S. Pat. & Tm. Off." or the letter R enclosed within a circle, thus ®; and in any suit for infringement under this chapter by such a registrant failing to give such notice of registration, no profits and no damages shall be recovered under the provisions of this chapter unless the defendant had actual notice of the registration. (As amended January 2, 1975, Public Law 93-596, sec. 1, 2, 88 Stat. 1949.)

§ 1112. Classification of goods and services; registration in plurality of classes [Section 30]

The Commissioner may establish a classification of goods and services, for convenience of Patent and Trademark Office administration, but not to limit or extend the applicant's rights. The applicant may file an application to register a mark for any or all of the goods and services upon or in connection with which he is actually using the mark: *Provided,* That when such goods or services fall within a plurality of classes, a fee equaling the sum of the fees for filing an application in each class shall be paid, and the Commissioner may issue a single certificate of registration for such mark. (As amended January 2, 1975, Public Law 93-596, sec. 1, 88 Stat. 1949.)

§ 1113. Fees [Section 31]

(a) The Commissioner will establish fees for the filing and processing of an application for the registration of a trademark or other mark and for all other services performed by and materials furnished by the Patent and Trademark Office related to trademarks and other marks. However, no fee for the filing or processing of an application for the registration of a trademark or other mark or for the renewal or assignment of a trademark or other mark will be adjusted more than once every three years. No fee established under this section will take effect prior to sixty days following notice in the Federal Register.

(b) The Commissioner may waive the payment of any fee for any service or material related to trademarks or other marks in connection with an occasional request made by a department or agency of the Government, or any officer thereof. The Indian Arts and Crafts Board will not be charged any fee to register Government trademarks of genuineness and quality for Indian products or for products of particular Indian tribes and groups. (As amended July 24, 1965, Public Law 89-83, sec. 3, 79 Stat. 260; January 2, 1975, Public Law 93-596, sec. 1, 88 Stat. 1949; August 27, 1982, Public Law 97-247, sec. 3, 96 Stat. 319; September 8, 1982, Public Law 97-256, sec 103, 96 Stat. 816.)

§ 1114. Remedies, infringement; innocent infringement by printers and publishers [Section 32]

(1) Any person who shall, without the consent of the registrant—

(a) use in commerce any reproduction, counterfeit, copy, or colorable imitation of a registered mark in connection with the sale, offering for sale, distribution, or advertising of any goods or services on or in connection with which such use is likely to cause confusion, or to cause mistake, or to deceive; or

(b) reproduce, counterfeit, copy, or colorably imitate a registered mark and apply such reproduction, counterfeit, copy, or colorable imitation to labels, signs, prints, packages, wrappers, receptacles or advertisements intended to be used in commerce upon or in connection with the sale, offering for sale, distribution, or advertising of goods or services on or in connection with which such use is likely to cause confusion or to cause mistake, or to deceive;

shall be liable in a civil action by the registrant for the remedies hereinafter provided. Under subsection (b) of this section, the registrant shall not be entitled to recover profits or damages unless the acts have been committed with knowledge that such imitation is intended to be used to cause confusion, or to cause mistake, or to deceive.

(2) Notwithstanding any other provision of this chapter, the remedies given to the owner of the right infringed shall be limited as follows: (a) Where an infringer is engaged solely in the business of printing the mark for others and establishes that he was an innocent infringer the owner of the right infringed shall be entitled as against such infringer only to an injunction against future printing; (b) where the infringement complained of is contained in or is part of paid advertising matter in a newspaper, magazine, or other similar periodical the remedies of the owner of the right infringed as against the publisher or distributor of such newspaper, magazine, or other similar periodical shall be confined to an injunction against the presentation of such advertising matter in future issues of such newspapers, magazines, or other similar periodical: *Provided,* That these limitations shall apply only to innocent infringers; (c) injunction relief shall not be available to the owner of the right infringed in respect of

an issue of a newspaper, magazine, or other similar periodical containing infringing matter when restraining the dissemination of such infringing matter in any particular issue of such periodical would delay the delivery of such issue after the regular time therefor, and such delay would be due to the method by which publication and distribution of such periodical is customarily conducted in accordance with sound business practice, and not to any method or device adopted for the evasion of this section or to prevent or delay the issuance of an injunction or restraining order with respect to such infringing matter. (July 5, 1946, c. 540, Title VI, sec. 32, 60 Stat. 437; October 9, 1962, Public Law 87-772, sec. 17, 76 Stat. 773.)

§ 1115. Registration on principal register as evidence of exclusive right to use mark; defenses [Section 33]

(a) Any registration issued under the Act of March 3, 1881, or the Act of February 20, 1905, or of a mark registered on the principal register provided by this chapter and owned by a party to an action shall be admissible in evidence and shall be prima facie evidence of registrant's exclusive right to use the registered mark in commerce on the goods or services specified in the registration subject to any conditions or limitations stated therein, but shall not preclude an opposing party from proving any legal or equitable defense or defect which might have been asserted if such mark had not been registered.

(b) If the right to use the registered mark has become incontestable under section 1065 of this title, the registration shall be conclusive evidence of the registrant's exclusive right to use the registered mark in commerce on or in connection with the goods or services specified in the affidavit filed under the provisions of said section 1065 subject to any conditions or limitations stated therein except when one of the following defenses or defect is established:

(1) That the registration or the incontestable right to use the mark was obtained fraudulently; or

(2) That the mark has been abandoned by the registrant; or

(3) That the registered mark is being used, by or with the permission of the registrant or a person in privity with the registrant, so as to misrepresent the source of the goods or services in connection with which the mark is used; or

(4) That the use of the name, term, or device charged to be an infringement is a use, otherwise than as a trade or service mark, of the party's individual name in his own business, or of the individual name of anyone in privity with such party, or of a term or device which is descriptive of and used fairly and in good faith only to describe to users the goods or services of such party, or their geographic origin; or

(5) That the mark whose use by a party is charged as an infringement was adopted without knowledge of the registrant's prior use and has been continuously used by such party or those in privity with him from a date prior to registration of the mark under this chapter or publication of the registered mark under subsection (c) of section 1062 of this title: *Provided, however,* That this defense or defect shall apply only for the area in which such continuous prior use is proved; or

(6) That the mark whose use is charged as an infringement was registered and used prior to the registration under this chapter or publication under subsection (c) of section 1062 of this title of the registered mark of the registrant, and not abandoned: *Provided, however,* That this defense or defect shall apply only for the area in which the mark was used prior to such registration or such publication of the registrant's mark; or

(7) That the mark has been or is being used to violate the antitrust laws of the United States. (July 5, 1946, c. 540, Title VI, sec. 33, 60 Stat. 438; October 9, 1962, Public Law 87-772, sec. 18, 76 Stat. 774.)

§ 1116. Injunctions; enforcement; notice to Commissioner [Section 34]

(a) The several courts vested with jurisdiction of civil actions arising under this chapter shall have power to grant injunctions, according to the principles of equity and upon such terms as the court may deem reasonable, to prevent the violation of any right of the registrant of a mark registered in the Patent and Trademark Office. Any such injunction may include a provision directing the defendant to file with the court and serve on the plaintiff within thirty days after the service on the defendant of such injunction, or such extended period as the court may direct, a report in writing under oath setting forth in detail the manner and form in which the defendant has complied with the injunction. Any such injunction granted upon hearing, after notice to the defendant, by any district court of the United States, may be served on the parties against whom such injunction is granted anywhere in the United States where they may be found, and shall be operative and may be enforced by proceedings to punish for contempt, or otherwise, by the court by which such injunction was granted, or by any other United States district court in whose jurisdiction the defendant may be found.

(b) The said courts shall have jurisdiction to enforce said injunction, as provided in this chapter, as fully as if the injunction had been granted by the district court in which it is sought to be enforced. The clerk of the court or judge granting the injunction shall, when required to do so by the court before which application to enforce said injunction is made, transfer without delay to said court a certified copy of all papers on file in his office upon which said injunction was granted.

(c) It shall be the duty of the clerks of such courts within one month after the filing of any action, suit, or proceeding arising under the provisions of this chapter to give notice thereof in writing to the Commissioner setting forth in order so far as known the names and addresses of the litigants and the designating number or numbers of the registration or registrations upon which the action, suit, or proceeding has been brought, and in the event any other registration be subsequently included in the action, suit, or proceeding by amendment, answer, or other pleading, the clerk shall give like notice thereof to the Commissioner, and within one month after the decision is rendered, appeal taken or a decree issued the clerk of the court shall give notice thereof to the Commissioner, and it shall be the duty of the Commissioner on receipt of such notice forthwith to endorse the same upon the file wrapper of the said registration or registrations and to incorporate the same as a part of the contents of said file wrapper. (July 5, 1946, c. 540, Title VI, sec. 34, 60 Stat. 439; January 2, 1975, Public Law 93-596, sec. 1, 88 Stat. 1949.)

(d) (1) (A) In the case of a civil action arising under section 32(1)(a) of this Act (15 U.S.C. 1114) or section 110 of the Act entitled "An Act to incorporate the United States Olympic Association", approved September 21, 1950 (36 U.S.C. 390) with respect to a violation that consists of using a counterfeit mark in connection with the sale, offering for sale, or distribution of goods or services, the court may, upon ex parte application, grant an order under subsection (a) of this section pursuant to this subsection providing for the seizue of goods and counterfeit marks involved in such violation and the means of making such marks, and records documenting the manufacture, sale, or receipt of things involved in such violation.

(B) As used in this subsection the term "counterfeit mark" means—

(i) a counterfeit of a mark that is registered on the principal register in the United States Patent and Trademark Office for such goods or services sold, offered for sale, or distributed and that is in use, whether or not the person against whom relief is sought knew such mark was so registered; or

(ii) a spurious designation that is identical with, or substantially indistinguishable from, a designation as to which the remedies of this Act are made available by reason of section 110 of the Act entitled "An Act to incorporate the United States Olympic Association", approved September 21, 1950 (36 U.S.C. 380);

but such term does not include any mark or designation used in connection with goods or services of which the manufacturer or producer was, at the time of the manufacture or production in question, authorized to use the mark or designation for the type of goods or services so manufactured or produced, by the holder of the right to use such mark or designation.

(2) The court shall not receive an application under this subsection unless the applicant has given such notice of the application as is reasonable under the circumstances to the United States attorney for the judicial district in which such order is sought. Such attorney may participate in the proceedings arising under such application if such proceedings may affect evidence of an offense against the United States. The court may deny such application if the court determines that the public interest in a potential prosecution so requires.

(3) The application for an order under this subsection shall—

(A) be based on an affidavit or the verified complaint establishing facts sufficient to support the findings of fact and conclusions of law required for such order; and

(B) contain the additional information required by paragraph (5) of this subsection to be set forth in such order.

(4) The court shall not grant such an application unless—

(A) the person obtaining an order under this subsection provides the security determined adequate by the court for the payment of such damages as any person may be entitled to recover as a result of a wrongful seizure or wrongful attempted seizure under this subsection; and

(B) the court finds that it clearly appears from specific facts that—

(i) an order other than an ex parte seizure order is not adequate to achieve the purposes of section 32 of this Act (15 U.S.C. 114);

(ii) the applicant has not publicized the requested seizure;

(iii) the applicant is likely to succeed in showing that the person against whom seizure would be ordered used a counterfeit mark in connection with the sale, offering for sale, or distribution of goods or services;

(iv) an immediate and irreparable injury will occur if such seizure is not ordered;

(v) the matter to be seized will be located at the place identified in the application;

(vi) the harm to the applicant of denying the application outweighs the harm to the legitimate interests of the person against whom seizure would be ordered of granting the application; and

(vii) the person against whom seizure would be ordered, or persons acting in concert with such person, would destroy, move, hide, or otherwise make such matter inaccessible to the court, if the applicant were to proceed on notice to such person.

(5) An order under this subsection shall set forth—

(A) the findings of fact and conclusions of law required for the order;

(B) a particular description of the matter to be seized, and a description of each place at which such matter is to be seized;

(C) the time period, which shall end not later than seven days after the date on which such order is issued, during which the seizure is to be made;

(D) the amount of security required to be provided under this subsection; and

(E) a date for the hearing required under paragraph (10) of this subsection.

(6) The court shall take appropriate action to protect the person against whom an order under this subsection is directed from publicity, by or at the behest of the plaintiff, about such order and any seizure under such order.

(7) Any materials seized under this subsection shall be taken into the custody of the court. The court shall enter an appropriate protective order with respect to discovery by the applicant of any records that have been seized. The protective order shall provide for appropriate procedures to assure that confidential information contained in such records is not improperly disclosed to the applicant.

(8) An order under this subsection, together with the supporting documents, shall be sealed until the person against whom the order is directed has an opportunity to contest such order, except that any person against whom such order is issued shall have access to such order and supporting documents after the seizure has been carried out.

(9) The court shall order that a United States marshal or other law enforcement officer is to serve a copy of the order under this subsection and then is to carry out the seizure under such order. The court shall issue orders, when appropriate, to protect the defendant from undue damage from the disclosure of trade secrets of other confidential information during

the course of the seizure, including, when appropriate, orders restricting the access of the applicant (or any agent or employee of the applicant) to such secrets or information.

(10) (A) The court shall hold a hearing, unless waived by all the parties, on the date set by the court in the order of seizure. The date shall be not sooner than ten days after the order is issued and not later than fifteen days after the order is issued, unless the applicant for the order shows good cause for another date or unless the party against whom such order is directed consents to another date for such hearing. At such hearing the party obtaining the order shall have the burden to prove that the facts supporting findings of fact and conclusions of law necessary to support such order are still in effect. If that party fails to meet that burden, the seizure order shall be dissolved or modified appropriately.

(B) In connection with a hearing under this paragraph, the court may make such orders modifying the time limits for discovery under the Rules of Civil Procedure as may be necessary to prevent the frustration of the purposes of such hearing.

(11) A person who suffers damage by reason of a wrongful seizure under this subsection has a cause of action against the applicant for the order under which such seizure was made, and shall be entitled to recover such relief as may be appropriate, including damages for lost profits, cost of materials, loss of good will, and punitive damages in instances where the seizure was sought in bad faith, and, unless the court finds extenuating circumstances, to recover a reasonable attorney's fee. The court in its discretion may award prejudgment interest on relief recovered under this paragraph, at an annual interest rate established under section 6621 of the Internal Revenue Code of 1954, commencing on the date of service of the claimant's pleading setting forth the claim under this paragraph and ending on the date such recovery is granted, or for such shorter time as the court deems appropriate. (Added October 12, 1984; Public Law 98-473, sec. 1503(a); 98 Stat. 2179.)

§ 1117. Recovery for violation of rights; profits, damages and costs; attorney fees [Section 35]

(a) When a violation of any right of the registrant of a mark registered in the Patent and Trademark Office shall have been established in any civil action arising under this chapter, the plaintiff shall be entitled, subject to the provisions of sections 1111 and 1114 of this title, and subject to the principles of equity, to recover (1) defendant's profits, (2) any damages sustained by the plaintiff, and (3) the costs of the action. The court shall assess such profits and damages or cause the same to be assessed under its direction. In assessing profits the plaintiff shall be required to prove defendant's sales only; defendant must prove all elements of cost or deduction claimed. In assessing damages the court may enter judgment, according to the circumstances of the case, for any sum above the amount found as actual damages, not exceeding three times such amount. If the court shall find that the amount of the recovery based on profits is either inadequate or excessive the court may in its discretion enter judgment for such sum as the court shall find to be just, according to the circumstances of the case. Such sum in either of the above circumstances shall constitute compensation and not a penalty. The court in exceptional cases may award reasonable attorney fees to the prevailing party. (July 5, 1946, c. 540, Title VI, sec. 35, 60 Stat. 439; October 9, 1962, Public Law 87-772, sec. 19, 76 Stat. 774; January 2, 1975, Public Law 93-596 sec. 1, 88 Stat. 1949, January 2, 1975, Public Law 93-600, sec. 3, 88 Stat 1955.)

(b) In assessing damages under subsection (a), the court shall, unless the court finds extenuating circumstances, enter judgment for three times such profits or damages, whichever is greater, together with a reasonable attorney's fee, in the case of any violation of section 32(1)(a) of this Act (15 U.S.C. 1114(1)(a)) or section 110 of the Act entitled "An Act to incorporate the United States Olympic Association", approved September 21, 1950 (36 U.S.C. 380) that consists of intentionally using a mark or designation, knowing such mark or designation is a counterfeit mark (as defined in section 34(d) of this Act (15 U.S.C. 1116(d)), in connection with the sale, offering for sale, or distribution of goods or services. In such cases, the court may in its discretion award prejudgment interest on such amount at an annual interest rate established under section 6621 of the Internal Revenue Code of 1954, commencing on the date of the service of the claimant's pleadings setting forth the claim for such entry and ending on the date such entry is made, or for such shorter time as the court deems appropriate. (Added October 12, 1984, Public Law 98-473, sec. 1503(2), 98 Stat. 2182.)

§ 1118. Destruction of infringing articles [Section 36]

In any action arising under this chapter, in which a violation of any right of the registrant of a mark registered in the Patent and Trademark Office shall have been established, the court may order that all labels, signs, prints, packages, wrappers, receptacles, and advertisements in the possession of the defendant, bearing the registered mark or any reproduction, counterfeit, copy, or colorable imitation thereof, and all plates, molds, matrices, and other means of making the same, shall be delivered up and destroyed. The party seeking an order under this section for destruction of articles seized under section 34(d) (15 U.S.C. 1116(d)) shall give ten days' notice to the United States attorney for the judicial district in which such order is sought (unless good cause is shown for lesser notice) and such United States attorney may, if such destruction may affect evidence of an offense against the United States, seek a hearing on such destruction or participate in any hearing otherwise to be held with respect to such destruction. (July 5, 1946, c. 540, Title VI, sec. 36, 60 Stat. 440; January 2, 1975, Public Law 93-596, sec. 1, 88 Stat. 1949; October 12, 1984, Public Law 98-473, sec. 1503(3), 98 Stat. 2182.)

§ 1119. Power of court over registration [Section 37]

In any action involving a registered mark the court may determine the right to registration, order the cancelation of registrations, in whole or in part, restore canceled registrations, and otherwise rectify the register with respect to the registrations of any party to the action. Decrees and orders shall be certified by the court to the Commissioner, who shall make appropriate entry upon the records of the patent and Trademark Office, and shall be controlled thereby. (July 5, 1946, c. 540, Title VI, sec. 37, 60 Stat. 440; January 2, 1975, Public Law 93-596, sec. 1, 88 Stat. 1949.)

§ 1120. Civil liability for false or fraudulent registration [Section 38]

Any person who shall procure registration in the Patent and Trademark Office of a mark by a false or fraudulent declaration or representation, oral or in writing, or by any false means, shall be liable in a civil action by any person injured thereby for any damages sustained in consequence thereof. (July 5, 1946, c. 540, Title VI, sec. 38, 60 Stat. 440; January 2, 1975, Public Law 93-596, sec. 1, 88 Stat. 1949.)

§ 1121. Jurisdiction of Federal courts [Section 39]

The district and territorial courts of the United States shall have original jurisdiction and the courts of appeal of the United States (other than the United States Court of Appeals for the Federal Circuit) shall have appellate jurisdiction, of all actions arising under this chapter, without regard to the amount in controversy or to diversity or lack of diversity of the citizenship of the parties. (July 5, 1946, c. 540, Title VI, sec. 39, 60 Stat. 440; June 25, 1948, c. 646, secs. 1, 32(a), 62 Stat. 870, 991; May 24, 1949, c. 139, sec. 127, 63 Stat. 107; April 2, 1982, Title I, sec. 148, 96 Stat. 46.)

(a) No State or other jurisdiction of the United States or any political subdivision or any agency thereof may require alteration of a registered mark, or require that additional trademarks, servicemarks, trade names, or corporate names that may be associated with or incorporated into the registered mark be displayed in the mark in a manner differing from the display of such additional trademarks, servicemarks, trade names, or corporate names contemplated by the registered mark as exhibited in the certificate of registration issued by the United States Patent and Trademark Office. (October 12, 1982, Public Law 97-296, 96 Stat. 1316.)

§ 1122. Repealed.

May 24, 1949, c. 139, sec. 142, 63 Stat. 109 [Section 40]

§ 1123. Rules and regulations for conduct of proceedings in Patent and Trademark Office [Section 41]

The Commissioner shall make rules and regulations, not inconsistent with law, for the conduct of proceedings in the Patent and Trademark Office under this chapter. (July 5, 1946, c. 540, Title VI, sec. 41, 60 Stat. 440; January 2, 1975, Public Law 93-596, sec. 1, 88 Stat. 1949.)

§ 1124.   Importation of goods bearing infringing marks or names forbidden [Section 42]

Except as provided in subsection (d) of section 526 of the Tariff Act of 1930 [19 USCS § 1526(d)], no article of imported merchandise which shall copy or simulate the name of the [any] domestic manufacture, or manufacturer, or trader, or of any manufacturer or trader located in any foreign country which, by treaty, convention, or law affords similar privileges to citizens of the United States, or which shall copy or simulate a trademark registered in accordance with the provisions of this Act [15 USCS §§ 1051 et seq.] or shall bear a name or mark calculated to induce the public to believe that the article is manufactured in the United States, or that it is manufactured in any foreign country or locality other than the country or locality in which it is in fact manufactured, shall be admitted to entry at any customhouse of the United States; and, in order to aid the officers of the customs in enforcing this prohibition, any domestic manufacturer or trader, and any foreign manufacturer or trader, who is entitled under the provisions of a treaty, conviction, delcaration, or agreement between the United States and any foreign country to the advantages afforded by law to citizens of the United States in respect to trademarks and commercial names, may require his name and residence, and the name of the locality in which his goods are manufactured, and a copy of the certificate of registration of his trademark, issued in accordance with the provisions of this Act [15 USCS §§ 1051 et seq.], to be recorded in books which shall be kept for this purpose in the Department of the Treasury, under such regulations as the Secretary of the Treasury shall prescribe, and may furnish to the Department facsimiles of his name, the name of the locality in which his goods are manufactured, or of his registered trademark, and thereupon the Secretary of the Treasury shall cause one or more copies of the same to be transmitted to each collector or other proper officer of customs. (As amended October 3, 1978, Public Law 95-410, Title II, sec. 211(b), 92 Stat. 903.)

§ 1125.   False designations of origin and false descriptions forbidden [Section 43]

(a) Any person who shall affix, apply, or annex, or use in connection with any goods or services, or any container or containers for goods, a false designation of origin, or any false description or representation, including words or other symbols tending falsely to describe or represent the same, and shall cause such goods or services to enter into commerce, and any person who shall with knowledge of the falsity of such designation of origin or description or representation cause or procure the same to be transported or used in commerce or deliver the same to any carrier to be transported or used, shall be liable to a civil action by any person doing business in the locality falsely indicated as that of origin or in the region in which said locality is situated, or by any person who believes that he is or is likely to be damaged by the use of any such false description or representation.

(b) Any goods marked or labeled in contravention of the provisions of this section shall not be imported into the United States or admitted to entry at any customhouse of the United States. The owner, importer, or consignee of goods refused entry at any customhouse under this section may have any recourse by protest or appeal that is given under the customs revenue laws or may have the remedy given by this chapter in cases involving goods refused entry or seized, (July 5, 1946, c. 540, Title VIII, sec. 43, 60 Stat. 441.)

§ 1126.   International conventions [Section 44]

Register of marks communicated by international bureaus

(a) The Commissioner shall keep a register of all marks communicated to him by the international bureaus provided for by the conventions for the protection of industrial property, trademarks, trade and commercial names, and the repression of unfair competition to which the United States is or may become a party, and upon the payment of the fees required by such conventions and the fees herein prescribed may place the marks so communicated upon such register. This register shall show a facsimile of the mark or trade or commercial name; the name, citizenship, and address of the registrant; the number, date, and place of the first registration of the mark, including the dates on which application for such registration was filed and granted and the term of such registration; a list of goods or services to which the mark is applied as shown by the registration in the country of origin, and such other data as may be useful concerning the mark. This register shall be a continuation of the register provided in section 1(a) of the Act of March 19, 1920.

(b) Any person whose country of origin is a party to any convention or treaty relating to trademarks, trade or commercial names, or the repression of unfair competition, to which the United States is also a party, or extends reciprocal rights to nationals of the United Sates by law, shall be entitled to the benefits of this section under the conditions expressed herein to the extent necessary to give effect to any provision of such convention, treaty or reciprocal law, in addition to the rights to which any owner of a mark is otherwise entitled by this chapter.

Prior registration in country of origin; country of origin defined

(c) No registration of a mark in the United States by a person described in subsection (b) of this section shall be granted until such mark has been registered in the country of origin of the applicant, unless the applicant alleges use in commerce.

For the purposes of this section, the country of origin of the applicant is the country in which he has a bona fide and effective industrial or commercial establishment, or if he has not such an establishment the country in which he is domiciled, or if he has not a domicile in any of the countries described in subsection (b) of this section, the country of which he is a national.

Right of priority

(d) An application for registration of a mark under sections 1051, 1052, 1053, 1054 or 1091 of this title, filed by a person described in subsection (b) of this section who has previously duly filed an application for registration of the same mark in one of the countries described in subsection (b) of this section shall be accorded the same force and effect as would be accorded to the same application if filed in the United States on the same date on which the application was first filed in such foreign country: *Provided,* That —

(1) the application in the United States is filed within six months from the date on which the application was first filed in the foreign country;

(2) the application conforms as nearly as practicable to the requirements of this chapter, but use in commerce need not be alleged.

(3) the rights acquired by third parties before the date of the filing of the first application in the foreign country shall in no way be affected by a registration obtained on an application filed under this subsection;

(4) nothing in this subsection shall entitle the owner of a registration granted under this section to sue for acts committed prior to the date on which his mark was registered in this country unless the registration is based on use in commerce.

In like manner and subject to the same conditions and requirements, the right provided in this section may be based upon a subsequent regularly filed application in the same foreign country, instead of the first filed foreign application: *Provided,* That any foreign application filed prior to such subsequent application has been withdrawn, abandoned, or otherwise disposed of, without having been laid open to public inspection and without leaving any rights outstanding, and has not served, nor thereafter shall serve, as a basis for claiming a right of priority.

Registration on principal or supplemental register;
copy of foreign registration

(e) A mark duly registered in the country of origin of the foreign applicant may be registered on the principal register if eligible, otherwise on the supplemental register in this chapter provided. The application therefor shall be accompanied by a certification or a certified copy of the registration in the country of origin of the applicant.

Domestic registration independent of foreign registration

(f) The registration of a mark under the provisions of subsections (c), (d), and (e) of this section by a person described in subsection (b) of this section shall be independent of the registration in the country of origin and the duration, validity, or transfer in the United States of such registration shall be governed by the provisions of this chapter.

Trade or commercial names of foreign nationals
protected without registration

(g) Trade names or commercial names of persons described in subsection (b) of this section shall be protected without the obligation of filing or registration whether or not they form parts of marks.

Protection of foreign nationals against unfair competition

(h) Any person designated in subsection (b) of this section as entitled to the benefits and subject to the provisions of this chapter shall be entitled to effective protection against unfair competition, and the remedies provided in this chapter for infringement of marks shall be available so far as they may be appropriate in repressing acts of unfair competition.

Citizens or residents of United States entitled to benefits of section

(i) Citizens or residents of the United States shall have the same benefits as are granted by this section to persons described in subsection (b) of this section. (July 5, 1946, c. 540, Title IX, sec. 44, 60 Stat. 441; October 3, 1961, Public Law 87-333, sec. 2, 75 Stat. 748; Octobert 9, 1962, Public Law 87-772, sec. 20, 76 Stat. 774.)

§ 1127. Construction and definitions; intent of chapter [Section 45]

In the construction of this chapter, unless the contrary is plainly apparent from the context—

The United States includes and embraces all territory which is under its jurisdiction and control.

The word "commerce" means all commerce which may lawfully be regulated by Congress.

The term "principal register" refers to the register provided for by sections 1051 to 1072 of this title, and the term "supplemental register" refers to the register provided for by sections 1091 to 1096 of this title.

The term "person" and any other word or term used to designate the applicant or other entitled to a benefit or privilege or rendered liable under the provisions of this chapter includes a juristic person as well as a natural person. The term "juristic person" includes a firm, corporation, union, association, or other organization capable of suing and being sued in a court of law.

The terms "applicant" and "registrant" embrace the legal representatives, predecessors, successors and assigns of such applicant or registrant.

The term "Commissioner" means the Commissioner of Patents and Trademarks.

The term "related company" means any person who legitimately controls or is controlled by the registrant or applicant for registration in respect to the nature and quality of the goods or services in connection with which the mark is used.

The terms "trade name" and "commercial name" include individual names and surnames, firm names and trade names used by manufacturers, industrialists, merchants, agriculturists, and others to identify their businesses, vocations, or occupations; the names or titles lawfully adopted and used by persons, firms, associations, corporations, companies, unions, and any manufacturing, industrial, commercial, agricultural, or other organizations engaged in trade or commerce and capable of suing and being sued in a court of law.

The term "trademark" includes any word, name, symbol, or device or any combination thereof adopted and used by a manufacturer or merchant to identify and distinguish his goods, including a unique product, from those manufactured or sold by others and to indicate the source of the goods, even if that source is unknown.

The term "service mark" means a mark used in the sale or advertising of services to identify and distinguish the services of one person, including a unique service, from the services of others and to indicate the source of the services, even if that source is unknown. Titles, character names and other distinctive features of radio or television programs may be registered as service marks notwithstanding that they, or the programs, may advertise the goods of the sponsor.

The term "certification mark" means a mark used upon or in connection with the products or services of one or more persons other than the owner of the mark to certify regional or other origin, material, mode of manufacture, quality, accuracy or other characteristics of such goods or services or that the work or labor on the goods or services was performed by members of a union or other organization.

The term "collective mark" means a trademark or service mark used by the members of a cooperative, an association or other collective group or organization and includes marks used to indicate membership in a union, an association or other organization.

The term "mark" includes any trademark, service mark, collective mark, or certification mark entitled to registration under this chapter whether registered or not.

For the purposes of this chapter a mark shall be deemed to be used in commerce (a) on goods when it is placed in any manner on the goods or their containers or the displays associated therewith or on the tags or labels affixed thereto and the goods are sold or transported in commerce and (b) on services when it is used or displayed in the sale or advertising of services and the services are rendered in commerce, or the services are rendered in more than one State or in this and a foreign country and the person rendering the services is engaged in commerce in connection therewith.

A mark shall be deemed to be "adandoned"—

(a) When its use has been discontinued with intent not to resume. Intent not to resume may be inferred from circumstances. Nonuse for two consecutive years shall be prima facie abandonment.

(b) When any course of conduct of the registrant, including acts of omission as well as commission, causes the mark to lose its significance as an indication of origin. Purchaser motivation shall not be a test for determining abandonment under this subparagraph.

The term "colorable imitation" includes any mark which so resembles a registered mark as to be likely to cause confusion or mistake or to deceive.

The term "registered mark" means a mark registered in the United States Patent and Trademark Office under this chapter or under the Act of March 3, 1881, or the Act of February 20, 1905, or the Act of March 19, 1920. The phrase "marks registered in the Patent and Trademark Office" means registered marks.

The term "Act of March 3, 1881", "Act of February 20, 1905", or "Act of March 19, 1920," means the respective Act as amended.

A "counterfeit" is a spurious mark which is identical with, or substantially indistinguishable from, a registered mark.

Words used in the singular include the plural and vice versa.

The intent of this chapter is to regulate commerce within the control of Congress by making actionable the deceptive and misleading use of marks in such commerce; to protect registered marks used in such commerce from interference by State, or territorial legislation; to protect persons engaged in such commerce against unfair competition; to prevent fraud and deception in such commerce by the use of reproductions, copies, counterfeits, or colorable imitations of registered marks; and to provide rights and remedies stipulated by treaties and conventions respecting trademarks, trade names, and unfair competition entered into between the United States and foreign nations. (July 5, 1946, c. 540, Title X, sec. 45, 60 Stat. 443; October 9, 1962, Public Law 87-772, sec. 21, 76 Stat. 774; January 2, 1975, Public Law 93-596, sec. 1, 88 Stat. 1949; Amended November 8, 1984, Public Law 98-620, sec. 103, 98 Stat. 3336.)

*(*Ed. Note:* The following sections of the Trademark (Lanham) Act of 1946 were not incorporated in the U.S. Code.)

*§ 46(a). Time of taking effect—Repeal of prior acts

This Act shall be in force and take effect one year from its enactment, but except as otherwise herein specifically provided shall not affect any suit, proceeding, or appeal then pending. All Acts and parts of Acts inconsistent herewith are hereby repealed effective one year from the enactment hereof, including the following Acts insofar as they are inconsistent herewith: The Act of Congress approved March 3, 1881, entitled "An Act to authorize the registration of trademarks and protect the same"; the Act approved August 5, 1882, entitled "An Act relating to the registration of trademarks", the Act of February 20, 1905 (U.S.C., title 15, secs. 81 to 109, inclusive), entitled "An Act to authorize the registration of trademarks used in commerce with foreign nations or among the several States or with Indian tribes, and to protect the same", and the amendments thereto by the Acts of May 4, 1906 (U.S.C., title 15, secs. 131 and 132; 34 Stat. 169), March 2, 1907 (34 Stat. 1251, 1252), February 18, 1909 (35 Stat. 627, 628), February 18, 1911 (36 Stat. 918), January 8, 1913 (37 Stat. 649), June 7, 1924 (43 Stat. 647), March 4, 1925 (43 Stat. 1268, 1269), April 11, 1930 (46 Stat. 155), June 10, 1938 (Public, Numbered 586, Seventy-fifth Congress, ch. 332, third session); the Act of March 19, 1920 (U.S.C., title 15, secs. 121 to 128, inclusive), entitled "an Act to give effect to certain provisions of the convention for the protection of trademarks and commercial names made and signed in the city of Buenos Aires, in the Argentine Republic, August 20, 1910, and for other purposes", and the amendments thereto, including the Act of June 10, 1938 (Public, Numbered 586, Seventy-fifth Congress, ch. 332, third session): *Provided*, That this repeal shall not affect the validity of registrations granted or applied for under any of said Acts prior to the effective date of this Act, or rights or remedies thereunder except as provided in sections 8, 12, 14, 15, and 47 of this Act; but nothing contained in this Act shall be construed as limiting, restricting, modifying, or repealing any statute in force on the effective date of this Act which does not relate to trademarks, or as restricting or increasing the authority of any Federal departments or regulatory agency except as may be specifically provided in this Act.

§ 46(b). Existing registrations under prior acts

Acts of 1881 and 1905. Registrations now existing under the Act of March 3, 1881, or the Act of February 20, 1905, shall continue in full force and effect for the unexpired terms thereof and may be renewed under the provisions of section 9 of this Act. Such registrations and the renewals thereof shall be subject to and shall be entitled to the benefits of the provisions of this Act to the same extent and with the same force and effect as though registered on the principal register established by this Act except as limited in sections 8, 12, 14, and 15 of this Act. Marks registered under the "10-year proviso" of section 5 of the Act of February 20, 1905, as amended, shall be deemed to have become distinctive of the registrant's goods in commerce under paragraph (f) of section 2 of this Act and may be renewed under section 9 hereof as marks coming within said paragraph.

Act of 1920. Registrations now existing under the Act of March 19, 1920, shall expire 6 months after the effective date of this Act, or twenty years from the dates of their registrations, whichever date is later. Such registrations shall be subject to and entitled to the benefits of the provisions of this Act relating to marks registered on the supplemental register established by this Act, and may not be renewed unless renewal is required to support foreign registrations. In that event renewal may be effected on the supplemental register under the provisions of section 9 of this Act.

Subject to registration under this Act. Marks registered under previous Acts may, if eligible, also be registered under this Act.

§ 47(a). Applications pending on effective date of Act

All applications for registration pending in the Patent and Trademark Office at the effective date of this Act may be amended, if practicable, to bring them under the provisions of this Act. The prosecution of such applications so amended and the grant of registrations thereon shall be proceeded with in accordance with the provisions of this Act. If such amendments are not made, the prosecution of said applications shall be proceeded with and registrations thereon granted in accordance with the Acts under which said applications were filed, and said Acts are hereby continued in force to this extent for this purpose only, notwithstanding the foregoing general repeal thereof.

§ 47(b). Appeals pending on effective date of Act

In any case in which an appeal is pending before the United States Court of Customs and Patent Appeals or any United States Circuit Court of Appeals or the United States Court of Appeals for the District of Columbia or the United States Supreme Court at the effective date of this Act, the court, if it be of the opinion that the provisions of this Act are applicable to the subject matter of the appeal, may apply such provision or may remand the case to the Commissioner or to the district court for the taking of additional evidence or a new trial or for reconsideration of the decision on the record as made, as the appellate court may deem proper.

§ 48. Prior acts not repealed

Section 4 of the Act of January 5, 1905 (U.S.C., title 36, sec. 4), as amended, entitled "An Act to incorporate the National Red Cross," and section 7 of the Act of June 15, 1916 (U.S.C., title 36, sec. 27), entitled "An Act to incorporate the Boy Scouts of America, and for other purposes," and the Act of June 20, 1936 (U.S.C., title 22, sec. 248), entitled "An Act to prohibit the commercial use of the coat of arms of the Swiss Confederation," are not repealed or affected by this Act.

NOTE: The first and third of the laws referred to in this section have been repealed and replaced by sections 706 and 708, respectively, of U.S.C., Title 18, Crimes and Criminal Procedure, enacted June 25, 1948, effective September 1, 1948.

§ 49. Preservation of existing rights

Nothing herein shall adversely affect the rights or the enforcement of rights in marks acquired in good faith prior to the effective date of this Act.

§ 50. Severability

If any provision of this Act or the application of such provision to any person or circumstance is held invalid, the remainder of the Act shall not be affected thereby.

Code of Federal Regulations

TRADEMARKS

PART 2—RULES OF PRACTICE IN TRADEMARK CASES

Sec.

AUTHORITY: 15 U.S.C. 1123; 35 U.S.C. 6, unless otherwise noted.

SOURCE: 30 FR 13193, Oct. 16, 1965, unless otherwise noted.

§ 2.1 Sections of part 1 applicable.

Sections 1.1 to 1.26 of this chapter are applicable to trademark cases except such parts thereof which specifically refer to patents and except § 1.22 to the extent that it is inconsistent with §§ 2.85(e), 2.101(d), 2.111(c) or § 2.162(d). Other sections of part 1 incorporated by reference or referred to in particular sections of this part are also applicable to trademark cases.

[51 FR 28709, Aug. 11, 1986]

§ 2.2 Definitions.

(a) *The Act* as used in this part means the Trademark Act of 1946, 60 Stat. 427, as amended, codified in 15 U.S.C. 1051 et seq.

(b) *Entity* as used in this part includes both natural and juristic persons.

[54 FR 37588, Sept. 11, 1989]

§ 2.6 Trademark fees.

The following fees and charges are established by the Patent and Trademark Office for trademark cases:

(a) For filing an application, per class ... $175.00
(b) For filing an application for renewal of a registration, per class ... 300.00
(c) For filing to publish a mark under section 12(c), per class ... 100.00
(d) For issuing a new certificate of registration upon request of assignee ... 100.00
(e) For a certificate of correction of registrant's error ... 100.00
(f) For filing a disclaimer to a registration ... 100.00
(g) For filing an amendment to a registration ... 100.00
(h) For filing an affidavit under § 8 of the Act, per class ... 100.00
(i) For filing an affidavit under § 15 of the Act, per class ... 100.00
(j) For filing a combined affidavit under §§ 8 and 15 of the Act, per class ... 200.00
(k) For petitions to the Commissioner ... 100.00
(l) For filing petition to cancel or notice of opposition, per class ... 200.00
(m) For ex parte appeal to the Trademark Trial and Appeal Board, per class ... 100.00
(n) For printed copy of registered mark, copy only ... 1.50
  Copy showing title and/or status ... 6.50
(o) For certifying trademark records, per certificate ... 3.50
  For expedited handling of such certification, per record requested ... 25.00
(p) For photocopies or other reproductions of records, drawings, or printed material, per page of the material copied ... 0.30
(q) For recording trademark assignments and agreements or other papers relating to the property in a registration or application, per mark ... 8.00
(r) For abstracts of title to each registration or application, including the search ... 12.00
(s) For special service handling of late filed fees in connection with a renewal ... 100.00
(t) For items and services that the Commissioner finds may be supplied, for which fees are not specified, such charges as may be determined by the Commissioner with respect to each such item or service ... actual cost
(u) For filing an amendment to allege use under section 1(c) of the Act or a statement of use under section 1(d)(1) of the Act, per class ... 100.00
(v) For filing a request under section 1(d)(2) of the Act for a six-month extension of time for filing a statement of use under section 1(d)(1) of the Act, per class ... 100.00
(w) Marginal cost, paid in advance, for each hour of terminal session time, including print time, using T-Search capabilities, prorated for the actual time used. The Commissioner may waive the payment by an individual for access to T-Search upon a showing of need or hardship, and if such waiver is in the public interest ... 40.00
(x) Marginal cost, for each printed page generated from the T-Search terminal ... 0.10

(35 U.S.C. 6; 15 U.S.C. 1113, 1123)

[47 FR 41282, Sept. 17, 1982, as amended at 51 FR 28057, Aug. 4, 1986; 54 FR 6904, Feb. 15, 1989; 54 FR 37588, Sept. 11, 1989; 54 FR 50949, Dec. 11, 1989]

REPRESENTATION BY ATTORNEYS OR OTHER AUTHORIZED PERSONS

AUTHORITY: Secs. 2.11 to 2.19 also issued under 35 U.S.C. 31, 32.

§ 2.11 Applicants may be represented by an attorney.

The owner of a trademark may file and prosecute his or her own application for registration of such trademark, or he or she may be represented by an attorney or other individual authorized to practice in trademark cases under § 10.14 of this subchapter. The Patent and Trademark Office cannot aid in the selection of an attorney or other representative.

[50 FR 5171, Feb. 6, 1985]

§ 2.12—2.16 [Reserved]

§ 2.17 Recognition for representation.

(a) When an attorney as defined in § 10.1(c) of this subchapter acting in a representative capacity appears in person or signs a paper in practice before the Patent and Trademark Office in a trademark case, his or her personal appearance or signature shall constitute a representation to the Patent and Trademark Office that, under the provisions of § 10.14 and the law he or she is authorized to represent the particular party in whose behalf he or she acts. Further proof of authority to act in a representative capacity may be required.

(b) Before any non-lawyer will be allowed to take action of any kind in any application or proceeding, a written authorization from the applicant, party to the proceeding, or other person entitled to prosecute such application or proceeding must be filed therein.

[30 FR 13193, Oct. 16, 1965, as amended at 50 FR 5171, Feb. 6, 1985]

§ 2.18 Correspondence, with whom held.

Correspondence will be sent to the applicant or a party to a proceeding at its address unless papers are transmitted by an attorney at law, or a written power of attorney is filed, or written authorization of other person entitled to be recognized is filed, or the applicant or party designates in writing another address to which correspondence is to be sent, in which event correspondence will be sent to the attorney at law transmitting the papers, or to the attorney at law designated in the power of attorney, or to the other person designated in the written authorization, or to the address designated by the applicant or party for correspondence. Correspondence will continue to be sent to such address until the applicant or party, or the attorney at law or other authorized representative of the applicant or party, indicates in writing that correspondence is to be sent to another address. Correspondence will be sent to the domestic representative of a foreign applicant unless the application is being prosecuted by an attorney at law or other qualified person duly authorized, in which event correspondence will be sent to the attorney at law or other qualified person duly authorized. Double correspondence will not be undertaken by the Patent and Trademark Office, and if more than one attorney at law or other authorized representative appears or signs a paper, the Office reply will be sent to the address already established in the file until another correspondence address is specified by the applicant or party or by the attorney or other authorized representative of the applicant or party.

[54 FR 37588, Sept. 11, 1989]

§ 2.19 Revocation of power of attorney or of other authorization to represent; withdrawal.

(a) Authority to represent an applicant or a party to a proceeding may be revoked at any stage in the proceedings of a case upon notification to the Commissioner; and when it is so revoked, the Office will communicate directly with the applicant or party to the proceeding or with such other qualified person as may be authorized. The Patent and Trademark Office will notify the person affected of the revocation of his or her authorization.

(b) An individual authorized to represent an applicant or party in a trademark case may withdraw upon application to and approval by the Commissioner.

[50 FR 5171, Feb. 6, 1985]

DECLARATIONS

§ 2.20 Declarations in lieu of oaths.

The applicant or member of the firm or an officer of the corporation or association making application for registration or filing a document in the Patent and Trademark Office relating to a mark may, in lieu of the oath, affidavit, verification, or sworn statement required from him, in those instances prescribed in the individual rules, file a declaration that all statements made of his own knowledge are true and that all statements made on information and belief are believed to be true, if, and only if, the declarant is, on the same paper, warned that willful false statements and the like are punishable by fine or imprisonment, or both (18 U.S.C. 1001), and may jeopardize the validity of the application or document or any registration resulting therefrom.

[31 FR 5261, Apr. 1, 1966]

APPLICATION FOR REGISTRATION

AUTHORITY: Secs. 2.21 to 2.47 also issued under sec. 1, 60 Stat. 427; 15 U.S.C. 1051.

§ 2.21 Requirements for receiving a filing date.

(a) Materials submitted as an application for registration of a mark will not be accorded a filing date as an application until all of the following elements are received:

(1) Name of the applicant;

(2) A name and address to which communications can be directed;

(3) A drawing of the mark sought to be registered substantially meeting all the requirements of §2.52;

(4) An identification of goods or services;

(5) A basis for filing:

(i) A date of first use of the mark in commerce, and at least one specimen or facsimile of the mark as used, in an application under section 1(a) of the Act, or

(ii) A claim of a bona fide intention to use the mark in commerce and a certification or certified copy of the foreign registration on which the application is based in an application under section 44(e) of the Act, or

(iii) A claim of a bona fide intention to use the mark in commerce and a claim of the benefit of a prior foreign application in an application filed in accordance with section 44(d) of the Act, or

(iv) A claim of a bona fide intention to use the mark in commerce in an application under section 1(b) of the Act;

(6) A verification or declaration in accordance with § 2.33(b) signed by the applicant;

(7) The required filing fee for at least one class of goods or services. Compliance with one or more of the rules relating to the elements specified above may be required before the application is further processed.

(b) The filing date of the application is the date on which all of the elements set forth in paragraph (a) of this section are received in the Patent and Trademark Office.

(c) If the papers and fee submitted as an application do not satisfy all of the requirements specified in paragraph (a) of this section, the papers will not be considered to constitute an application and will not be given a filing date. The Patent and Trademark Office will return the papers and any fee submitted therewith to the person who submitted the papers. The Office will notify the person to whom the papers are returned of the defect or defects which prevented their being considered to be an application.

[47 FR 38695, Sept. 2, 1982, as amended at 51 FR 29921, Aug. 21, 1986; 54 FR 37588, Sept. 11, 1989]

§ 2.23 Serial number.

Applications will be given a serial number as received, and the applicant will be informed of the serial number and the filing date of the application.

[37 FR 931, Jan. 21, 1972]

§ 2.24 Designation of representative by foreign applicant.

If an applicant is not domiciled in the United States, the applicant must designate by a written document filed in the Patent and Trademark Office the name and address of some person resident in the United States on whom may be served notices or process in proceedings affecting the mark. If this document does not accompany or form part of the application, it will be required and registration refused unless it is supplied. Official communications of the Patent and Trademark Office will be addressed to the domestic representative unless the application is being prosecuted by an attorney at law or other qualified person duly authorized, in which event Official communications will be sent to the attorney at law or other qualified person duly authorized. The mere designation of a domestic representative does not authorize the person designated to prosecute the application unless qualified under paragraph (a), (b) or (c) of § 10.14 of this subchapter and authorized under § 2.17(b).

[54 FR 37588, Sept. 11, 1989]

§ 2.25 Papers not returnable.

After an application is filed the papers will not be returned for any purpose whatever; but the Office will furnish copies to the applicant upon request and payment of the fee.

§ 2.26 Use of old drawing in new application.

In an application filed in place of an abandoned or rejected application, or in an application for reregistration (§ 2.158), a new complete application is required, but the old drawing, if suitable, may be used. The application must be accompanied by a request for the transfer of the drawing, and by a permanent photographic copy, or an order for such copy, of the drawing to be placed in the original file. A drawing so transferred, or to be transferred, cannot be amended.

§ 2.27 Pending trademark application index; access to applications.

(a) An index of pending applications including the name and address of the applicant, a reproduction or description of the mark, the goods or services with which the mark is used, the class number, the dates of use, and the serial number and filing date of the application will be available for public inspection as soon as practicable after filing.

(b) Except as provided in paragraph (e) of this section, access to the file of a particular pending application will be permitted prior to publication under § 2.80 upon written request.

(c) Decisions of the Commissioner and the Trademark Trial and Appeal Board in applications and proceedings relating thereto are published or available for inspection or publication.

(d) Except as provided in paragraph (e) of this section, after a mark has been registered, or published for opposition, the file of the application and all proceedings relating thereto are available for public inspection and copies of the papers may be furnished upon paying the fee therefor.

(e) Anything ordered to be filed under seal pursuant to a protective order issued or made by any court or by the Trademark Trial and Appeal Board in any proceeding involving an application or a registration shall be kept confidential and shall not be made available for public inspection or copying unless otherwise ordered by the court or the Board, or unless the party protected by the order voluntarily discloses the matter subject thereto. When possible, only confidential portions of filings with the Board shall be filed under seal.

[36 FR 25406, Dec. 31, 1971, as amended at 48 FR 23134, May 23, 1983; 48 FR 27225, June 14, 1983]

THE WRITTEN APPLICATION

§ 2.31 Application must be in English.

The application must be in the English language and plainly written on but one side of the paper. It is preferable that the application be on letter-size (i.e., 8½ inches, 21.6 cm., by 11 inches, 27.9 cm.) paper, typewritten double spaced, with at least a one and one-half inch (3.8 cm.) margin on the left-hand side and top of the page.

[54 FR 37589, Sept. 11, 1989]

§ 2.32 Application to be signed and sworn to or include a declaration by applicant.

(a) The application must be made to the Commissioner of Patents and Trademarks and must be signed and verified (sworn to) or include a declaration in accordance with § 2.20 by the applicant or by a member of the firm or an officer of the corporation or association applying.

(b) Re-executed papers or a statement which is verified or which includes a declaration in accordance with § 2.20 of continued use of the mark may be required when the application has not been filed in the Patent and Trademark Office within a reasonable time after the date of execution.

(c) The signature to the application must be the correct name of the applicant, since the name will appear in the certificate of registration precisely as it is signed to the application. The name of the applicant, wherever it appears in the papers of the application, will be made to agree with the name as signed.

§ 2.33 **Requirements for written application.**

(a)(1) The application shall include a request for registration and shall specify:

(i) The name of the applicant;

(ii) The citizenship of the applicant; if the applicant is a partnership, the state or nation under the laws of which the partnership is organized and the names and citizenship of the general partners or, if the applicant is a corporation or association, the state or nation under the laws of which the corporation or association is organized;

(iii) The domicile and post office address of the applicant;

(iv) In an application under section 1(a) of the Act, that the applicant has adopted and is using the mark shown in the accompanying drawing, or, in an application under section 1(b) or 44 of the Act, that the applicant has a bona fide intention to use the mark shown in the accompanying drawing in commerce;

(v) In an application under section 1(a) of the Act, the particular goods or services on or in connection with which the mark is used or, in an application under section 1(b) or 44 of the Act, the particular goods or services on or in connection with which the applicant has a bona fide intention to use the mark, which in an application under section 44 may not exceed the scope of the goods or services covered by the foreign application or registration;

(vi) The class of goods or services according to the official classification, if known to the applicant;

(vii) In an application under section 1(a) of the Act, the date of applicant's first use of the mark as a trademark or service mark on or in connection with goods or services specified in the application and the date of applicant's first use in commerce of the mark as a trademark or service mark on or in connection with goods or services specified in the application, specifying the nature of such commerce (see § 2.38);

(viii) In an application under section 44(e) of the Act for registration of a mark duly registered in the applicant's country of origin, as that term is defined in section 44(c), accompanying the application, a certificate of the trademark office of the applicant's country of origin showing that the mark has been registered in such country and also showing the mark, the goods or services for which the mark is registered, the date of filing of the application on the basis of which registration was granted and that said registration is in full force and effect and, if the certificate is not in the English language, a translation thereof;

(ix) In an application claiming the benefit of a foreign application in accordance with section 44(d) of the Act, compliance with the requirements of § 2.39;

(x) In an application under section 1(a) of the Act, the mode, manner or method of applying, affixing or otherwise using the mark on or in connection with the goods or services specified or, in an application under section 1(b) of the Act, the intended mode, manner or method of applying, affixing or otherwise using the mark on or in connection with the goods or services specified.

(2) If more than one item of goods or services is specified in the application, the dates of use required in paragraph (a)(1)(vii) of this section need be for only one of the items specified, provided the particular item to which the dates apply is designated.

(3) The word *commerce* as used throughout this part means commerce

which may lawfully be regulated by Congress, as specified in section 45 of the Act.

(b)(1) In an application under section 1(a) of the Act, the application must include averments to the effect that the applicant is believed to be the owner of the mark sought to be registered; that the mark is in use in commerce, specifying the nature of such commerce; that no other entity, to the best of the declarant's knowledge and belief, has the right to use such mark in commerce, either in the identical form or in such near resemblance as to be likely, when applied to the goods or services of such other entity, to cause confusion, or to cause mistake, or to deceive; that the specimens or facsimiles show the mark as used on or in connection with the goods or services; and that the facts set forth in the application are true; or

(2) In an application under section 1(b) or 44 of the Act, the application must include averments to the effect that the applicant is believed to be the owner of the mark sought to be registered; that the applicant has a bona fide intention to use the mark in commerce on or in connection with the specified goods or services; that no other entity, to the best of the declarant's knowledge and belief, has the right to use such mark in commerce, either in the identical form or in such near resemblance as to be likely, when applied to the goods or services of such other entity, to cause confusion, or to cause mistake, or to deceive; and that the facts set forth in the application are true.

(c) For an application for the registration of a mark for goods or services falling within multiple classes, see § 2.86.

(d) An applicant may not file under both sections 1(a) and 1(b) of the Act in a single application, nor may an applicant in an application under section 1(a) of the Act amend that application to seek registration under section 1(b) of the Act.

[51 FR 28709, Aug. 11, 1986, as amended at 54 FR 37589, Sept. 11, 1989; 54 FR 46231, Nov. 2, 1989]

§ 2.35 Description of mark.

A description of the mark, which must be acceptable to the Examiner of Trademarks, may be included in the application, and must be included if required by the examiner. If the mark is displayed in color or a color combination, the colors should be described in the application.

§ 2.36 Identification of prior registrations.

Prior registrations of the same or similar marks owned by the applicant should be identified in the application.

§ 2.37 Authorization for representation; U.S. representative.

The authorization of a qualified person to represent applicant (§ 2.17(b)) and the designation of a domestic representative (§ 2.24) may be included as a paragraph or paragraphs in the application.

[41 FR 758, Jan. 5, 1976]

§ 2.38 Use by predecessor or by related companies.

(a) If the first use, the date of which is required by paragraph (a)(1)(vii) of § 2.33, was by a predecessor in title, or by a related company (sections 5 and 45 of the Act), and such use inures to the benefit of the applicant, the date of such first use may be asserted with a statement that such first use was by the predecessor in title or by the related company as the case may be.

(b) If the mark is not in fact being used by the applicant but is being used by one or more related companies whose use inures to the benefit of the applicant under section 5 of the Act, such facts must be indicated in the application.

(c) The Office may require such details concerning the nature of the relationship and such proofs as may be necessary and appropriate for the purpose of showing that the use by related companies inures to the benefit of the applicant and does not affect the validity of the mark.

(Sec. 5, 60 Stat. 429; 15 U.S.C. 1055)

[30 FR 13193, Oct. 16, 1965, as amended at 54 FR 37589, Sept. 11, 1989]

§ 2.39 Priority claim based on foreign application.

(a) An application claiming the benefit of a foreign application in accordance with section 44(d) of the Act shall specify the filing date and country of the first regularly filed foreign application or, if the application is based upon a subsequent regularly filed application in the same foreign country, the application shall so state and shall show that any prior filed application has been withdrawn, abandoned or otherwise disposed of, without having been laid open to public inspection and without having any rights outstanding, and has not served as a basis for claiming a right of priority.

(b) Before the application can be approved for publication, a basis for registration under section 1(a), 1(b) or 44(e) of the Act must be established.

[54 FR 37589, Sept. 11, 1989]

§ 2.41 Proof of distinctiveness under section 2(f).

(a) When registration is sought of a mark which would be unregistrable by reason of section 2(e) of the Act but which is said by applicant to have become distinctive in commerce of the goods or services set forth in the application, applicant may, in support of registrability, submit with the application, or in response to a request for evidence or to a refusal to register, affidavits, or declarations in accordance with § 2.20, depositions, or other appropriate evidence showing duration, extent and nature of use in commerce and advertising expenditures in connection therewith (identifying types of media and attaching typical advertisements), and affidavits, or declarations in accordance with § 2.20, letters or statements from the trade or public, or both, or other appropriate evidence tending to show that the mark distinguishes such goods.

(b) In appropriate cases, ownership of one or more prior registrations on the Principal Register or under the Act of 1905 of the same mark may be accepted as prima facie evidence of distinctiveness. Also, if the mark is said to have become distinctive of applicant's goods by reason of substantially exclusive and continuous use in commerce thereof by applicant for the five years before the date on which the claim of distinctiveness is made, a showing by way of statements which are verified or which include declarations in accordance with § 2.20, in the application may, in appropriate cases, be accepted as prima facie evidence of distinctiveness. In each of these situations, however, further evidence may be required.

[54 FR 37590, Sept. 11, 1989]

§ 2.42 Concurrent use.

An application for registration as a lawful concurrent user shall specify and contain all the elements required by the preceding sections. The applicant in addition shall state in the application the area, the goods, and the mode of use for which applicant seeks registration; and also shall state, to the extent of the applicant's knowledge, the concurrent lawful use of the mark by others, setting forth their names and addresses; registrations issued to or applications filed by such others, if any; the areas of such use; the goods on or in connection with which such use is made; the mode of such use; and the periods of such use.

[54 FR 34897, Aug. 22, 1989]

§ 2.43 Service mark.

In an application to register a service mark, the application shall specify and contain all the elements required by the preceding sections for trademarks, but shall be modified to relate to services instead of to goods wherever necessary.

(Sec. 3, 60 Stat. 429; 15 U.S.C. 1052)

§ 2.44 Collective mark.

(a) In an application to register a collective mark under section 1(a) of the Act, the application shall specify and contain all applicable elements required by the preceding sections for trademarks, but shall, in addition, specify the class of persons entitled to use the mark, indicating their relationship to the applicant, and the nature of the applicant's control over the use of the mark.

(b) In an application to register a collective mark under section 1(b) or

44 of the Act, the application shall specify and contain all applicable elements required by the preceding sections for trademarks, but shall, in addition, specify the class of persons intended to be entitled to use the mark, indicating what their relationship to the applicant will be, and the nature of the control applicant intends to exercise over the use of the mark.

[54 FR 37590, Sept. 11, 1989]

§ 2.45   Certification mark.

(a) In an application to register a certification mark under section 1(a) of the Act, the application shall specify and contain all applicable elements required by the preceding sections for trademarks. It shall, in addition, specify the manner in which and the conditions under which the certification mark is used; it shall allege that the applicant exercises legitimate control over the use of the mark and that the applicant is not engaged in the production or marketing of the goods or services to which the mark is applied.

(b) In an application to register a certification mark under section 1(b) or 44 of the Act, the application shall specify and contain all applicable elements required by the preceding sections for trademarks. It shall, in addition, specify the manner in which and the conditions under which the certification mark is intended to be used; it shall allege that the applicant intends to exercise legitimate control over the use of the mark and that the applicant will not engage in the production or marketing of the goods or services to which the mark is applied.

[54 FR 37590, Sept. 11, 1989]

§ 2.46   Principal Register.

All applications will be treated as seeking registration on the Principal Register unless otherwise stated in the application. Service marks, collective marks, and certification marks, registrable in accordance with the applicable provisions of section 2 of the Act, are registered on the Principal Register.

§ 2.47   Supplemental Register.

(a) In an application to register on the Supplemental Register under sec-tion 23 of the Act, the application shall so indicate and shall specify that the mark has been in lawful use in commerce, specifying the nature of such commerce, by the applicant.

(b) In an application to register on the Supplemental Register under section 44 of the Act, the application shall so indicate. The statement of lawful use in commerce may be omitted.

(c) A mark in an application to register on the Principal Register under section 1(b) of the Act is eligible for registration on the Supplemental Register only after an acceptable amendment to allege use under § 2.76 or statement of use under § 2.88 has been timely filed.

(d) An application for registration on the Supplemental Register must conform to the requirements for registration on the Principal Register under section 1(a) of the Act, so far as applicable.

[54 FR 37590, Sept. 11, 1989]

DRAWING

AUTHORITY: Secs. 2.51 to 2.55 also issued under sec. 1, 60 Stat. 427; 15 U.S.C. 1051.

§ 2.51   Drawing required.

(a)(1) In an application under section 1(a) of the Act, the drawing of the trademark shall be a substantially exact representation of the mark as used on or in connection with the goods; or

(2) In an application under section 1(b) of the Act, the drawing of the trademark shall be a substantially exact representation of the mark as intended to be used on or in connection with the goods specified in the application, and once an amendment to allege use under § 2.76 or a statement of use under § 2.88 has been filed, the drawing of the trademark shall be a substantially exact representation of the mark as used on or in connection with the goods; or

(3) In an application under section 44 of the Act, the drawing of the trademark shall be a substantially exact representation of the mark as it appears in the drawing in the registration certificate of a mark duly regis-

tered in the country of origin of the applicant.

(b)(1) In an application under section 1(a) of the Act, the drawing of a service mark shall be a substantially exact representation of the mark as used in the sale or advertising of the services; or

(2) In an application under section 1(b) of the Act, the drawing of a service mark shall be a substantially exact representation of the mark as intended to be used in the sale or advertising of the services specified in the application and, once an amendment to allege use under § 2.76 or a statement of use under § 2.88 has been filed, the drawing of the service mark shall be a substantially exact representation of the mark as used in the sale or advertising of the services; or

(3) In an application under section 44 of the Act, the drawing of a service mark shall be a substantially exact representation of the mark as it appears in the drawing in the registration certificate of a mark duly registered in the country of origin of applicant.

(c) The drawing of a mark may be dispensed with in the case of a mark not capable of representation by a drawing, but in any such case the application must contain an adequate description of the mark.

(d) Broken lines should be used in the drawing of a mark to show placement of the mark on the goods, or on the packaging, or to show matter not claimed as part of the mark, or both, as appropriate. In an application to register a mark with three-dimensional features, the drawing shall depict the mark in perspective in a single rendition.

(e) If the application is for the registration of only a word, letter or numeral, or any combination thereof, not depicted in special form, the drawing may be the mark typed in capital letters on paper, otherwise complying with the requirements of § 2.52.

[54 FR 37590, Sept. 11, 1989]

§ 2.52 **Requirements for drawings.**

(a) *Character of drawing.* All drawings, except as otherwise provided, must be made with the pen or by a process which will provide high definition upon reproduction. A photolithographic reproduction or printer's proof copy may be used if otherwise suitable. Every line and letter, including color lining and lines used for shading, must be black. All lines must be clean, sharp, and solid, and must not be fine or crowded. Gray tones or tints may not be used for surface shading or any other purpose. The requirements of this paragraph are not necessary in the case of drawings permitted and filed in accordance with paragraph (e) of § 2.51.

(b) *Paper and ink.* The drawing must be made upon paper which is flexible, strong, smooth, nonshiny, white and durable. A good grade of bond paper is suitable; however, water marks should not be prominent. India ink or its equivalent in quality must be used for pen drawings to secure perfectly black solid lines. The use of white pigment to cover lines is not acceptable.

(c) *Size of paper and margins.* The size of the sheet on which a drawing is made must be 8 to 8½ inches (20.3 to 21.6 cm.) wide and 11 inches (27.9 cm.) long. One of the shorter sides of the sheet should be regarded as its top. It is preferable that the drawing be 2.5 inches (6.1 cm.) high and/or wide, but in no case may it be larger than 4 inches (10.3 cm.) high and 4 inches (10.3 cm) wide. If the amount of detail in the mark precludes a reduction to this size, such detail may be verbally described in the body of the application. There must be a margin of at least 1 inch (2.5 cm.) on the sides and bottom of the paper and at least 1 inch (2.5 cm.) between the drawing and the heading.

(d) *Heading.* Across the top of the drawing, beginning one inch (2.5 cm.) from the top edge and not exceeding one third of the sheet, there must be placed a heading, listing in separate lines, applicant's complete name; applicant's post office address; the dates of first use of the mark and first use of the mark in commerce in an application under section 1(a) of the Act; the priority filing date of the relevant foreign application in an application claiming the benefit of a prior foreign application in accordance with section 44(d) of the Act; and the goods or services recited in the application or a typical item of the goods or services if a number of items are recited in the application. This heading should be typewritten. If the drawing is in special form, the heading should include a description of the essential elements of the mark.

(e) *Linings for color.* Where color is a feature of a mark, the color or colors employed may be designated by means of conventional linings as shown in the following color chart:

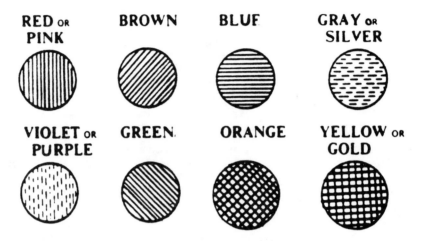

[51 FR 29921, Aug. 21, 1986, as amended at 54 FR 37591, Sept. 11, 1989; 54 FR 46231, Nov. ?, 1989]

§ 2.53   Transmission of drawings.

Drawings transmitted to the Patent and Trademark Office, other than those typed in accordance with § 2.51(e), should be sent flat, protected by a sheet of heavy binder's board, or should be rolled for transmission in a suitable mailing tube to prevent mutilation or folding.

[54 FR 37591, Sept. 11, 1989; 54 FR 46231, Nov. 2, 1989]

§ 2.56   Specimens.

An application under section 1(a) of the Act, an amendment to allege use under § 2.76, and a statement of use under § 2.88 must each include three specimens of the trademark as used on or in connection with the goods in commerce. The specimens shall be duplicates of the labels, tags, or containers bearing the trademark, or the displays associated with the goods and bearing the trademark (or if the nature of the goods makes use of such specimens impracticable then on documents associated with the goods or their sale), when made of suitable flat material and of a size not to exceed 8½ inches (21.6 cm.) wide and 11 inches (27.9 cm.) long.

[54 FR 37591, Sept. 11, 1989]

§ 2.57   Facsimiles.

(a) When, due to the mode of applying or affixing the trademark to the goods, or to the manner of using the mark on the goods, or to the nature of the mark, specimens as above stated cannot be furnished, three copies of a suitable photograph or other acceptable reproduction, not to exceed 8½ inches (21.6 cm.) wide and 11 inches (27.9 cm.) long, and clearly and legibly showing the mark a all matter used in connection therewith, shall be furnished.

(b) A purported facsimile which is merely a reproduction of the drawing submitted to comply with § 2.51 will not be considered to be a facsimile depicting the mark as used on or in connection with the goods or in connection with the services.

[54 FR 37591, Sept. 11, 1989]

§ **2.58 Specimens or facsimiles in the case of a service mark.**

(a) In the case of service marks, specimens or facsimiles as specified in §§ 2.56 and 2.57, of the mark as used in the sale or advertising of the services shall be furnished unless impossible because of the nature of the mark or the manner in which it is used, in which event some other representation acceptable to the Commissioner must be submitted.

(b) In the case of service marks not used in printed or written form, three audio cassette tape recordings will be accepted.

[30 FR 13193, Oct. 16, 1965, as amended at 51 FR 29922, Aug. 21, 1986]

EXAMINATION OF APPLICATION AND ACTION BY APPLICANTS

AUTHORITY: Secs. 2.61 to 2.69 also issued under sec. 12, 60 Stat. 432; 15 U.S.C. 1062.

§ **2.59 Filing substitute specimens.**

(a) In an application under section 1(a) of the Act, the applicant may submit substitute specimens of the mark as used on or in connection with the goods, or in the sale or advertising of the services, provided that any substitute specimens submitted are supported by applicant's affidavit or declaration in accordance with § 2.20 verifying that the substitute specimens were in use in commerce at least as early as the filing date of the application. The verification requirement shall not apply if the specimens are duplicates or facsimiles, such as photographs, of specimens already of record in the application.

(b) In an application under section 1(b) of the Act, after filing either an amendment to allege use under § 2.76 or a statement of use under § 2.88, the applicant may submit substitute specimens of the mark as used on or in connection with the goods, or in the sale or advertising of the services, provided that the use in commerce of any sub-stitute specimens submitted is supported by applicant's affidavit or declaration in accordance with § 2.20. In the case of a statement of use under § 2.88, the applicant must verify that the substitute specimens were in use in commerce prior to the filing of the statement of use or prior to the expiration of the time allowed to applicant for filing a statement of use.

[54 FR 37591, Sept. 11, 1989]

§ **2.61 Action by examiner.**

(a) Applications for registration, including amendments to allege use under section 1(c) of the Act, and statements of use under section 1(d) of the Act, will be examined and, if the applicant is found not entitled to registration for any reason, applicant will be notified and advised of the reasons therefor and of any formal requirements or objections.

(b) The examiner may require the applicant to furnish such information and exhibits as may be reasonably necessary to the proper examination of the application.

(c) Whenever it shall be found that two or more parties whose interests are in conflict are represented by the same attorney, each party and also the attorney shall be notified of this fact.

[30 FR 13193, Oct. 16, 1965, as amended at 37 FR 2880, Feb. 9, 1972; 54 FR 37592, Sept. 11, 1989]

§ **2.62 Period for response.**

The applicant has six months from the date of mailing of any action by the examiner to respond thereto. Such response may be made with or without amendment and must include such proper action by the applicant as the nature of the action and the condition of the case may require.

§ **2.63 Reexamination.**

(a) After response by the applicant, the application will be reexamined or reconsidered. If registration is again refused or any formal requirement[s] is repeated, but the examiner's action is not stated to be final, the applicant may respond again.

(b) After reexamination the applicant may respond by filing a timely petition to the Commissioner for relief from a formal requirement if: (1) The requirement is repeated, but the examiner's action is not made final, and the subject matter of the requirement is appropriate for petition to the Commissioner (see § 2.146(b)); or (2) the examiner's action is made final and such action is limited to subject matter appropriate for petition to the Commissioner. If the petition is denied, the applicant shall have until six months from the date of the Office action which repeated the requirement or made it final or thirty days from the date of the decision on the petition, whichever date is later, to comply with the requirement. A formal requirement which is the subject of a petition decided by the Commissioner may not subsequently be the subject of an appeal to the Trademark Trial and Appeal Board.

[48 FR 23134, May 23, 1983]

§ 2.64 Final action.

(a) On the first or any subsequent reexamination or reconsideration the refusal of the registration or the insistence upon a requirement may be stated to be final, whereupon applicant's response is limited to an appeal, or to a compliance with any requirement, or to a petition to the Commissioner if permitted by § 2.63(b).

(b) During the period between a final action and expiration of the time for filing an appeal, the applicant may request the examiner to reconsider the final action. The filing of a request for reconsideration will not extend the time for filing an appeal or petitioning the Commissioner, but normally the examiner will reply to a request for reconsideration before the end of the six-month period if the request is filed within three months after the date of the final action. Amendments accompanying requests for reconsideration after final action will be entered if they comply with the rules of practice in trademark cases and the Act of 1946.

(c)(1) If an applicant in an application under section 1(b) of the Act files an amendment to allege use under § 2.76 during the six-month response period after issuance of a final action, the examiner shall examine the amendment. The filing of such an amendment will not extend the time for filing an appeal or petitioning the Commissioner.

(2) If the amendment to allege use under § 2.76 is acceptable in all respects, the applicant will be notified of its acceptance.

(3) If, as a result of the examination of the amendment to allege use under § 2.76, the applicant is found not entitled to registration for any reason not previously stated, applicant will be notified and advised of the reasons and of any formal requirements or refusals. The Trademark Examining Attorney shall withdraw the final action previously issued and shall incorporate all unresolved refusals or requirements previously stated in the new non-final action.

[48 FR 23134, May 23, 1983, as amended at 54 FR 37592, Sept. 11, 1989]

§ 2.65 Abandonment.

(a) If an applicant fails to respond, or to respond completely, within six months after the date an action is mailed, the application shall be deemed to have been abandoned. A timely petition to the Commissioner pursuant to §§ 2.63(b) and 2.146 is a response which avoids abandonment of an application.

(b) When action by the applicant filed within the six-month response period is a bona fide attempt to advance the examination of the application and is substantially a complete response to the examiner's action, but consideration of some matter or compliance with some requirement has been inadvertently omitted, opportunity to explain and supply the omission may be given before the question of abandonment is considered.

(c) If an applicant in an application under section 1(b) of the Act fails to timely file a statement of use under § 2.88, the application shall be deemed to be abandoned.

[48 FR 23134, May 23, 1983, as amended at 54 FR 37592, Sept. 11, 1989]

§ 2.66 Revival of abandoned applications.

(a) An application abandoned for failure to timely respond, or for failure to timely file a statement of use under § 2.88 in an application under section 1(b) of the Act, may be revived as a pending application if it is shown to the satisfaction of the Commissioner that the delay was unavoidable.

(b) A petition to revive an application abandoned for failure to timely respond must be accompanied by:

(1) The required fee,

(2) A showing which is verified or which includes a declaration in accordance with § 2.20 of the causes of the delay, and

(3) The proposed response, unless a response has been previously filed.

(c) A petition to revive an application abandoned for failure to timely file a statement of use under § 2.88 in an application under section 1(b) of the Act must be accompanied by:

(1) The required petition fee,

(2) A showing which is verified or which includes a declaration in accordance with § 2.20 of the causes of the delay,

(3) The required fees for the number of requests (in accordance with § 2.89 for extensions of time to file a statement of use) which should have been filed if the application had not been abandoned, and

(4) Either a statement of use in accordance with § 2.88 (unless the same has been previously filed) or a request in accordance with § 2.89 for an extension of time to file a statement of use.

(d) The petition must be filed promptly. No petition to revive will be granted in an application under section 1(b) of the Act if granting the petition would permit the filing of a statement of use more than 36 months after the issuance of a notice of allowance under section 13(b)(2) of the Act.

[54 FR 37592, Sept. 11, 1989]

§ 2.67 Suspension of action by the Patent and Trademark Office.

Action by the Patent and Trademark Office may be suspended for a reasonable time for good and sufficient cause. The fact that a proceeding is pending before the Patent and Trademark Office or a court which is relevant to the issue of registrability of the applicant's mark, or the fact that the basis for registration is, under the provisions of section 44(e) of the Act, registration of the mark in a foreign country and the foreign application is

still pending, will be considered prima facie good and sufficient cause. An applicant's request for a suspension of action under this section filed within the 6-month response period (see § 2.62) may be considered responsive to the previous Office action. The first suspension is within the discretion of the Examiner of Trademarks and any subsequent suspension must be approved by the Commissioner.

[37 FR 3898, Feb. 24, 1972]

§ 2.68 Express abandonment (withdrawal) of application.

An application may be expressly abandoned by filing in the Patent and Trademark Office a written statement of abandonment or withdrawal of the application signed by the applicant, or the attorney or other person representing the applicant. Except as provided in § 2.135, the fact that an application has been expressly abandoned shall not, in any proceeding in the Patent and Trademark Office, affect any rights that the applicant may have in the mark which is the subject of the abandoned application.

[54 FR 34897, Aug. 22, 1989]

§ 2.69 Compliance with other laws.

When the sale or transportation of any product for which registration of a trademark is sought is regulated under an Act of Congress, the Patent and Trademark Office may make appropriate inquiry as to compliance with such Act for the sole purpose of determining lawfulness of the commerce recited in the application.

[54 FR 37592, Sept. 11, 1989]

§ 2.71 Amendments to correct informalities.

(a) The application may be amended to correct informalities, or to avoid objections made by the Patent and Trademark Office, or for other reasons arising in the course of examination.

(b) The identification of goods or services may be amended to clarify or limit the identification, but additions will not be permitted.

(c) If the verification or declaration filed with the application is defective, the defect may be corrected only by the submission of a substitute or supplemental verification or declaration in accordance with § 2.20. A verification or declaration required under §§ 2.21(a)(6), 2.76(e)(3) or 2.88(e)(3), to be properly signed, must be signed by the applicant, a member of the applicant firm, or an officer of the applicant corporation or association. A verification or declaration which is signed by a person having color of authority to sign, is acceptable for the purpose of determining the timely filing of the paper. Persons having color of authority to sign are those who have first-hand knowledge of the truth of the statements in the verification or declaration and who also have actual or implied authority to act on behalf of the applicant. However, a properly signed substitute verification or declaration must be submitted before the application will be approved for publication or registration, as the case may be.

(d)(1) No amendment to the dates of use will be permitted unless the amendment is supported by applicant's affidavit or declaration in accordance with § 2.20 and by such showing as may be required.

(2) In an application under section 1(a) of the Act, no amendment to specify a date of use which is subsequent to the filing date of the application will be permitted.

(3) In an application under section 1(b) of the Act, after the filing of a statement of use under § 2.88, no amendment will be permitted to the statement of use to recite dates of use which are subsequent to the expiration of the time allowed to applicant for filing a statement of use.

[54 FR 37592, Sept. 11, 1989]

§ 2.72 Amendments to description or drawing of the mark.

(a) Amendments may not be made to the description or drawing of the mark if the character of the mark is materially altered. The determination of whether a proposed amendment materially alters the character of the mark will be made by comparing the proposed amendment with the description or drawing of the mark as originally filed.

(b) In applications under section 1(a) of the Act, amendments to the description or drawing of the mark may be permitted only if warranted by the specimens (or facsimiles) as originally filed, or supported by additional specimens (or facsimiles) and a supplemental affidavit or declaration in accordance with § 2.20 alleging that the mark shown in the amended drawing was in use prior to the filing date of the application.

(c) In applications under section 1(b) of the Act, amendments to the description or drawing of the mark, which are filed after submission of an amendment to allege use under § 2.76 or a statement of use under § 2.88, may be permitted only if warranted by the specimens (or facsimiles) filed, or supported by additional specimens (or facsimiles) and a supplemental affidavit or declaration in accordance with § 2.20 alleging that the mark shown in the amended drawing is in use in commerce. In the case of a statement of use under § 2.88, applicant must verify that the mark shown in the amended drawing was in use in commerce prior to the filing of the statement of use or prior to the expiration of the time allowed to applicant for filing a statement of use.

(d) In applications under section 44 of the Act, amendments to the description or drawing of the mark may be permitted only if warranted by the description or drawing of the mark in the foreign registration certificate.

[54 FR 37593, Sept. 11, 1989]

§ 2.73 Amendment to recite concurrent use.

(a) An application under section 1(a) of the Act may be amended so as to be treated as an application for a concurrent registration, provided the application as amended satisfies the requirements of § 2.42. The examiner will determine whether the application, as amended, is acceptable.

(b) An application under section 1(b) of the Act may not be amended so as to be treated as an application for a concurrent registration until an acceptable amendment to allege use under § 2.76 or statement of use under § 2.88 has been filed in the application, after which time such an amendment may be made, provided the application as amended satisfies the requirements of § 2.42. The examiner will determine whether the application, as amended, is acceptable.

[54 FR 37593, Sept. 11, 1989]

§ 2.74 Form of amendment.

(a) In every amendment the exact word or words to be stricken out or inserted in the application must be specified and the precise point indicated where the deletion or insertion is to be made. Erasures, additions, insertions, or mutilations of the papers and records must not be made by the applicant or his attorney or agent.

(b) When an amendatory clause is amended, it must be wholly rewritten so that no interlineation or erasure will appear in the clause, as finally amended, when the application is passed to registration. If the number or nature of the amendments shall render it otherwise difficult to consider the case or to arrange the papers for printing or copying, or when otherwise desired to clarify the record, the examiner may require the entire statement to be rewritten.

§ 2.75 Amendment to change application to different register.

(a) An application for registration on the Principal Register under section 1(a) or 44 of the Act may be changed to an application for registration on the Supplemental Register and vice versa by amending the application to comply with the rules relating to the appropriate register, as the case may be.

(b) An application under section 1(b) of the Act may be amended to change the application to a different register only after submission of an acceptable amendment to allege use under § 2.76 or statement of use under § 2.88. When such an application is changed from the Principal Register to the Supplemental Register, the effective filing date of the application is the date of the filing of the allegation of use under section 1(c) or 1(d) of the Act.

[54 FR 37593, Sept. 11, 1989]

§ 2.76 Amendment to allege use.

(a) An application under section 1(b) of the Act may be amended to allege use of the mark in commerce under section 1(c) of the Act at any time between the filing of the application and the date the examiner approves the mark for publication or the date of expiration of the six-month response period after issuance of a final action. Thereafter, an allegation of use may be submitted only as a statement of use under § 2.88 after the issuance of a notice of allowance under section 13(b)(2) of the Act. If an amendment to allege use is filed outside the time period specified in this paragraph, it will be returned to the applicant.

(b) A complete amendment to allege use must include:

(1) A verified statement that the applicant is believed to be the owner of the mark sought to be registered and that the mark is in use in commerce, specifying the date of the applicant's first use of the mark and first use of the mark in commerce, the type of commerce, those goods or services specified in the application on or in connection with which the mark is in use in commerce and the mode or manner in which the mark is used on or in connection with such goods or services;

(2) Three specimens or facsimiles, conforming to the requirements of §§ 2.56, 2.57 and 2.58, of the mark as used in commerce; and

(3) The fee prescribed in § 2.6.

(c) An amendment to allege use may be filed only when the applicant has made use of the mark in commerce on or in connection with all of the goods or services, as specified in the application, for which applicant will seek registration in that application unless the amendment to allege use is accompanied by a request in accordance with § 2.87 to divide out from the application the goods or services to which the amendment pertains. If more than one item of goods or services is specified in the amendment to allege use, the dates of use required in paragraph (b)(1) of this section need be for only one of the items specified in each class, provided the particular item to which the dates apply is designated.

(d) The title "Amendment to allege use under § 2.76" should appear at the top of the first page of the paper.

(e) The Office will review a timely filed amendment to allege use to determine whether it meets the following minimum requirements:

(1) The fee prescribed in § 2.6;

(2) At least one specimen or facsimile of the mark as used in commerce; and

(3) A verification or declaration signed by the applicant stating that the mark is in use in commerce.

(f) A timely filed amendment to allege use which meets the minimum requirements specified in paragraph (e) of this section will be examined in accordance with §§ 2.61 through 2.69. If, as a result of the examination of the amendment to allege use, applicant is found not entitled to registration for any reason not previously stated, applicant will be so notified and advised of the reasons and of any formal requirements or refusals. The notification shall restate or incorporate by reference all unresolved refusals or requirements previously stated. The amendment to allege use may be amended in accordance with §§ 2.59 and 2.71 through 2.75. If the amendment to allege use is acceptable in all respects, the applicant will be notified of its acceptance. The filing of such an amendment shall not constitute a response to any outstanding action by the Trademark Examining Attorney.

(g) If the amendment to allege use is filed within the permitted time period but does not meet the minimum requirements specified in paragraph (e) of this section, applicant will be notified of the deficiency. The deficiency may be corrected provided the mark has not been approved for publication or the six-month response period after issuance of a final action has not expired. If an acceptable amendment to correct the deficiency is not filed prior to approval of the mark for publication or prior to the expiration of the six-month response period after issuance of a final action, the amendment will not be examined.

(h) An amendment to allege use may be withdrawn for any reason prior to approval of a mark for publication or

expiration of the six-month response period after issuance of a final action.

[54 FR 37593, Sept. 11, 1989]

§ 2.77 Amendments between notice of allowance and statement of use.

An application under section 1(b) of the Act may not be amended during the period between the issuance of the notice of allowance under section 13(b)(2) of the Act and the filing of a statement of use under § 2.88, except to delete specified goods or services. Other amendments filed during this period will be placed in the application file and considered when the statement of use is examined.

[54 FR 37594, Sept. 11, 1989]

PUBLICATION AND POST PUBLICATION

§ 2.80 Publication for opposition.

If, on examination or reexamination of an application for registration on the Principal Register, it appears that the applicant is entitled to have his mark registered, the mark will be published in the *Official Gazette* for opposition. The mark will also be published in the case of an application to be placed in interference or concurrent use proceedings, if otherwise registrable.

[41 FR 758, Jan. 5, 1976]

§ 2.81 Post publication.

(a) Except in an application under section 1(b) of the Act for which no amendment to allege use under § 2.76 has been submitted and accepted, if no opposition is filed within the time permitted or all oppositions filed are dismissed, and if no interference is declared and no concurrent use proceeding is instituted, the application will be prepared for issuance of the certificate of registration as provided in § 2.151.

(b) In an application under section 1(b) of the Act for which no amendment to allege use under § 2.76 has been submitted and accepted, if no opposition is filed within the time permitted or all oppositions filed are dismissed, and if no interference is declared, a notice of allowance will issue. The notice of allowance will state the serial number of the application, the name of the applicant, the correspondence address, the mark, the identification of goods or services, and the issue date of the notice of allowance. The mailing date that appears on the notice of allowance will be the issue date of the notice of allowance. Thereafter, the applicant shall submit a statement of use as provided in § 2.88.

[54 FR 37594, Sept. 11, 1989]

§ 2.82 Marks on Supplemental Register published only upon registration.

In the case of an application for registration on the Supplemental Register the mark will not be published for opposition but if it appears, after examination or reexamination, that the applicant is entitled to have the mark registered, a certificate of registration will issue as provided in § 2.151. The mark will be published in the "Official Gazette" when registered.

[54 FR 37594, Sept. 11, 1989]

§ 2.83 Conflicting marks.

(a) Whenever an application is made for registration of a mark which so resembles another mark or marks pending registration as to be likely to cause confusion or mistake or to deceive, the mark with the earliest effective filing date will be published in the "Official Gazette" for opposition if eligible for the Principal Register, or issued a certificate of registration if eligible for the Supplemental Register.

(b) In situations in which conflicting applications have the same effective filing date, the application with the earliest date of execution will be published in the "Official Gazette" for opposition or issued on the Supplemental Register.

(c) Action on the conflicting application which is not published in the *Official Gazette* for opposition or not issued on the Supplemental Register will be suspended by the Examiner of Trademarks until the published or issued application is registered or abandoned.

[37 FR 2880, Feb. 9, 1972, as amended at 54 FR 37594, Sept. 11, 1989]

§ 2.84 Jurisdiction over published applications.

(a) The examiner may exercise jurisdiction over an application up to the date the mark is published in the "Official Gazette." After publication of an application under section 1(a) or 44 of the Act the examiner may, with the permission of the Commissioner, exercise jurisdiction over the application. After publication of an application under section 1(b) of the Act, the examiner may exercise jurisdiction over the application after the issuance of the notice of allowance under section 13(b)(2) of the Act. After publication, and prior to issuance of a notice of allowance in an application under section 1(b), the examiner may, with the permission of the Commissioner, exercise jurisdiction over the application.

(b) After publication, but before the printing of the certificate of registration in an application under section 1(a) or 44 of the Act, or before the printing of the notice of allowance in an application under section 1(b) of the Act, an application which is not the subject of an *inter partes* proceeding before the Trademark Trial and Appeal Board may be amended if the amendment does not necessitate republication of the mark or issuance of an Office action. Otherwise, an amendment to such an application may be submitted only upon petition to the Commissioner to restore jurisdiction of the application to the examiner for consideration of the amendment and further examination. The amendment of an application which is the subject of an *inter partes* proceeding before the Trademark Trial and Appeal Board is governed by § 2.133.

[54 FR 37594, Sept. 11, 1989]

§ 2.85 Classification schedules.

(a) Section 6.1 of part 6 of this chapter specifies the system of classification for goods and services which applies for all statutory purposes to trademark applications filed in the Patent and Trademark Office on or after September 1, 1973, and to registrations issued on the basis of such applications. It shall not apply to applications filed on or before August 31,

1973, nor to registrations issued on the basis of such applications.

(b) With respect to applications filed on or before August 31, 1973, and registrations issued thereon, including older registrations issued prior to that date, the classification system under which the application was filed will govern for all statutory purposes, including, inter alia, the filing of petitions to revive, appeals, oppositions, petitions for cancellation, affidavits under section 8 and renewals, even though such petitions to revive, appeals, etc., are filed on or after September 1, 1973.

(c) Section 6.2 of part 6 of this chapter specifies the system of classification for goods and services which applies for all statutory purposes to all trademark applications filed in the Patent and Trademark Office on or before August 31, 1973, and to registrations issued on the basis of such applications, except when the registration may have been issued under a classification system prior to that set forth in § 6.2. Moreover, this classification will also be utilized for facilitating trademark searches until all pending and registered marks in the search file are organized on the basis of the international system of classification.

(d) Renewals filed on registrations issued under a prior classification system will be processed on the basis of that system.

(e) Where the amount of the fee received on filing an appeal in connection with an application or on an application for renewal or in connection with a petition for cancellation is sufficient for at least one class of goods or services but is less than the required amount because multiple classes in an application or registration are involved, the appeal or renewal application or petition for cancellation will not be refused on the ground that the amount of the fee was insufficient if the required additional amount of the fee is received in the Patent and Trademark Office within the time limit set forth in the notification of this defect by the Office, or if action is sought only for the number of classes equal to the number of fees submitted.

(f) Sections 6.3 and 6.4 specify the system of classification which applies to certification marks and collective membership marks.

(g) Classification schedules shall not limit or extend the applicant's rights.

(35 U.S.C. 6; 15 U.S.C. 1113, 1123)

[38 FR 14681, June 4, 1973, as amended at 39 FR 16885, May 10, 1974; 47 FR 41282, Sept. 17, 1982]

§ 2.86 Application may include multiple goods or services comprised in single class or multiple classes.

(a) An application may recite more than one item of goods, or more than one service, comprised in a single class, provided the goods or services are specifically identified and the applicant either has used the mark on or in connection with all of the specified goods or services, or has a bona fide intention to use the mark on or in connection with all of the specified goods or services.

(b) An application also may be filed to register the same mark for goods and/or services comprised in multiple classes, provided the goods or services are specifically identified; a fee equaling the sum of the fees for filing an application in each class is submitted; and the application includes either dates of use and three specimens for each class, or a statement of a bona fide intention to use the mark on or in connection with all of the goods or services specified in each class. An amendment to allege use under § 2.76 or a statement of use under § 2.88, filed in a multiple class application under section 1(b) of the Act, must include, for each class, the required fee, dates of use and three specimens. A single certificate of registration for the mark shall be issued, unless the application is divided pursuant to § 2.87.

(c) The applicant may not allege use as to certain goods or services and a bona fide intention to use as to other goods or services in the same application, regardless of the number of classes contained therein.

[54 FR 37594, Sept. 11, 1989]

§ 2.87 Dividing an application.

(a) An application may be physically divided into two or more separate applications upon submission by the applicant of a request therefor, in accordance with paragraph (c) of this section. In the case of a request to divide out some, but not all, of the goods or services in a class, a fee for each new separate application to be created by the division must be submitted. Any outstanding time period for action by the applicant in the original application at the time of the division will be applicable to each new separate application created by the division.

(b) A request to divide an application may be filed at any time between the filing of the application and the date the Trademark Examining Attorney approves the mark for publication or the date of expiration of the six-month response period after issuance of a final action; or during an opposition, upon motion granted by the Trademark Trial and Appeal Board. Additionally, a request to divide an application under section 1(b) of the Act may be filed with a statement of use under § 2.88 or at any time between the filing of a statement of use and the date the Trademark Examining Attorney approves the mark for registration or the date of expiration of the six-month response period after issuance of a final action.

(c) A request to divide an application should be made in a separate paper from any other amendment or response in the application. The title "Request to divide application." should appear at the top of the first page of the paper.

[54 FR 37595, Sept. 11, 1989]

POST NOTICE OF ALLOWANCE

§ 2.88 Filing statement of use after notice of allowance.

(a) In an application under section 1(b) of the Act, a statement of use, required under section 1(d) of the Act, must be filed within six months after issuance of a notice of allowance under section 13(b)(2) of the Act, or within an extension of time granted under § 2.89. A statement of use that is filed prior to issuance of a notice of allowance is premature, will not be considered, and will be returned to the applicant.

(b) A complete statement of use must include:

(1) A verified statement that the applicant is believed to be the owner of the mark sought to be registered and that the mark is in use in commerce, specifying the date of the applicant's first use of the mark and first use of the mark in commerce, the type of commerce, those goods or services specified in the notice of allowance on or in connection with which the mark is in use in commerce and the mode or manner in which the mark is used on or in connection with such goods or services;

(2) Three specimens or facsimiles, conforming to the requirements of §§ 2.56, 2.57 and 2.58, of the mark as used in commerce; and

(3) The fee prescribed in § 2.6.

(c) The statement of use may be filed only when the applicant has made use of the mark in commerce on or in connection with all of the goods or services, as specified in the notice of allowance, for which applicant will seek registration in that application, unless the statement of use is accompanied by a request in accordance with § 2.87 to divide out from the application the goods or services to which the statement of use pertains. If more than one item of goods or services is specified in the statement of use, the dates of use required in paragraph (b)(1) of this section need be for only one of the items specified in each class, provided the particular item to which the dates apply is designated.

(d) The title "Statement of use under § 2.88." should appear at the top of the first page of the paper.

(e) The Office will review a timely filed statement of use to determine whether it meets the following minimum requirements:

(1) The fee prescribed in § 2.6;

(2) At least one specimen or facsimile of the mark as used in commerce;

(3) A verification or declaration signed by the applicant stating that the mark is in use in commerce.

(f) A timely filed statement of use which meets the minimum requirements specified in paragraph (e) of this section will be examined in accordance with §§ 2.61 through 2.69. If, as a result of the examination of the statement of use, applicant is found not entitled to registration, applicant will be notified and advised of the reasons and of any formal requirements or refusals. The statement of use may be amended in accordance with §§ 2.59 and 2.71 through 2.75. If the statement of use is acceptable in all respects, the applicant will be notified of its acceptance.

(g) If the statement of use does not meet the minimum requirements specified in paragraph (e) of this section, applicant will be notified of the deficiency. If the time permitted for applicant to file a statement of use has not expired, applicant may correct the deficiency. After the filing of a statement of use during a permitted time period for such filing, the applicant may not withdraw the statement to return to the previous status of awaiting submission of a statement of use, regardless of whether it is in compliance with paragraph (e) of this section.

(h) The failure to timely file a statement of use which meets the minimum requirements specified in paragraph (e) of this section shall result in the abandonment of the application.

(i)(1) The goods or services specified in a statement of use must conform to those goods or services identified in the notice of allowance. An applicant may specify the goods or services by stating "those goods or services identified in the notice of allowance" or, if appropriate, "those goods or services identified in the notice of allowance except * * *" followed by an identification of the goods or services to be deleted.

(2) If any goods or services specified in the notice of allowance are omitted from the identification of goods or services in the statement of use, the Trademark Examining Attorney shall inquire about the discrepancy and permit the applicant to amend the statement of use to include any omitted goods or services, provided that the amendment is supported by a verification that the mark was in use in commerce, on or in connection with each of the goods or services sought to be included, prior to the expiration of the time allowed to applicant for filing a statement of use.

(3) The statement of use may be accompanied by a separate request to amend the identification of goods or services in the application, as stated in the notice of allowance, in accordance with § 2.71(b).

(j) The statement of use may be accompanied by a separate request to amend the drawing in the application, in accordance with §§ 2.51 and 2.72.

[54 FR 37595, Sept. 11, 1989]

§ 2.89 Extensions of time for filing a statement of use.

(a) The applicant may request a six-month extension of time to file the statement of use required under § 2.88 by submitting:

(1) A written request, before the expiration of the six-month period following the issuance of a notice of allowance under section 13(b)(2) of the Act;

(2) The fee prescribed in § 2.6; and

(3) A verified statement by the applicant that the applicant has a continued bona fide intention to use the mark in commerce, specifying those goods or services identified in the notice of allowance on or in connection with which the applicant has a continued bona fide intention to use the mark in commerce.

(b) The applicant may request further six-month extensions of time for filing the statement of use by submitting:

(1) A written request, prior to the expiration of a previously granted extension of time;

(2) The fee prescribed in § 2.6;

(3) A verified statement by the applicant that the applicant has a continued bona fide intention to use the mark in commerce, specifying those goods or services identified in the notice of allowance on or in connection with which the applicant has a continued bona fide intention to use the mark in commerce; and

(4) A showing of good cause, as specified in paragraph (d) of this section.

(c) Extensions of time under paragraph (b) of this section will be granted only in six-month increments and may not aggregate more than 24 months.

(d) The showing required by paragraph (b)(4) of this section must include:

(1) An allegation that the applicant has not yet made use of the mark in commerce on all the goods or services specified in the notice of allowance on or in connection with which the applicant has a continued bona fide intention to use the mark in commerce, and

(2) A statement of applicant's ongoing efforts to make use of the mark in commerce on or in connection with each of the goods or services specified in the verified statement of continued bona fide intention to use required under paragraph (b) of this section. Those efforts may include, without limitation, product or service research or development, market research, manufacturing activities, promotional activities, steps to acquire distributors, steps to obtain required governmental approval, or other similar activities. In the alternative, a satisfactory explanation for the failure to make such efforts must be submitted.

(e)(1) At the time of the filing of a statement of use, or during any time remaining in the existing six-month period in which a statement of use is filed, applicant may file one request, in accordance with paragraph (a) or (b) of this section, for a six-month extension of time for filing a statement of use, provided that the time requested would not extend beyond 36 months from the issuance of the notice of allowance. Thereafter, applicant may not request any further extensions of time.

(2) A request for an extension of time that is filed at the time of the filing of a statement of use, or during any time remaining in the existing six-month period in which a statement of use is filed, must comply with all the requirements of paragraph (a) of this section, if it is applicant's first extension request, or paragraph (b) of this section, if it is a second or subsequent extension request. However, in a request under paragraph (b) of this section, applicant may satisfy the requirement for a showing of good cause by asserting that applicant believes that it has made valid use of the mark in commerce, as evidenced by the submitted statement of use, but that if the statement of use is found by the Patent and Trademark Office to be fatally defective, applicant will need additional time in which to file a new statement of use.

(f) The goods or services specified in a request for an extension of time for filing a statement of use must conform to those goods or services identified in the notice of allowance. Any goods or services specified in the notice of allowance which are omitted from the identification of goods or services in the request for extension of time will be presumed to be deleted and the applicant may not thereafter request that the deleted goods or services be reinserted in the application. If appropriate, an applicant may specify the goods or services by stating "those goods or services identified in the notice of allowance" or "those goods or services identified in the notice of allowance except * * *" followed by an identification of the goods or services to be deleted.

(g) The applicant will be notified of the grant or denial of a request for an extension of time, and of the reasons for a denial. Failure to notify the applicant of the grant or denial of the request prior to the expiration of the existing period or requested extension does not relieve the applicant of the responsibility of timely filing a statement of use under § 2.88. If, after denial of an extension request, there is time remaining in the existing six-month period for filing a statement of use, applicant may submit a substitute request for extension of time. Otherwise, the only recourse available after denial of a request for an extension of time is a petition to the Commissioner in accordance with §§ 2.66 or 2.146. A petition from the denial of a request for an extension of time to file a statement of use shall be filed within one month from the date of mailing of the denial of the request. If the petition is granted, the term of the requested six-month extension which was the subject of the petition will run from the date of the expiration of the previously existing six-month period for filing a statement of use.

[54 FR 37595, Sept. 11, 1989]

INTERFERENCES AND CONCURRENT USE
PROCEEDINGS

AUTHORITY: Secs. 2.91 to 2.99 also issued under secs. 16, 17, 60 Stat. 434; 15 U.S.C. 1066, 1067.

§ 2.91 Declaration of interference.

(a) An interference will not be declared between two applications or between an application and a registration except upon petition to the Commissioner. Interferences will be declared by the Commissioner only upon a showing of extraordinary circumstances which would result in a party being unduly prejudiced without an interference. In ordinary circumstances, the availability of an opposition or cancellation proceeding to the party will be deemed to remove any undue prejudice.

(b) Registrations and applications to register on the Supplemental Register, registrations under the Act of 1920, and registrations of marks the right to use of which has become incontestable are not subject to interference.

[37 FR 2881, Feb. 9, 1972, as amended at 54 FR 34897, Aug. 22, 1989]

§ 2.92 Preliminary to interference.

An interference which has been declared by the Commissioner will not be instituted by the Trademark Trial and Appeal Board until the Examiner of Trademarks has determined that the marks which are to form the subject matter of the controversy are registrable, and all of the marks have been published in the Official Gazette for opposition.

[54 FR 34897, Aug. 22, 1989]

§ 2.93 Institution of interference.

An interference is instituted by the mailing of a notice of interference to the parties. The notice shall be sent to each applicant, in care of the applicant's attorney or other representative of record, if any, and if one of the parties is a registrant, the notice shall be sent to the registrant or the registrant's assignee of record. The notice shall give the name and address of every adverse party and of the adverse party's attorney or other authorized representative, if any, together with the serial number and date of filing and publication of each of the applications, or the registration number and date of issuance of each of the registrations, involved.

[54 FR 34897, Aug. 22, 1989]

§§ 2.94—2.95 [Reserved]

§ 2.96 Issue; burden of proof.

The issue in an interference between applications is normally priority of use, but the rights of the parties to registration may also be determined. The party whose application involved in the interference has the latest filing date is the junior party and has the burden of proof. When there are more than two parties to an interference, a party shall be a junior party to and shall have the burden of proof as against every other party whose application involved in the interference has an earlier filing date. If the involved applications of any parties have the same filing date, the application with the latest date of execution will be deemed to have the latest filing date and that applicant will be the junior party. The issue in an interference between an application and a registration shall be the same, but in the event the final decision is adverse to the registrant, a registration to the applicant will not be authorized so long as the interfering registration remains on the register.

[48 FR 23135, May 23, 1983; 48 FR 27225 June 14, 1983]

§ 2.97 [Reserved]

§ 2.98 Adding party to interference.

A party may be added to an interference only upon petition to the Commissioner by that party. If an application which is or might be the subject of a petition for addition to an interference is not added, the examiner may suspend action on the application pending termination of the interference proceeding.

[48 FR 23135, May 23, 1983]

§ 2.99 Application to register as concurrent user.

(a) An application for registration as a lawful concurrent user will be examined in the same manner as other applications for registration.

(b) When it is determined that the mark is ready for publication, the applicant may be required to furnish as many copies of his application, specimens and drawing as may be necessary for the preparation of notices for each applicant, registrant or user specified as a concurrent user in the application for registration.

(c) Upon receipt of the copies required by paragraph (b) of this section, the examiner shall forward the application for concurrent use registration for publication in the *Official Gazette* as provided by § 2.80. If no opposition is filed, or if all oppositions that are filed are dismissed or withdrawn, the Trademark Trial and Appeal Board shall prepare a notice for the applicant for concurrent use registration and for each applicant, registrant or user specified as a concurrent user in the application. The notices for the specified parties shall state the name and address of the applicant and of the applicant's attorney or other authorized representative, if any, together with the serial number and filing date of the application.

(d)(1) The notices shall be sent to each applicant, in care of his attorney or other authorized representative, if any, to each user, and to each registrant. A copy of the application shall be forwarded with the notice to each party specified in the application.

(2) An answer to the notice is not required in the case of an applicant or registrant whose application or registration is specified as a concurrent user in the application, but a statement, if desired, may be filed within forty days after the mailing of the notice; in the case of any other party specified as a concurrent user in the application, an answer must be filed within forty days after the mailing of the notice.

(3) If an answer, when required, is not filed, judgment will be entered precluding the specified user from claiming any right more extensive than that acknowledged in the application(s) for concurrent use registration, but the applicant(s) will remain with the burden of proving entitlement to registration(s).

(e) The applicant for a concurrent use registration has the burden of proving entitlement thereto. If there are two or more applications for concurrent use registration involved in a proceeding, the party whose application has the latest filing date is the junior party. A party whose application has a filing date between the filing dates of the earliest involved application and the latest involved application is a junior party to every party whose involved application has an earlier filing date. If any applications have the same filing date, the application with the latest date of execution will be deemed to have the latest filing date and that applicant will be the junior party. A person specified as an excepted user in a concurrent use application but who has not filed an application shall be considered a party senior to every party that has an application involved in the proceeding.

(f) When a concurrent use registration is sought on the basis that a court of competent jurisdiction has finally determined that the parties are entitled to use the same or similar marks in commerce, a concurrent use registration proceeding will not be instituted if all of the following conditions are fulfilled:

(1) The applicant is entitled to registration subject only to the concurrent lawful use of a party to the court proceeding; and

(2) The court decree specifies the rights of the parties; and

(3) A true copy of the court decree is submitted to the examiner; and

(4) The concurrent use application complies fully and exactly with the court decree; and

(5) The excepted use specified in the concurrent use application does not involve a registration, or any involved registration has been restricted by the Commissioner in accordance with the court decree.

If any of the conditions specified in this paragraph is not satisfied, a concurrent use registration proceeding shall be prepared and instituted as provided in paragraphs (a) through (e) of this section.

(g) Registrations and applications to register on the Supplemental Register and registrations under the Act of 1920 are not subject to concurrent use registration proceedings. Applications to register under section 1(b) of the Act of 1946 are subject to concurrent use registration proceedings only after an acceptable amendment to allege use under § 2.76 or statement of use under § 2.88 has been filed.

(h) The Trademark Trial and Appeal Board will consider and determine concurrent use rights only in the context of a concurrent use registration proceeding.

[48 FR 23135, May 23, 1983; 48 FR 27225, June 14, 1983; 54 FR 37596, Sept. 11, 1989]

OPPOSITION

AUTHORITY: Secs. 2.101 to 2.106 also issued under secs. 13, 17, 60 Stat. 433, 434; 15 U.S.C. 1063, 1067.

§ 2.101   Filing an opposition.

(a) An opposition proceeding is commenced by the filing of an opposition in the Patent and Trademark Office.

(b) Any entity which believes that it would be damaged by the registration of a mark on the Principal Register may oppose the same by filing an opposition, which should be addressed to the Trademark Trial and Appeal Board. The opposition need not be verified, and may be signed by the opposer or the opposer's attorney or other authorized representative.

(c) The opposition must be filed within thirty days after publication (§ 2.80) of the application being opposed or within an extension of time (§ 2.102) for filing an opposition.

(d)(1) The opposition must be accompanied by the required fee for each party joined as opposer for each class in the application for which registration is opposed (see § 2.6(1)). If no fee, or a fee insufficient to pay for one person to oppose the registration of a mark in at least one class, is submitted within thirty days after publication of the mark to be opposed or within an extension of time for filing an opposition, the opposition will not be refused if the required fee(s) is submitted to the Patent and Trademark Office within the time limit set in the notification of this defect by the Office.

(2) If the fees submitted are sufficient to pay for one person to oppose registration in at least one class but are insufficient for an opposition against all of the classes in the application, and the particular class or classes against which the opposition is filed are not specified, the Office will issue a written notice allowing opposer until a set time in which to submit the required fee(s) or to specify the class or classes opposed. If the required fee(s) is not submitted, or the specification made, within the time set in the notice, the opposition will be presumed to be against the class or classes in ascending order, beginning with the lowest numbered class and including the number of classes in the application for which the fees submitted are sufficient to pay the fee due for each class.

(3) If persons are joined as party opposers, and the fees submitted are sufficient to pay for one person to oppose registration in at least one class but are insufficient for each named party opposer, the Office will issue a written notice allowing the named party opposers until a set time in which to submit the required fee(s) or to specify the opposer(s) to which the submitted fees apply. If the required fee(s) is not submitted, or the specification made, within the time set in the notice, the first named party will be presumed to be the party opposer and additional parties will be deemed to be party opposers to the extent that the fees submitted are sufficient to pay the fee due for each party opposer. If persons are joined as party opposers against the registration of a mark in more than one class, the fees submitted are insufficient, and no specification of opposers and classes is made within the time set in the written notice issued by the Office, the fees submitted will be applied first on behalf of the first-named opposer against as many of the classes in the application as the submitted fees are sufficient to pay, and any excess will be applied on behalf of the second-named party to the opposition against the classes in the application in ascending order.

[48 FR 3976, Jan. 28, 1983, as amended at 51 FR 28709, Aug. 11, 1986; 54 FR 37596, Sept. 11, 1989]

§ 2.102 Extension of time for filing an opposition.

(a) Any person who believes that he would be damaged by the registration of a mark on the Principal Register may file a written request to extend the time for filing an opposition. The written request may be signed by the potential opposer or by an attorney at law or other person authorized, in accordance with § 2.12 (b) and (c) and § 2.17(b), to represent the potential opposer.

(b) The written request to extend the time for filing an opposition must identify the potential opposer with reasonable certainty. Any opposition filed during an extension of time should be in the name of the person to whom the extension was granted, but an opposition may be accepted if the person in whose name the extension was requested was misidentified through mistake or if the opposition is filed in the name of a person in privity with the person who requested and was granted the extension of time.

(c) The written request to extend the time for filing an opposition must be filed in the Patent and Trademark Office before the expiration of thirty days from the date of publication or within any extension of time previously granted, should specify the period of extension desired, and should be addressed to the Trademark Trial and Appeal Board. A first extension of time for not more than thirty days will be granted upon request. Further extensions of time may be granted by the Board for good cause. In addition, extensions of time to file an opposition aggregating more than 120 days from the date of publication of the application will not be granted except upon (1) a written consent or stipulation signed by the applicant or its authorized representative, or (2) a written request by the potential opposer or its authorized representative stating that the applicant or its authorized representative has consented to the request, and including proof of service on the applicant or its authorized representative, or (3) a showing of extraordinary circumstances, it being considered that a potential opposer has an adequate alternative remedy by a petition for cancellation.

(d) Every request to extend the time for filing a notice of opposition should be submitted in triplicate (original plus two copies).

[48 FR 3976 Jan. 28, 1983]

§ 2.104 Contents of opposition.

(a) The opposition must set forth a short and plain statement showing why the opposer believes it would be damaged by the registration of the opposed mark and state the grounds for opposition. A duplicate copy of the opposition, including exhibits, shall be filed with the opposition.

(b) Oppositions to different applications owned by the same party may be joined in a consolidated opposition when appropriate, but the required fee must be included for each party joined as opposer for each class in which registration is opposed in each application against which the opposition is filed.

[54 FR 34897, Aug. 22, 1989]

§ 2.105 Notification of opposition proceeding[s].

When an opposition in proper form has been filed and the correct fee(s) have been submitted, a notification shall be prepared by the Trademark Trial and Appeal Board, which shall identify the title and number of the proceeding and the application involved and shall designate a time, not less than thirty days from the mailing date of the notification, within which an answer must be filed. A copy of the notification shall be forwarded to the attorney or other authorized representative of the opposer, if any, or to the opposer. The duplicate copy of the opposition and exhibits shall be forwarded with a copy of the notification to the attorney or other authorized representative of the applicant, if any, or to the applicant.

[48 FR 23136, May 23, 1983]

§ 2.106 Answer.

(a) If no answer is filed within the time set, the opposition may be decided as in case of default.

(b)(1) An answer shall state in short and plain terms the applicant's defenses to each claim asserted and shall admit or deny the averments upon which the opposer relies. If the applicant is without knowledge or information sufficient to form a belief as to the truth of an averment, applicant shall so state and this will have the effect of a denial. Denials may take any of the forms specified in Rule 8(b) of the Federal Rules of Civil Procedure. An answer may contain any defense, including the affirmative defenses of unclean hands, laches, estoppel, acquiescence, fraud, mistake, prior judgment, or any other matter constituting an avoidance or affirmative defense. When pleading special matters, the Federal Rules of Civil Procedure shall be followed. A reply to an affirmative defense need not be filed. When a defense attacks the validity of a registration pleaded in the opposition, paragraph (b)(2) of this section shall govern. A pleaded registration is a registration identified by number and date of issuance in an original notice of opposition or in any amendment thereto made under Rule 15, Federal Rules of Civil Procedure.

(2)(i) A defense attacking the validity of any one or more of the registrations pleaded in the opposition shall be a compulsory counterclaim if grounds for such counterclaim exist at the time when the answer is filed. If grounds for a counterclaim are known to the applicant when the answer to the opposition is filed, the counterclaim shall be pleaded with or as part of the answer. If grounds for a counterclaim are learned during the course of the opposition proceeding, the counterclaim shall be pleaded promptly after the grounds therefor are learned. A counterclaim need not be filed if it is the subject of another proceeding between the same parties or anyone in privity therewith.

(ii) An attack on the validity of a registration pleaded by an opposer will not be heard unless a counterclaim or separate petition is filed to seek the cancellation of such registration.

(iii) The provisions of §§ 2.111 through 2.115, inclusive, shall be applicable to counterclaims. A time, not less than thirty days, will be designated within which an answer to the counterclaim must be filed.

(iv) The times for pleading, discovery, testimony, briefs or oral argument will be reset or extended when necessary, upon motion by a party, to enable a party fully to present or meet a counterclaim or separate petition for cancellation of a registration.

(c) The opposition may be withdrawn without prejudice before the answer is filed. After the answer is filed, the opposition may not be withdrawn without prejudice except with the written consent of the applicant or the applicant's attorney or other authorized representative.

[30 FR 13193, Oct. 16, 1965, as amended at 46 FR 6940, Jan. 22, 1981; 48 FR 23136, May 23, 1983; 54 FR 34897, Aug. 22, 1989]

§ 2.107   Amendment of pleadings in an opposition proceeding.

Pleadings in an opposition proceeding may be amended in the same manner and to the same extent as in a civil action in a United States district court.

[48 FR 23136, May 23, 1983]

CANCELLATION

AUTHORITY: Secs. 2.111 to 2.114 also issued under secs. 14, 17, 24, 60 Stat. 433, 434, 436; 15 U.S.C. 1064, 1067, 1092.

§ 2.111   Filing petition for cancellation.

(a) A cancellation proceeding is commenced by the timely filing of a petition for cancellation, together with the required fee, in the Patent and Trademark Office.

(b) Any entity which believes that it is or will be damaged by a registration may file a petition, which should be addressed to the Trademark Trial and Appeal Board, to cancel the registration in whole or in part. The petition need not be verified, and may be signed by the petitioner or the petitioner's attorney or other authorized representative. The petition may be filed at any time in the case of registrations on the Supplemental Register or under the Act of 1920, or registrations under the Act of 1881 or the Act of 1905 which have not been published under section 12(c) of the Act, or on any ground specified in section 14 (c) or (e) of the Act. In all other cases the petition and the required fee must be filed within five years from the date of registration of the mark under the Act or from the date of publication under section 12(c) of the Act.

(c)(1) The petition must be accompanied by the required fee for each class in the registration for which cancellation is sought (see §§ 2.6(l) and 2.85(e)). If the fees submitted are insufficient for a cancellation against all of the classes in the registration, and the particular class or classes against which the cancellation is filed are not specified, the Office will issue a written notice allowing petitioner until a set time in which to submit the required fee(s) (provided that the five-year period, if applicable, has not expired) or to specify the class or classes sought to be cancelled. If the required fee(s) is not submitted, or the specification made, within the time set in the notice, the cancellation will be presumed to be against the class or classes in ascending order, beginning with the lowest numbered class, and including the number of classes in the registration for which the fees submitted are sufficient to pay the fee due for each class.

(2) If persons are joined as party petitioners, each must submit a fee for each class for which cancellation is sought. If the fees submitted are insufficient for each named party petitioner, the Office will issue a written notice allowing the named party petitioners until a set time in which to submit the required fee(s) (provided that the five-year period, if applicable, has not expired) or to specify the petitioner(s) to which the submitted fees apply. If the required fee(s) is not submitted, or the specification made, within the time set in the notice, the first named party will be presumed to be the party petitioner and additional parties will be deemed to be party petitioners to the extent that the fees submitted are sufficient to pay the fee due for each party petitioner. If persons are joined as party petitioners against a registration sought to be cancelled in more than one class, the fees submitted are insufficient, and no specification of parties and classes is made within the time set in the written notice issued by the Office, the fees submitted will be applied first on behalf of the first-named petitioner against as many of the classes in the registration as the submitted fees are sufficient to pay, and any excess will be applied on behalf of the second-named party to the petition against the classes in the registration in ascending order.

(3) The filing date of the petition is the date of receipt in the Patent and Trademark Office of the petition together with the required fee. If the amount of the fee filed with the petition is sufficient to pay for at least one person to petition to cancel one class of goods or services but is less than the required amount because multiple party petitioners and/or multiple classes in the registration for which cancellation is sought are involved, and the required additional amount of the fee is filed within the time limit set in the notification of the defect by the Office, the filing date of the petition with respect to the additional party petitioners and/or classes is the date of receipt in the Patent and Trademark Office of the additional fees.

[48 FR 3976 Jan. 28, 1983, as amended at 54 FR 37596, Sept. 11, 1989]

§2.112 **Contents of petition for cancellation.**

(a) The petition to cancel must set forth a short and plain statement showing why the petitioner believes it is or will be damaged by the registration, state the grounds for cancellation, and indicate, to the best of petitioner's knowledge, the name and address of the current owner of the registration. A duplicate copy of the petition, including exhibits, shall be filed with the petition.

(b) Petitions to cancel different registrations owned by the same party may be joined in a consolidated petition when appropriate, but the required fee must be included for each party joined as petitioner for each class sought to be cancelled in each registration against which the petition to cancel is filed.

[48 FR 3977 Jan. 28, 1983, as amended at 51 FR 28710, Aug. 11, 1986; 54 FR 34897, Aug. 22, 1989]

§ 2.113 Notification of cancellation proceeding.

When a petition for cancellation has been filed in proper form (see §§ 2.111 and 2.112), a notification shall be prepared by the Trademark Trial and Appeal Board, which shall identify the title and number of the proceeding and the registration or registrations involved and shall designate a time, not less than thirty days from the mailing date of the notification, within which an answer must be filed. A copy of the notification shall be forwarded to the attorney or other authorized representative of the petitioner, if any, or to the petitioner. The duplicate copy of the petition for cancellation and exhibits shall be forwarded with a copy of the notification to the respondent (see § 2.118), who shall be the party shown by the records of the Patent and Trademark Office to be the current owner of the registration or registrations sought to be cancelled, except that the Board, in its discretion, may join or substitute as respondent a party who makes a showing of a current ownership interest in such registration or registrations. When the party identified by the petitioner, pursuant to § 2.112(a), as the current owner of the registration or registrations is not the record owner thereof, a courtesy copy of the petition for cancellation shall be forwarded with a copy of the notification to the alleged current owner, which may file a motion to be joined or substituted as respondent. If the petition is found to be defective as to form, the party filing the petition shall be so advised and allowed a reasonable time for correcting the informality.

[54 FR 34897, Aug. 22, 1989; 54 FR 38041, Sept. 14, 1989]

§ 2.114 Answer.

(a) If no answer is filed within the time set, the petition may be decided as in case of default.

(b)(1) An answer shall state in short and plain terms the respondent's defenses to each claim asserted and shall admit or deny the averments upon which the petitioner relies. If the respondent is without knowledge or information sufficient to form a belief as to the truth of an averment, respondent shall so state and this will have the effect of a denial. Denials may take any of the forms specified in Rule 8(b) of the Federal Rules of Civil Procedure. An answer may contain any defense, including the affirmative defenses of unclean hands, laches, estoppel, acquiescence, fraud, mistake, prior judgment, or any other matter constituting an avoidance or affirmative defense. When pleading special matters, the Federal Rules of Civil Procedure shall be followed. A reply to an affirmative defense need not be filed. When a defense attacks the validity of a registration pleaded in the petition, paragraph (b)(2) of this section shall govern. A pleaded registration is a registration identified by number and date of issuance in an original petition for cancellation or in any amendment thereto made under Rule 15, Federal Rules of Civil Procedure.

(2)(i) A defense attacking the validity of any one or more of the registrations pleaded in the petition shall be a compulsory counterclaim if grounds for such counterclaim exist at the time when the answer if filed. If grounds for a counterclaim are known to respondent when the answer to the petition is filed, the counterclaim shall be pleaded with or as part of the answer. If grounds for a counterclaim are learned during the course of the cancellation proceeding, the counterclaim shall be pleaded promptly after the grounds therefor are learned. A counterclaim need not be filed if it is the subject of another proceeding between the same parties or anyone in privity therewith.

(ii) An attack on the validity of a registration pleaded by a petitioner for cancellation will not be heard unless a counterclaim or separate petition is filed to seek the cancellation of such registration.

(iii) The provisions of §§ 2.111 through 2.115, inclusive, shall be applicable to counterclaims. A time, not less than thirty days, will be designated within which an answer to the counterclaim must be filed.

(iv) The times for pleading, discovery, testimony, briefs, or oral argument will be reset or extended when necessary, upon motion by a party, to enable a party fully to present or meet a counterclaim or separate petition for cancellation of a registration.

(c) The petition for cancellation may be withdrawn without prejudice before the answer is filed. After the answer is filed, the petition may not be withdrawn without prejudice except with the written consent of the registrant or the registrant's attorney or other authorized representative.

[30 FR 13193, Oct. 16, 1965, as amended at 46 FR 6940, Jan. 22, 1981; 46 FR 11548, Feb. 9, 1981; 51 FR 28710, Aug. 11, 1986; 54 FR 34898, Aug. 22, 1989]

§ 2.115 Amendment of pleadings in a cancellation proceeding.

Pleadings in a cancellation proceeding may be amended in the same manner and to the same extent as in a civil action in a United States district court.

[48 FR 23136, May 23, 1983]

PROCEDURE IN INTER PARTES
PROCEEDINGS

AUTHORITY: Secs. 2.116 to 2.136 also issued under sec. 17, 60 Stat. 434; 15 U.S.C. 1067.

§ 2.116 Federal Rules of Civil Procedure.

(a) Except as otherwise provided, and wherever applicable and appropriate, procedure and practice in inter partes proceedings shall be governed by the Federal Rules of Civil Procedure.

(b) The opposer in an opposition proceeding or the petitioner in a cancellation proceeding shall be in the position of plaintiff, and the applicant in an opposition proceeding or the respondent in a cancellation proceeding shall be in the position of defendant. A party that is a junior party in an interference proceeding or in a concurrent use registration proceeding shall be in the position of plaintiff against every party that is senior, and the party that is a senior party in an interference proceeding or in a concurrent use registration proceeding shall be a defendant against every party that is junior.

(c) The opposition or the petition for cancellation and the answer corre-

spond to the complaint and answer in a court proceeding.

(d) The assignment of testimony periods corresponds to setting a case for trial in court proceedings.

(e) The taking of depositions during the assigned testimony periods corresponds to the trial in court proceedings.

(f) Oral hearing corresponds to oral summation in court proceedings.

[30 FR 13193, Oct. 16, 1965. Redesignated and amended at 37 FR 7606, Apr. 18, 1972; 48 FR 23136, May 23, 1983]

§ 2.117 Suspension of proceedings.

(a) Whenever it shall come to the attention of the Trademark Trial and Appeal Board that parties to a pending case are engaged in a civil action which may be dispositive of the case, proceedings before the Board may be suspended until termination of the civil action.

(b) Whenever there is pending, at the time when the question of the suspension of proceedings is raised, a motion which is potentially dispositive of the case, the motion may be decided before the question of suspension is considered.

(c) Proceedings may also be suspended, for good cause, upon motion or a stipulation of the parties approved by the Board.

[48 FR 23136, May 23, 1983]

§ 2.118 Undelivered Office notices.

When the notices sent by the Patent and Trademark Office to any registrant are returned to the Office undelivered, or when one of the parties resides abroad and his representative in the United States is unknown, additional notice may be given by publication in the *Official Gazette* for such period of time as the Commissioner may direct.

§ 2.119 Service and signing of papers.

(a) Every paper filed in the Patent and Trademark Office in inter partes cases, including notice of appeal, must be served upon the other parties except the notice of interference (§ 2.93), the notification of opposition (§ 2.105), the petition for cancellation (§ 2.113), and the notice of a concurrent use proceeding (§ 2.99), which are mailed by the Patent and Trademark Office. Proof of such service must be made before the paper will be considered by the Office. A statement signed by the attorney or other authorized representative, attached to or appearing on the original paper when filed, clearly stating the date and manner in which service was made will be accepted as prima facie proof of service.

(b) Service of papers must be on the attorney or other authorized representative of the party if there be such or on the party if there is no attorney or other authorized representative, and may be made in any of the following ways:

(1) By delivering a copy of the paper to the person served;

(2) By leaving a copy at the usual place of business of the person served, with someone in the person's employment;

(3) When the person served has no usual place of business, by leaving a copy at the person's residence, with a member of the person's family over 14 years of age and of discretion;

(4) Transmission by the "Express Mail Post Office to Addressee" service of the United States Postal Service or by first-class mail, which may also be certified or registered;

(5) Transmission by overnight courier.

Whenever it shall be satisfactorily shown to the Commissioner that none of the above modes of obtaining service or serving the paper is practicable, service may be by notice published in the *Official Gazette.*

(c) When service is made by first-class mail, "Express Mail," or overnight courier, the date of mailing or of delivery to the overnight courier will be considered the date of service. Whenever a party is required to take some action within a prescribed period after the service of a paper upon the party by another party and the paper is served by first-class mail, "Express Mail," or overnight courier, 5 days shall be added to the prescribed period.

(d) If a party to an inter partes proceeding is not domiciled in the United States and is not represented by an attorney or other authorized representa-

tive located in the United States, the party must designate by written document filed in the Patent and Trademark Office the name and address of a person resident in the United States on whom may be served notices or process in the proceeding. In such cases, official communications of the Patent and Trademark Office will be addressed to the domestic representative unless the proceeding is being prosecuted by an attorney at law or other qualified person duly authorized under § 10.14(c) of this subchapter. The mere designation of a domestic representative does not authorize the person designated to prosecute the proceeding unless qualified under § 10.14(a), or qualified under paragraph (b) or (c) of § 10.14 and authorized under § 2.17(b).

(e) Every paper filed in an inter partes proceeding, and every request for an extension of time to file an opposition, must be signed by the party filing it, or by the party's attorney or other authorized representative, but an unsigned paper will not be refused consideration if a signed copy is submitted to the Patent and Trademark Office within the time limit set in the notification of this defect by the Office.

[37 FR 7606, Apr. 18, 1972, as amended at 41 FR 760, Jan. 5, 1976; 54 FR 34898, Aug. 22, 1989; 54 FR 38041, Sept. 14, 1989]

§ 2.120 Discovery.

(a) *In general.* The provisions of the Federal Rules of Civil Procedure relating to discovery shall apply in opposition, cancellation, interference and concurrent use registration proceedings except as otherwise provided in this section. The Trademark Trial and Appeal Board will specify the closing date for the taking of discovery. The opening of discovery is governed by the Federal Rules of Civil Procedure.

(b) *Discovery deposition within the United States.* The deposition of a natural person shall be taken in the Federal judicial district where the person resides or is regularly employed or at any place on which the parties agree by stipulation. The responsibility rests wholly with the party taking discovery to secure the attendance of a proposed deponent other than a party or anyone who, at the time set for the taking of the deposition, is an officer, director, or managing agent of a party, or a person designated under Rule 30(b)(6) or Rule 31(a) of the Federal Rules of Civil Procedure. See 35 U.S.C. 24.

(c) *Discovery deposition in foreign countries.* (1) The discovery deposition of a natural person residing in a foreign country who is a party or who, at the time set for the taking of the deposition, is an officer, director, or managing agent of a party, or a person designated under Rule 30(b)(6) or Rule 31(a) of the Federal Rules of Civil Procedure, shall, if taken in a foreign country, be taken in the manner prescribed by § 2.124 unless the Trademark Trial and Appeal Board, upon motion for good cause, orders or the parties stipulate, that the deposition be taken by oral examination.

(2) Whenever a foreign party is or will be, during a time set for discovery, present within the United States or any territory which is under the control and jurisdiction of the United States, such party may be deposed by oral examination upon notice by the party seeking discovery. Whenever a foreign party has or will have, during a time set for discovery, an officer, director, managing agent, or other person who consents to testify on its behalf, present within the United States or any territory which is under the control and jurisdiction of the United States, such officer, director, managing agent, or other person who consents to testify in its behalf may be deposed by oral examination upon notice by the party seeking discovery. The party seeking discovery may have one or more officers, directors, managing agents, or other persons who consent to testify on behalf of the adverse party, designated under Rule 30(b)(6) of the Federal Rules of Civil Procedure. The deposition of a person under this paragraph shall be taken in the Federal judicial district where the witness resides or is regularly employed, or, if the witness neither resides nor is regularly employed in a Federal judicial district, where the witness is at the time of the deposition. This paragraph does not preclude the taking of a discovery deposition of a foreign party by any other procedure provided by paragraph (c)(1) of this section.

(d) *Interrogatories; request for production.* (1) The total number of written interrogatories which a party may serve upon another party pursuant to Rule 33 of the Federal Rules of Civil Procedure, in a proceeding, shall not exceed seventy-five, counting subparts, except that the Trademark Trial and Appeal Board, in its discretion, may allow additional interrogatories upon motion therefor showing good cause, or upon stipulation of the parties. A motion for leave to serve additional interrogatories must be accompanied by a copy of the interrogatories, if any, which have already been served by the moving party, and by a copy of the interrogatories proposed to be served. If a party upon which interrogatories have been served believes that the number of interrogatories served exceeds the limitation specified in this paragraph, and is not willing to waive this basis for objection, the party shall, within the time for (and instead of) serving answers and objections to the interrogatories, file a motion for a protective order, accompanied by a copy of the interrogatories which together are said to exceed the limitation.

(2) The production of documents and things under the provisions of Rule 34 of the Federal Rules of Civil Procedure will be made at the place where the documents and things are usually kept, or where the parties agree, or where and in the manner which the Trademark Trial and Appeal Board, upon motion, orders.

(e) *Motion for an order to compel discovery.* If a party fails to designate a person pursuant to Rule 30(b)(6) or Rule 31(a) of the Federal Rules of Civil Procedure, or if a party, or such designated person, or an officer, director or managing agent of a party fails to attend a deposition or fails to answer any question propounded in a discovery deposition, or any interrogatory, or fails to produce and permit the inspection and copying of any document or thing, the party seeking discovery may file a motion before the Trademark Trial and Appeal Board for an order to compel a designation, or attendance at a deposition, or an answer, or production and an opportunity to inspect and copy. The motion shall include a copy of the request for designation or of the relevant portion of the discovery deposition; or a copy of the interrogatory with any answer or objection that was made; or a copy of the request for production, any proffer of production or objection to production in response to the request, and a list and brief description of the documents or things that were not produced for inspection and copying. The motion must be supported by a written statement from the moving party that such party or the attorney therefor has made a good faith effort, by conference or correspondence, to resolve with the other party or the attorney therefor the issues presented in the motion and has been unable to reach agreement. If issues raised in the motion are subsequently resolved by agreement of the parties, the moving party should inform the Board in writing of the issues in the motion which no longer require adjudication.

(f) *Motion for a protective order.* Upon motion by a party from whom discovery is sought, and for good cause, the Trademark Trial and Appeal Board may make any order which justice requires to protect a party from annoyance, embarrassment, oppression, or undue burden or expense, including one or more of the types of orders provided by clauses (1) through (8), inclusive, of Rule 26(c) of the Federal Rules of Civil Procedure. If the motion for a protective order is denied in whole or in part, the Board may, on such conditions (other than an award of expenses to the party prevailing on the motion) as are just, order that any party provide or permit discovery.

(g) *Sanctions.* (1) If a party fails to comply with an order of the Trademark Trial and Appeal Board relating to discovery, including a protective order, the Board may make any appropriate order, including any of the orders provided in Rule 37(b)(2) of the Federal Rules of Civil Procedure, except that the Board does not have authority to hold any person in contempt or to award any expenses to any party. The Board may impose against a party any of the sanctions provided by this subsection in the event that said party or any attorney, agent, or designated witness of that party fails to comply with a protective order made pursuant to Rule 26(c) of the Federal Rules of Civil Procedure.

(2) If a party, or an officer, director, or managing agent of a party, or a person designated under Rule 30(b)(6) or 31(a) of the Federal Rules of Civil Procedure to testify on behalf of a party, fails to attend the party's or person's discovery deposition, after being served with proper notice, or fails to provide any response to a set of interrogatories or to a set of requests for production of documents and things, and such party or the party's attorney or other authorized representative informs the party seeking discovery that no response will be made thereto, the Board may make any appropriate order, as specified in paragraph (g)(1) of this section.

(h) *Request for admissions.* Requests for admissions shall be governed by Rule 36 of the Federal Rules of Civil Procedure except that the Trademark Trial and Appeal Board does not have authority to award any expenses to any party. A motion by a party to determine the sufficiency of an answer or objection to a request made by that party for an admission shall include a copy of the request for admission and any exhibits thereto and of the answer or objection. The motion must be supported by a written statement from the moving party that such party or the attorney therefor has made a good faith effort, by conference or correspondence, to resolve with the other party or the attorney therefor the issues presented in the motion and has been unable to reach agreement. If issues raised in the motion are subsequently resolved by agreement of the parties, the moving party should inform the Board in writing of the issues in the motion which no longer require adjudication.

(i) *Telephone and pre-trial conferences.* (1) Whenever it appears to the Trademark Trial and Appeal Board that a motion filed in an inter partes proceeding is of such nature that its resolution by correspondence is not practical, the Board may, upon its own initiative or upon request made by one or both of the parties, resolve the motion by telephone conference.

(2) Whenever it appears to the Trademark Trial and Appeal Board that questions or issues arising during the interlocutory phase of an inter partes proceeding have become so complex that their resolution by correspondence or telephone conference is not practical and that resolution would be likely to be facilitated by a conference in person of the parties or their attorneys with a Member or Attorney-Examiner of the Board, the Board may, upon its own initiative or upon motion made by one or both of the parties, request that the parties or their attorneys, under circumstances which will not result in undue hardship for any party, meet with the Board at its offices for a pre-trial conference.

(j) *Use of discovery deposition, answer to interrogatory, or admission.*

(1) The discovery deposition of a party or of anyone who at the time of taking the deposition was on officer, director or managing agent of a party, or a person designated by a party pursuant to Rule 30(b)(6) or Rule 31(a) of the Federal Rules of Civil Procedure, may be offered in evidence by an adverse party.

(2) Except as provided in paragraph (j)(1) of this section, the discovery deposition of a witness, whether or not a party, shall not be offered in evidence unless the person whose deposition was taken is, during the testimony period of the party offering the deposition, dead; or out of the United States (unless it appears that the absence of the witness was procured by the party offering the deposition); or unable to testify because of age, illness, infirmity, or imprisonment; or cannot be served with a subpoena to compel attendance at a testimonial deposition; or there is a stipulation by the parties; or upon a showing that such exceptional circumstances exist as to make it desirable, in the interest of justice, to allow the deposition to be used. The use of a discovery deposition by any party under this paragraph will be allowed only by stipulation of the parties approved by the Trademark Trial and Appeal Board, or by

order of the Board on motion, which shall be filed at the time of the purported offer of the deposition in evidence, unless the motion is based upon a claim that such exceptional circumstances exist as to make it desirable, in the interest of justice, to allow the deposition to be used, in which case the motion shall be filed promptly after the circumstances claimed to justify use of the deposition became known.

(3)(i) A discovery deposition, an answer to an interrogatory, or an admission to a request for admission, which may be offered in evidence under the provisions of paragraph (j) of this section may be made of record in the case by filing the deposition or any part thereof with any exhibit to the part that is filed, or a copy of the interrogatory and answer thereto with any exhibit made part of the answer, or a copy of the request for admission and any exhibit thereto and the admission (or a statement that the party from which an admission was requested failed to respond thereto), together with a notice of reliance. The notice of reliance and the material submitted thereunder should be filed during the testimony period of the party which files the notice of reliance. An objection made at a discovery deposition by a party answering a question subject to the objection will be considered at final hearing.

(ii) A party which has obtained documents from another party under Rule 34 of the Federal Rules of Civil Procedure may not make the documents of record by notice of reliance alone, except to the extent that they are admissible by notice of reliance under the provisions of § 2.122(e).

(4) If only part of a discovery deposition is submitted and made part of the record by a party, an adverse party may introduce under a notice of reliance any other part of the deposition which should in fairness be considered so as to make not misleading what was offered by the submitting party. A notice of reliance filed by an adverse party must be supported by a written statement explaining why the adverse party needs to rely upon each additional part listed in the adverse party's notice, failing which the Board, in its

discretion, may refuse to consider the additional parts.

(5) An answer to an interrogatory, or an admission to a request for admission, may be submitted and made part of the record by only the inquiring party except that, if fewer than all of the answers to interrogatories, or fewer than all of the admissions, are offered in evidence by the inquiring party, the responding party may introduce under a notice of reliance any other answers to interrogatories, or any other admissions, which should in fairness be considered so as to make not misleading what was offered by the inquiring party. The notice of reliance filed by the responding party must be supported by a written statement explaining why the responding party needs to rely upon each of the additional discovery responses listed in the responding party's notice, failing which the Board, in its discretion, may refuse to consider the additional responses.

(6) Paragraph (j) of this section will not be interpreted to preclude the reading or the use of a discovery deposition, or answer to an interrogatory, or admission as part of the examination or cross-examination of any witness during the testimony period of any party.

(7) When a discovery deposition, or a part thereof, or an answer to an interrogatory, or an admission, has been made of record by one party in accordance with the provisions of paragraph (j)(3) of this section, it may be referred to by any party for any purpose permitted by the Federal Rules of Evidence.

(8) Requests for discovery, responses thereto, and materials or depositions obtained through the discovery process should not be filed with the Board except when submitted with a motion relating to discovery, or in support of or response to a motion for summary judgment, or under a notice of reliance during a party's testimony period. Papers or materials filed in violation of this paragraph may be returned by the Board.

[48 FR 23136, May 23, 1983, as amended at 54 FR 34898, Aug. 22, 1989; 54 FR 38041, Sept. 14, 1989]

§ 2.121 Assignment of times for taking testimony.

(a)(1) The Trademark Trial and Appeal Board will issue a trial order assigning to each party the time for taking testimony. No testimony shall be taken except during the times assigned, unless by stipulation of the parties approved by the Board, or, upon motion, by order of the Board. Testimony periods may be rescheduled by stipulation of the parties approved by the Board, or upon motion granted by the Board, or by order of the Board. The resetting of the closing date for discovery will result in the rescheduling of the testimony periods without action by any party. The resetting of a party's time to respond to an outstanding request for discovery will not result in the automatic rescheduling of the discovery and/or testimony periods; such dates will be rescheduled only upon stipulation of the parties approved by the Board, or upon motion granted by the Board, or by order of the Board.

(2) The initial trial order will be mailed by the Board after issue is joined.

(b)(1) The Trademark Trial and Appeal Board will schedule a testimony period for the plaintiff to present its case in chief, a testimony period for the defendant to present its case and to meet the case of the plaintiff, and a testimony period for the plaintiff to present evidence in rebuttal.

(2) When there is a counterclaim, or when proceedings have been consolidated and one party is in the position of plaintiff in one of the involved proceedings and in the position of defendant in another of the involved proceedings, or when there is an interference or a concurrent use registration proceeding involving more than two parties, the Board will schedule testimony periods so that each party in the position of plaintiff will have a period for presenting its case in chief against each party in the position of defendant, each party in the position of defendant will have a period for presenting its case and meeting the case of each plaintiff, and each party in the position of plaintiff will have a period for presenting evidence in rebuttal.

(c) A testimony period which is solely for rebuttal will be set for fifteen days. All other testimony periods will be set for thirty days. The periods may be extended by stipulation of the parties approved by the Trademark Trial and Appeal Board, or upon motion granted by the Board, or by order of the Board.

(d) When parties stipulate to the rescheduling of testimony periods or to the rescheduling of the closing date for discovery and the rescheduling of testimony periods, a stipulation presented in the form used in a trial order, signed by the parties, or a motion in said form signed by one party and including a statement that every other party has agreed thereto, and submitted in one original plus as many photocopies as there are parties, will, if approved, be so stamped, signed, and dated, and the copies will be promptly returned to the parties.

[48 FR 23138, May 23, 1983; 48 FR 27226, June 14, 1983; 54 FR 34899, Aug. 22, 1989]

§ 2.122 **Matters in evidence.**

(a) *Rules of evidence.* The rules of evidence for proceedings before the Trademark Trial and Appeal Board are the Federal Rules of Evidence, the relevant provisions of the Federal Rules of Civil Procedure, the relevant provisions of Title 28 of the United States Code, and the provisions of this part of title 37 of the Code of Federal Regulations.

(b) *Application files.* (1) The file of each application or registration specified in a declaration of interference, of each application or registration specified in the notice of a concurrent use registration proceeding, of the application against which a notice of opposition is filed, or of each registration against which a petition or counterclaim for cancellation is filed forms part of the record of the proceeding without any action by the parties and reference may be made to the file for any relevant and competent purpose.

(2) The allegation in an application for registration, or in a registration, of a date of use is not evidence on behalf of the applicant or registrant; a date of use of a mark must be established by competent evidence. Specimens in the file of an application for registra-tion, or in the file of a registration, are not evidence on behalf of the applicant or registrant unless identified and introduced in evidence as exhibits during the period for the taking of testimony.

(c) *Exhibits to pleadings.* Except as provided in paragraph (d)(1) of this section, an exhibit attached to a pleading is not evidence on behalf of the party to whose pleading the exhibit is attached unless identified and introduced in evidence as an exhibit during the period for the taking of testimony.

(d) *Registrations.* (1) A registration of the opposer or petitioner pleaded in an opposition or petition to cancel will be received in evidence and made part of the record if the opposition or petition is accompanied by two copies of the registration prepared and issued by the Patent and Trademark Office showing both the current status of and current title to the registration. For the cost of a copy of a registration showing status and title, see § 2.6(n).

(2) A registration owned by any party to a proceeding may be made of record in the proceeding by that party by appropriate identification and introduction during the taking of testimony or by filing a notice of reliance, which shall be accompanied by a copy of the registration prepared and issued by the Patent and Trademark Office showing both the current status of and current title to the registration. The notice of reliance shall be filed during the testimony period of the party that files the notice.

(e) *Printed publications and official records.* Printed publications, such as books and periodicals, available to the general public in libraries or of general circulation among members of the public or that segment of the public which is relevant under an issue in a proceeding, and official records, if the publication of official record is competent evidence and relevant to an issue, may be introduced in evidence by filing a notice of reliance on the material being offered. The notice shall specify the printed publication (including information sufficient to identify the source and the date of the publication) or the official record and the pages to be read; indicate generally the relevance of the material being offered; and be accompanied by the official record or a copy thereof whose authenticity is established under the Federal Rules of Evidence, or by the printed publication or a copy of the relevant portion thereof. A copy of an official record of the Patent and Trademark Office need not be certified to be offered in evidence. The notice of reliance shall be filed during the testimony period of the party that files the notice.

(f) *Testimony from other proceedings.* By order of the Trademark Trial and Appeal Board, on motion, testimony taken in another proceeding, or testimony taken in a suit or action in a court, between the same parties or those in privity may be used in a proceeding, so far as relevant and material, subject, however, to the right of any adverse party to recall or demand the recall for examination or cross-examination of any witness whose prior testimony has been offered and to rebut the testimony.

[48 FR 23138, May 23, 1983, as amended at 54 FR 34899, Aug. 22, 1989; 54 FR 38041, Sept. 14, 1989]

§ 2.123   Trial testimony in inter partes cases.

(a)(1) The testimony of witnesses in inter partes cases may be taken by depositions upon oral examination as provided by this section or by depositions upon written questions as provided by § 2.124. If a party serves notice of the taking of a testimonial deposition upon written questions of a witness who is, or will be at the time of the deposition, present within the United States or any territory which is under the control and jurisdiction of the United States, any adverse party may, within fifteen days from the date of service of the notice, file a motion with the Trademark Trial and Appeal Board, for good cause, for an order that the deposition be taken by oral examination.

(2) A testimonial deposition taken in a foreign country shall be taken by deposition upon written questions as provided by § 2.124, unless the Board, upon motion for good cause, orders that the deposition be taken by oral examination, or the parties so stipulate.

(b) *Stipulations.* If the parties so stipulate in writing, depositions may be taken before any person authorized to administer oaths, at any place, upon any notice, and in any manner, and when so taken may be used like other depositions. By agreement of the parties, the testimony of any witness or witnesses of any party, may be submitted in the form of an affidavit by such witness or witnesses. The parties may stipulate what a particular witness would testify to if called, or the facts in the case of any party may be stipulated.

(c) *Notice of examination of witnesses.* Before the depositions of witnesses shall be taken by a party, due notice in writing shall be given to the opposing party or parties, as provided in § 2.119(b), of the time when and place where the depositions will be taken, of the cause or matter in which they are to be used, and the name and address of each witness to be examined; if the name of a witness is not known, a general description sufficient to identify the witness or the particular class or group to which the witness belongs, together with a satisfactory explanation, may be given instead. Depositions may be noticed for any reasonable time and place in the United States. A deposition may not be noticed for a place in a foreign country except as provided in paragraph (a)(2) of this section. No party shall take depositions in more than one place at the same time, nor so nearly at the same time that reasonable opportunity for travel from one place of examination to the other is not available.

(d) *Persons before whom depositions may be taken.* Depositions may be taken before persons designated by Rule 28 of the Federal Rules of Civil Procedure.

(e) *Examination of witnesses.* (1) Each witness before testifying shall be duly sworn according to law by the officer before whom his deposition is to be taken.

(2) The deposition shall be taken in answer to questions, with the questions and answers recorded in their regular order by the officer, or by some other person (who shall be subject to the provisions of Rule 28 of the

Federal Rules of Civil Procedure) in the presence of the officer except when the officer's presence is waived on the record by agreement of the parties. The testimony shall be taken stenographically and transcribed, unless the parties present agree otherwise. In the absence of all opposing parties and their attorneys or other authorized representatives, depositions may be taken in longhand, typewriting, or stenographically. Exhibits which are marked and identified at the deposition will be deemed to have been offered into evidence, without any formal offer thereof, unless the intention of the party marking the exhibits is clearly expressed to the contrary.

(3) Every adverse party shall have full opportunity to cross-examine each witness. If the notice of examination of witnesses which is served pursuant to paragraph (c) of this section is improper or inadequate with respect to any witness, an adverse party may cross-examine that witness under protest while reserving the right to object to the receipt of the testimony in evidence. Promptly after the testimony is completed, the adverse party, if he wishes to preserve the objection, shall move to strike the testimony from the record, which motion will be decided on the basis of all of the relevant circumstances. A motion to strike the testimony of a witness for lack of proper or adequate notice of examination must request the exclusion of the entire testimony of that witness and not only a part of that testimony.

(4) All objections made at the time of the examination to the qualifications of the officer taking the deposition, or to the manner of taking it, or to the evidence presented, or to the conduct of any party, and any other objection to the proceedings, shall be noted by the officer upon the deposition. Evidence objected to shall be taken subject to the objections.

(5) When the deposition has been transcribed, the deposition shall be carefully read over by the witness or by the officer to him, and shall then be signed by the witness in the presence of any officer authorized to administer oaths unless the reading and

the signature be waived on the record by agreement of all parties.

(f) *Certification and filing by officer.* The officer shall annex to the deposition his certificate showing:

(1) Due administration of the oath by the officer to the witness before the commencement of his deposition;

(2) The name of the person by whom the deposition was taken down, and whether, if not taken down by the officer, it was taken down in his presence;

(3) The presence or absence of the adverse party;

(4) The place, day, and hour of commencing and taking the deposition;

(5) The fact that the officer was not disqualified as specified in Rule 28 of the Federal Rules of Civil Procedure.

If any of the foregoing requirements are waived, the certificate shall so state. The officer shall sign the certificate and affix thereto his seal of office, if he has such a seal. Unless waived on the record by an agreement, he shall then, without delay, securely seal in an envelope all the evidence, notices, and paper exhibits, inscribe upon the envelope a certificate giving the number and title of the case, the name of each witness, and the date of sealing, address the package, and forward the same to the Commissioner of Patents and Trademarks. If the weight or bulk of an exhibit shall exclude it from the envelope, it shall, unless waived on the record by agreement of all parties, be authenticated by the officer and transmitted in a separate package marked and addressed as provided in this section.

(g) *Form of deposition.* (1) The pages of each deposition must be numbered consecutively, and the name of the witness plainly and conspicuously written at the top of each page. The deposition may be written on legal-size or letter-size paper, with a wide margin on the left-hand side of the page, and with the writing on one side only of the sheet. The questions propounded to each witness must be consecutively numbered unless paper with numbered lines is used, and each question must be followed by its answer.

(2) Exhibits must be numbered or lettered consecutively and each must

be marked with the number and title of the case and the name of the party offering the exhibit. Entry and consideration may be refused to improperly marked exhibits.

(3) Each deposition must contain an index of the names of the witnesses, giving the pages where their examination and cross-examination begin, and an index of the exhibits, briefly describing their nature and giving the pages at which they are introduced and offered in evidence.

(h) *Depositions must be filed.* All depositions which are taken must be duly filed in the Patent and Trademark Office. On refusal to file, the Office at its discretion will not further hear or consider the contestant with whom the refusal lies; and the Office may, at its discretion, receive and consider a copy of the withheld deposition, attested by such evidence as is procurable.

(i) *Inspection of depositions.* After the depositions are filed in the Office, they may be inspected by any party to the case, but they cannot be withdrawn for the purpose of printing. They may be printed by someone specially designated by the Office for that purpose, under proper restrictions.

(j) *Effect of errors and irregularities in depositions:* Rule 32(d) (1), (2), and (3) (A) and (B) of the Federal Rules of Civil Procedure shall apply to errors and irregularities in depositions. Notice will not be taken of merely formal or technical objections which shall not appear to have wrought a substantial injury to the party raising them; and in case of such injury it must be made to appear that the objection was raised at the time specified in said rule.

(k) *Objections to admissibility:* Subject to the provisions of paragraph (j) of this section, objection may be made to receiving in evidence any deposition, or part thereof, or any other evidence, for any reason which would require the exclusion of the evidence from consideration. Objections to the competency of a witness or to the competency, relevancy, or materiality of testimony must be raised at the time specified in Rule 32(d)(3)(A) of the Federal Rules of Civil Procedure. Such

objections will not be considered until final hearing.

(l) *Evidence not considered.* Evidence not obtained and filed in compliance with these sections will not be considered.

[37 FR 7607, Apr. 18, 1972, as amended at 41 FR 760, Jan. 5, 1976; 48 FR 23139, May 23, 1983; 54 FR 34899, Aug. 22, 1989; 54 FR 38041, Sept. 14, 1989]

§ 2.124 Depositions upon written questions.

(a) A deposition upon written questions may be taken before any person before whom depositions may be taken as provided by Rule 28 of the Federal Rules of Civil Procedure.

(b)(1) A party desiring to take a testimonial deposition upon written questions shall serve notice thereof upon each adverse party within ten days from the opening date of the testimony period of the party who serves the notice. The notice shall state the name and address of the witness. A copy of the notice, but not copies of the questions, shall be filed with the Trademark Trial and Appeal Board.

(2) A party desiring to take a discovery deposition upon written questions shall serve notice thereof upon each adverse party and shall file a copy of the notice, but not copies of the questions, with the Board. The notice shall state the name and address, if known, of the person whose deposition is to be taken. If the name of the person is not known, a general description sufficient to identify him or the particular class or group to which he belongs shall be stated in the notice, and the party from whom the discovery deposition is to be taken shall designate one or more persons to be deposed in the same manner as is provided by Rule 30(b)(6) of the Federal Rules of Civil Procedure.

(c) Every notice given under the provisions of paragraph (b) of this section shall be accompanied by the name or descriptive title of the officer before whom the deposition is to be taken.

(d)(1) Every notice served on any adverse party under the provisions of paragraph (b) of this section shall be accompanied by the written questions to be propounded on behalf of the party who proposes to take the deposition. Within twenty days from the date of service of the notice, any adverse party may serve cross questions upon the party who proposes to take the deposition; any party who serves cross questions shall also serve every other adverse party. Within ten days from the date of service of the cross questions, the party who proposes to take the deposition may serve redirect questions on every adverse party. Within ten days from the date of service of the redirect questions, any party who served cross questions may serve recross questions upon the party who proposes to take the deposition; any party who serves recross questions shall also serve every other adverse party. Written objections to questions may be served on a party propounding questions; any party who objects shall serve a copy of the objections on every other adverse party. In response to objections, substitute questions may be served on the objecting party within ten days of the date of service of the objections; substitute questions shall be served on every other adverse party.

(2) Upon motion for good cause by any party, or upon its own initiative, the Trademark Trial and Appeal Board may extend any of the time periods provided by paragraph (d)(1) of this section. Upon receipt of written notice that one or more testimonial depositions are to be taken upon written questions, the Trademark Trial and Appeal Board shall suspend or reschedule other proceedings in the matter to allow for the orderly completion of the depositions upon written questions.

(e) Within ten days after the last date when questions, objections, or substitute questions may be served, the party who proposes to take the deposition shall mail a copy of the notice and copies of all the questions to the officer designated in the notice; a copy of the notice and of all the questions mailed to the officer shall be served on every adverse party. The officer designated in the notice shall take the testimony of the witness in response to the questions and shall record each answer immediately after the corresponding question. The offi-

cer shall then certify the transcript and mail the transcript and exhibits to the party who took the deposition.

(f) The party who took the deposition shall promptly serve a copy of the transcript, copies of documentary exhibits, and duplicates or photographs of physical exhibits on every adverse party. It is the responsibility of the party who takes the deposition to assure that the transcript is correct (see §2.125(b)). If the deposition is a discovery deposition, it may be made of record as provided by §2.120(j). If the deposition is a testimonial deposition, the original, together with copies of documentary exhibits and duplicates or photographs of physical exhibits, shall be filed promptly with the Trademark Trial and Appeal Board.

(g) Objections to questions and answers in depositions upon written questions may be considered at final hearing.

[48 FR 23139, May 23, 1983]

§2.125 Filing and service of testimony.

(a) One copy of the transcript of testimony taken in accordance with §2.123, together with copies of documentary exhibits and duplicates or photographs of physical exhibits, shall be served on each adverse party within thirty days after completion of the taking of that testimony. If the transcript with exhibits is not served on each adverse party within thirty days or within an extension of time for the purpose, any adverse party which was not served may have remedy by way of a motion to the Trademark Trial and Appeal Board to reset such adverse party's testimony and/or briefing periods, as may be appropriate. If the deposing party fails to serve a copy of the transcript with exhibits on an adverse party after having been ordered to do so by the Board, the Board, in its discretion, may strike the deposition, or enter judgment as by default against the deposing party, or take any such other action as may be deemed appropriate.

(b) The party who takes testimony is responsible for having all typographical errors in the transcript and all errors of arrangement, indexing and form of the transcript corrected, on notice to each adverse party, prior to the filing of one certified transcript with the Trademark Trial and Appeal Board. The party who takes testimony is responsible for serving on each adverse party one copy of the corrected transcript or, if reasonably feasible, corrected pages to be inserted into the transcript previously served.

(c) One certified transcript and exhibits shall be filed promptly with the Trademark Trial and Appeal Board. Notice of such filing shall be served on each adverse party and a copy of each notice shall be filed with the Board.

(d) Each transcript shall comply with § 2.123(g) with respect to arrangement, indexing and form.

(e) Upon motion by any party, for good cause, the Trademark Trial and Appeal Board may order that any part of a deposition transcript or any exhibits that directly disclose any trade secret or other confidential research, development, or commercial information may be filed under seal and kept confidential under the provisions of § 2.27(e). If any party or any attorney or agent of a party fails to comply with an order made under this paragraph, the Board may impose any of the sanctions authorized by § 2.120(g).

[48 FR 23140, May 23, 1983, as amended at 54 FR 34900, Aug. 22, 1989]

§ 2.126 [Reserved]

§ 2.127 Motions.

(a) Every motion shall be made in writing, shall contain a full statement of the grounds, and shall embody or be accompanied by a brief. A brief in response to a motion shall be filed within fifteen days from the date of service of the motion unless another time is specified by the Trademark Trial and Appeal Board or the time is extended by order of the Board on motion for good cause. When a party fails to file a brief in response to a motion, the Board may treat the motion as conceded. An oral hearing will not be held on a motion except on order by the Board.

(b) Any request for reconsideration or modification of an order or decision issued on a motion must be filed within thirty days from the date thereof. A brief in response must be filed within fifteen days from the date of service of the request.

(c) Interlocutory motions, requests, and other matters not actually or potentially dispositive of a proceeding may be acted upon by a single Member of the Trademark Trial and Appeal Board or by an Attorney-Examiner of the Board to whom authority so to act has been delegated.

(d) When any party files a motion to dismiss, or a motion for judgment on the pleadings, or a motion for summary judgment, or any other motion which is potentially dispositive of a proceeding, the case will be suspended by the Trademark Trial and Appeal Board with respect to all matters not germane to the motion and no party should file any paper which is not germane to the motion. If the case is not disposed of as a result of the motion, proceedings will be resumed pursuant to an order of the Board when the motion is decided.

(e)(1) A motion for summary judgment should be filed prior to the commencement of the first testimony period, as originally set or as reset, and the Trademark Trial and Appeal Board, in its discretion, may deny as untimely any motion for summary judgment filed thereafter.

(2) For purposes of summary judgment only, a discovery deposition, or an answer to an interrogatory, or a document or thing produced in response to a request for production, or an admission to a request for admission, will be considered by the Trademark Trial and Appeal Board if any party files, with the party's brief on the summary judgment motion, the deposition or any part thereof with any exhibit to the part that is filed, or a copy of the interrogatory and answer thereto with any exhibit made part of the answer, or a copy of the request for production and the documents or things produced in response thereto, or a copy of the request for admission and any exhibit thereto and the admission (or a statement that the party from which an admission was requested failed to respond thereto).

(f) The Board does not have authority to hold any person in contempt, or to award attorneys' fees or other expenses to any party.

[48 FR 23140, May 23, 1983, as amended at 54 FR 34900, Aug. 22, 1989]

§ 2.128 Briefs at final hearing.

(a)(1) The brief of the party in the position of plaintiff shall be due not later than sixty days after the date set for the close of rebuttal testimony. The brief of the party in the position of defendant, if filed, shall be due not later than thirty days after the due date of the first brief. A reply brief by the party in the position of plaintiff, if filed, shall be due not later than fifteen days after the due date of the defendant's brief.

(2) When there is a counterclaim, or when proceedings have been consolidated and one party is in the position of plaintiff in one of the involved proceedings and in the position of defendant in another of the involved proceedings, or when there is an interference or a concurrent use registration proceeding involving more than two parties, the Trademark Trial and Appeal Board will set the due dates for the filing of the main brief, and the answering brief, and the rebuttal brief by the parties.

(3) When a party in the position of plaintiff fails to file a main brief, an order may be issued allowing plaintiff until a set time, not less than fifteen days, in which to show cause why the Board should not treat such failure as a concession of the case. If plaintiff fails to file a response to the order, or files a response indicating that he has lost interest in the case, judgment may be entered against plaintiff.

(b) Briefs shall be submitted in typewritten or printed form, double spaced, in at least pica or eleven-point type, on letter-size paper Each brief shall contain an alphabetical index of cases cited therein. Without prior leave of the Trademark Trial and Appeal Board, a main brief on the case shall not exceed fifty-five pages in length in its entirety, including the table of contents, index of cases, description of the record, statement of the issues, recitation of facts, argument, and summary; and a reply brief shall not exceed twenty-five pages in its entirety. Three legible copies, on good quality paper, of each brief shall be filed.

[48 FR 23140, May 23, 1983; 48 FR 27226, June 14, 1983; 54 FR 34900, Aug. 22, 1989]

§ 2.129 Oral argument; reconsideration.

(a) If a party desires to have an oral argument at final hearing, the party shall request such argument by a separate notice filed not later than ten days after the due date for the filing of the last reply brief in the proceeding. Oral arguments will be heard by at least three Members of the Trademark Trial and Appeal Board at the time specified in the notice of hearing. If any party appears at the specified time, that party will be heard. If the Board is prevented from hearing the case at the specified time, a new hearing date will be set. Unless otherwise permitted, oral arguments in an inter partes case will be limited to thirty minutes for each party. A party in the position of plaintiff may reserve part of the time allowed for oral argument to present a rebuttal argument.

(b) The date or time of a hearing may be reset, so far as is convenient and proper, to meet the wishes of the parties and their attorneys or other authorized representatives.

(c) Any request for rehearing or reconsideration or modification of a decision issued after final hearing must be filed within one month from the date of the decision. A brief in response must be filed within fifteen days from the date of service of the request. The times specified may be extended by order of the Trademark Trial and Appeal Board on motion for good cause.

(d) When a party to an inter partes proceeding before the Trademark Trial and Appeal Board cannot prevail without establishing constructive use pursuant to section 7(c) of the Act in an application under section 1(b) of the Act, the Trademark Trial and Appeal Board will enter a judgment in favor of that party, subject to the party's establishment of constructive use. The time for filing an appeal or for commencing a civil action under section 21 of the Act shall run from the date of the entry of the judgment.

[48 FR 23141, May 23, 1983; 54 FR 29554, July 13, 1989; 54 FR 34900, Aug. 22, 1989; 54 FR 37597, Sept. 11, 1989]

§ 2.130 New matter suggested by Examiner of Trademarks.

If, during the pendency of an inter partes case, facts appear which, in the opinion of the Examiner of Trademarks, render the mark of any applicant involved unregistrable, the attention of the Trademark Trial and Appeal Board shall be called thereto. The Board may suspend the proceeding and refer the application to the Examiner of Trademarks for his determination of the question of registrability, following the final determination of which the application shall be returned to the Board for such further inter partes action as may be appropriate. The consideration of such facts by the Examiner of Trademarks shall be ex parte, but a copy of the action of the examiner will be furnished to the parties to the inter partes proceeding.

§ 2.131 Remand after decision in inter partes proceeding.

If, during an inter partes proceeding, facts are disclosed which appear to render the mark of an applicant unregistrable, but such matter has not been tried under the pleadings as filed by the parties or as they might be deemed to be amended under Rule 15(b) of the Federal Rules of Civil Procedure to conform to the evidence, the Trademark Trial and Appeal Board, in lieu of determining the matter in the decision on the proceeding, may refer the application to the examiner for reexamination in the event the applicant ultimately prevails in the inter partes proceeding. Upon receiving the application, the examiner shall withhold registration pending reexamination of the application in the light of the reference by the Board. If, upon reexamination, the examiner finally refuses registration to the applicant, an appeal may be taken as provided by §§ 2.141 and 2.142.

[48 FR 23141, May 23, 1983]

§ 2.132 Involuntary dismissal for failure to take testimony.

(a) If the time for taking testimony by any party in the position of plaintiff has expired and that party has not taken testimony or offered any other evidence, any party in the position of defendant may, without waiving the right to offer evidence in the event the motion is denied, move for dismissal on the ground of the failure of the plaintiff to prosecute. The party in the position of plaintiff shall have fifteen days from the date of service of the motion to show cause why judgment should not be rendered against him. In the absence of a showing of good and sufficient cause, judgment may be rendered against the party in the position of plaintiff. If the motion is denied, testimony periods will be reset for the party in the position of defendant and for rebuttal.

(b) If no evidence other than a copy or copies of Patent and Trademark Office records is offered by any party in the position of plaintiff, any party in the position of defendant may, without waiving the right to offer evidence in the event the motion is denied, move for dismissal on the ground that upon the law and the facts the party in the position of plaintiff has shown no right to relief. The party in the position of plaintiff shall have fifteen days from the date of service of the motion to file a brief in response to the motion. The Trademark Trial and Appeal Board may render judgment against the party in the position of plaintiff, or the Board may decline to render judgment until all of the evidence is in the record. If judgment is not rendered, testimony periods will be reset for the party in the position of defendant and for rebuttal.

(c) A motion filed under paragraph (a) or (b) of this section must be filed before the opening of the testimony period of the moving party, except that the Trademark Trial and Appeal Board may in its discretion grant a motion under paragraph (a) even if the motion was filed after the opening of the testimony period of the moving party.

[48 FR 23141, May 23, 1983, as amended at 51 FR 28710, Aug. 11, 1986]

§ 2.133 Amendment of application or registration during proceedings.

(a) An application involved in a proceeding may not be amended in substance nor may a registration be amended or disclaimed in part, except with the consent of the other party or parties and the approval of the Trademark Trial and Appeal Board, or except upon motion.

(b) If, in an inter partes proceeding, the Trademark Trial and Appeal Board finds that a party whose application or registration is the subject of the proceeding is not entitled to registration in the absence of a specified restriction to the involved application or registration, the Trademark Trial and Appeal Board will allow the party time in which to file a request that the application or registration be amended to conform to the findings of the Trademark Trial and Appeal Board, failing which judgment will be entered against the party.

(c) Geographic limitations will be considered and determined by the Trademark Trial and Appeal Board only in the context of a concurrent use registration proceeding.

(d) A plaintiff's pleaded registration will not be restricted in the absence of a counterclaim to cancel the registration in whole or in part, except that a counterclaim need not be filed if the registration is the subject of another proceeding between the same parties or anyone in privity therewith.

[54 FR 37597, Sept. 11, 1989]

§ 2.134 Surrender or voluntary cancellation of registration.

(a) After the commencement of a cancellation proceeding, if the respondent applies for cancellation of the involved registration under section 7(d) of the Act of 1946 without the written consent of every adverse party to the proceeding, judgment shall be entered against the respondent. The written consent of an adverse party may be signed by the adverse party or by the adverse party's attorney or other authorized representative.

(b) After the commencement of a cancellation proceeding, if it comes to the attention of the Trademark Trial and Appeal Board that the respondent has permitted his involved registration to be cancelled under section 8 of the Act of 1946 or has failed to renew his involved registration under section 9 of the Act of 1946, an order may be issued allowing respondent until a set time, not less than fifteen days, in which to show cause why such cancellation or failure to renew should not be deemed to be the equivalent of a cancellation by request of respondent without the consent of the adverse party and should not result in entry of judgment against respondent as provided by paragraph (a) of this section. In the absence of a showing of good and sufficient cause, judgment may be entered against respondent as provided by paragraph (a) of this section.

[48 FR 23141, May 23, 1983, as amended at 54 FR 34900, Aug. 22, 1989]

§ 2.135 Abandonment of application or mark.

After the commencement of an opposition, concurrent use, or interference proceeding, if the applicant files a written abandonment of the application or of the mark without the written consent of every adverse party to the proceeding, judgment shall be entered against the applicant. The written consent of an adverse party may be signed by the adverse party or by the adverse party's attorney or other authorized representative.

[54 FR 34900, Aug. 22, 1989]

§ 2.136 Status of application on termination of proceeding.

On termination of a proceeding involving an application, the application, if the judgment is not adverse, returns to the status it had before the institution of the proceedings. If the judgment is adverse to the applicant, the application stands refused without further action and all proceedings thereon are considered terminated.

APPEALS

§ 2.141 Ex parte appeals from the Examiner of Trademarks.

Every applicant for the registration of a mark may, upon final refusal by the Examiner of Trademarks, appeal to the Trademark Trial and Appeal Board upon payment of the prescribed fee for each class in the application for which an appeal is taken. An appeal which includes insufficient fees to cover all classes in the application should specify the particular class or classes in which an appeal is taken. A second refusal on the same grounds may be considered as final by the applicant for purpose of appeal.

[41 FR 760, Jan. 5, 1976]

§ 2.142 Time and manner of ex parte appeals.

(a) Any appeal filed under the provisions of § 2.141 must be filed within six months from the date of final refusal or the date of the action from which the appeal is taken. An appeal is taken by filing a notice of appeal and paying the appeal fee.

(b)(1) The brief of appellant shall be filed within sixty days from the date of appeal. If the brief is not filed within the time allowed, the appeal may be dismissed. The examiner shall, within sixty days after the brief of appellant is sent to the examiner, file with the Trademark Trial and Appeal Board a written brief answering the brief of appellant and shall mail a copy of the brief to the appellant. The appellant may file a reply brief within twenty days from the date of mailing of the brief of the examiner.

(2) Briefs shall be submitted in type-written or printed form, double spaced, in at least pica or eleven-point type, on letter-size paper. Without prior leave of the Trademark Trial and Appeal Board, a brief shall not exceed twenty-five pages in length in its entirety.

(c) All requirements made by the examiner and not the subject of appeal shall be complied with prior to the filing of an appeal.

(d) The record in the application should be complete prior to the filing of an appeal. The Trademark Trial and Appeal Board will ordinarily not consider additional evidence filed with the Board by the appellant or by the examiner after the appeal is filed. After an appeal is filed, if the appellant or the examiner desires to introduce additional evidence, the appellant or the examiner may request the Board to suspend the appeal and to remand the application for further examination.

(e)(1) If the appellant desires an oral hearing, a request therefor should be made by a separate notice filed not later than ten days after the due date for a reply brief. Oral argument will be heard by at least three Members of the Trademark Trial and Appeal Board at the time specified in the notice of hearing, which may be reset if the Board is prevented from hearing the argument at the specified time or, so far as is convenient and proper, to meet the wish of the appellant or his attorney or other authorized representative.

(2) If the appellant requests an oral argument, the examiner who issued the refusal of registration or the requirement from which the appeal is taken, or in lieu thereof another examiner from the same examining division as designated by the supervisory attorney thereof, shall present an oral argument. If no request for an oral hearing is made by the appellant, the appeal will be decided on the record and briefs.

(3) Oral argument will be limited to twenty minutes by the appellant and ten minutes by the examiner. The appellant may reserve part of the time allowed for oral argument to present a rebuttal argument.

(f)(1) If, during an appeal from a refusal of registration, it appears to the Trademark Trial and Appeal Board that an issue not previously raised may render the mark of the appellant unregistrable, the Board may suspend the appeal and remand the application to the examiner for further examination to be completed within thirty days.

(2) If the further examination does not result in an additional ground for refusal of registration, the examiner shall promptly return the application to the Board, for resumption of the appeal, with a written statement that further examination did not result in an additional ground for refusal of registration.

(3) If the further examination does result in an additional ground for refusal of registration, the examiner and appellant shall proceed as provided by §§ 2.61, 2.62, 2.63 and 2.64. If the ground for refusal is made final, the examiner shall return the application to the Board, which shall thereupon issue an order allowing the appellant sixty days from the date of the order to file a supplemental brief limited to

the additional ground for the refusal of registration. If the supplemental brief is not filed by the appellant within the time allowed, the appeal may be dismissed.

(4) If the supplemental brief of the appellant is filed, the examiner shall, within sixty days after the supplemental brief of the appellant is sent to the examiner, file with the Board a written brief answering the supplemental brief of appellant and shall mail a copy of the brief to the appellant. The appellant may file a reply brief within twenty days from the date of mailing of the brief of the examiner.

(5) If an oral hearing on the appeal had been requested prior to the remand of the application but not yet held, an oral hearing will be set and heard as provided in paragraph (e) of this section. If an oral hearing had been held prior to the remand or had not been previously requested by the appellant, an oral hearing may be requested by the appellant by a separate notice filed not later than ten days after the due date for a reply brief on the additional ground for refusal of registration. If the appellant files a request for an oral hearing, one will be set and heard as provided in paragraph (e) of this section.

(6) If, during an appeal from a refusal of registration, it appears to the examiner that an issue not involved in the appeal may render the mark of the appellant unregistrable, the examiner may, by written request, ask the Board to suspend the appeal and to remand the application to the examiner for further examination. If the request is granted, the examiner and appellant shall proceed as provided by §§ 2.61, 2.62, 2.63 and 2.64. After the additional ground for refusal of registration has been withdrawn or made final, the examiner shall return the application to the Board, which shall resume proceedings in the appeal and take further appropriate action with respect thereto.

(g) An application which has been considered and decided on appeal will not be reopened except for the entry of a disclaimer under section 6 of the Act of 1946 or upon order of the Commissioner, but a petition to the Commissioner to reopen an application will

be considered only upon a showing of sufficient cause for consideration of any matter not already adjudicated.

[48 FR 23141, May 23, 1983, as amended at 54 FR 34901, Aug. 22, 1989]

§ 2.144 Reconsideration of decision on ex parte appeal.

Any request for rehearing or reconsideration, or modification of the decision, must be filed within one month from the date of the decision. Such time may be extended by the Trademark Trial and Appeal Board upon a showing of sufficient cause.

[54 FR 29554, July 13, 1989]

§ 2.145 Appeal to court and civil action.

(a) Appeal to U.S. Court of Appeals for the Federal Circuit. An applicant for registration, or any party to an interference, opposition, or cancellation proceeding or any party to an application to register as a concurrent user, hereinafter referred to as inter partes proceedings, who is dissatisfied with the decision of the Trademark Trial and Appeal Board and any registrant who has filed an affidavit or declaration under section 8 of the Act or who has filed an application for renewal and is dissatisfied with the decision of the Commissioner (§§ 2.165, 2.184), may appeal to the U.S. Court of Appeals for the Federal Circuit. The appellant must take the following steps in such an appeal:

(1) In the Patent and Trademark Office give written notice of appeal to the Commissioner (see paragraphs (b) and (d) of this section);

(2) In the court, file a copy of the notice of appeal and pay the fee for appeal, as provided by the rules of the Court.

(b) *Notice of appeal.* (1) When an appeal is taken to the U.S. Court of Appeals for the Federal Circuit, the appellant shall give notice thereof in writing to the Commissioner, which notice shall be filed in the Patent and Trademark Office, within the time specified in paragraph (d) of this section. The notice shall specify the party or parties taking the appeal and shall designate the decision or part thereof appealed from.

(2) In inter partes proceedings, the notice must be served as provided in § 2.119.

(3) The notice, if mailed to the Office, shall be addressed as follows: Box 8, Commissioner of Patents and Trademarks, Washington, DC 20231.

(c) *Civil action.* (1) Any person who may appeal to the U.S. Court of Appeals for the Federal Circuit (paragraph (a) of this section), may have remedy by civil action under section 21(b) of the Act. Such civil action must be commenced within the time specified in paragraph (d) of this section.

(2) Any applicant or registrant in an ex parte case who takes an appeal to the U.S. Court of Appeals for the Federal Circuit waives any right to proceed under section 21(b) of the Act.

(3) Any adverse party to an appeal taken to the U.S. Court of Appeals for the Federal Circuit by a defeated party in an inter partes proceeding may file a notice with the Commissioner within twenty days after the filing of the defeated party's notice of appeal to the court (paragraph (b) of this section), electing to have all further proceedings conducted as provided in section 21(b) of the Act. The notice of election must be served as provided in § 2.119. The certificate of mailing practice of § 1.8 is not available for filing a notice of election. See § 1.8(a)(2)(viii).

(4) A party to a proceeding before the Trademark Trial and Appeal Board which commences a civil action, pursuant to section 21(b) of the Act, seeking review of a decision of the Board should file written notice thereof in the Patent and Trademark Office, addressed to the Board, within one month after the expiration of the time for appeal or civil action, in order to avoid premature termination of the Board proceeding.

(d) *Time for appeal or civil action.* (1) The time for filing the notice of appeal to the U.S. Court of Appeals for the Federal Circuit (paragraph (b) of this section), or for commencing a civil action (paragraph (c) of this section), is two months from the date of the decision of the Trademark Trial and Appeal Board or the Commissioner, as the case may be. If a request for rehearing or reconsideration or modification of the decision is filed within the time specified in §§ 2.127(b), 2.129(c) or § 2.144, or within any extension of time granted thereunder, the time for filing an appeal or commencing a civil action shall expire two months after action on the request. In inter partes cases, the time for filing a cross-action or a notice of a cross-appeal expires (i) 14 days after service of the notice of appeal or the summons and complaint or (ii) two months from the date of the decision of the Trademark Trial and Appeal Board or the Commissioner, whichever is later. The certificate of mailing practice of § 1.8 is not available for filing a notice of appeal or cross-appeal. See § 1.8(a)(2)(ix).

(2) The times specified in this section in days are calendar days. The times specified herein in months are calendar months except that one day shall be added to any two-month period which includes February 28. If the last day of time specified for an appeal, or commencing a civil action falls on a Saturday, Sunday or Federal holiday in the District of Columbia, the time is extended to the next day which is neither a Saturday, Sunday nor a Federal holiday.

(3) If a party to an inter partes proceeding has taken an appeal to the U.S. Court of Appeals for the Federal Circuit and an adverse party has filed notice under section 21(a)(1) of the Act electing to have all further proceedings conducted under section 21(b) of the Act, the time for filing a civil action thereafter is specified in section 21(a)(1) of the Act. The time for filing a cross-action expires 14 days after service of the summons and complaint.

(e) *Extensions of time to commence judicial review.* The Commissioner may extend the time for filing an appeal or commencing a civil action (1) for good cause shown if requested in writing before the expiration of the period for filing an appeal or commencing a civil action, or (2) upon written request after the expiration of the period for filing an appeal or commencing a civil action upon a showing that the failure to act was the result of excusable neglect.

[47 FR 47382, Oct. 26, 1982, as amended at 51 FR 28710, Aug. 11, 1986; 53 FR 16414, May 9, 1988; 54 FR 29554, July 13, 1989; 54 FR 34901, Aug. 22, 1989]

PETITIONS AND ACTIONS BY THE COMMISSIONER

§ 2.146 Petitions to the Commissioner.

(a) Petition may be taken to the Commissioner: (1) From any repeated or final formal requirement of the examiner in the ex parte prosecution of an application if permitted by § 2.63(b); (2) in any case for which the Act of 1946, or Title 35 of the United States Code, or this part of Title 37 of the *Code of Federal Regulations* specifies that the matter is to be determined directly or reviewed by the Commissioner; (3) to invoke the supervisory authority of the Commissioner in appropriate circumstances; (4) in any case not specifically defined and provided for by this part of Title 37 of the *Code of Federal Regulations*; (5) in an extraordinary situation, when justice requires and no other party is injured thereby, to request a suspension or waiver of any requirement of the rules not being a requirement of the Act of 1946.

(b) Questions of substance arising during the ex parte prosecution of applications, including, but not limited to, questions arising under sections 2, 3, 4, 5, 6 and 23 of the Act of 1946, are not considered to be appropriate subject matter for petitions to the Commissioner.

(c) Every petition to the Commissioner shall include a statement of the facts relevant to the petition, the points to be reviewed, the action or relief that is requested, and the requisite fee (see § 2.6). Any brief in support of the petition shall be embodied in or accompany the petition. When facts are to be proved in ex parte cases (as in a petition to revive an abandoned application), the proof in the form of affidavits or declarations in accordance with § 2.20, and any exhibits, shall accompany the petition.

(d) A petition on any matter not otherwise specifically provided for shall be filed within sixty days from the date of mailing of the action from which relief is requested.

(e)(1) A petition from the denial of a request for an extension of time to file a notice of opposition shall be filed within fifteen days from the date of mailing of the denial of the request and shall be served on the attorney or other authorized representative of the applicant, if any, or on the applicant. Proof of service of the petition shall be made as provided by § 2.119(a). The applicant may file a response within fifteen days from the date of service of the petition and shall serve a copy of the response on the petitioner, with proof of service as provided by § 2.119(a). No further paper relating to the petition shall be filed.

(2) A petition from an interlocutory order of the Trademark Trial and Appeal Board shall be filed within thirty days after the date of mailing of the order from which relief is requested. Any brief in response to the petition shall be filed, with any supporting exhibits, within fifteen days from the date of service of the petition. Petitions and responses to petitions, and any papers accompanying a petition or response, under this subsection shall be served on every adverse party pursuant to § 2.119(a).

(f) An oral hearing will not be held on a petition except when considered necessary by the Commissioner.

(g) The mere filing of a petition to the Commissioner will not act as a stay in any appeal or inter partes proceeding that is pending before the Trademark Trial and Appeal Board nor stay the period for replying to an Office action in an application except when a stay is specifically requested and is granted or when §§ 2.63(b) and 2.65 are applicable to an ex parte application.

(h) Authority to act on petitions, or on any petition, may be delegated by the Commissioner.

[48 FR 23142, May 23, 1983; 48 FR 27226, June 14, 1983]

§ 2.147 [Reserved]

§ 2.148 Commissioner may suspend certain rules.

In an extraordinary situation, when justice requires and no other party is injured thereby, any requirement of the rules in this part not being a requirement of the statute may be suspended or waived by the Commissioner.

CERTIFICATE

§ 2.151 Certificate.

When the requirements of the law and of the rules have been complied with, and the Patent and Trademark Office has adjudged a mark registrable, a certificate will be issued to the effect that the applicant has complied with the law and that he is entitled to registration of his mark on the Principal Register or on the Supplemental Register, as the case may be. The certificate will state the date on which the application for registration was filed in the Patent and Trademark Office, the act under which the mark is registered, the date of issue and the number of the certificate. Attached to the certificate and forming a part thereof will be a reproduction of the mark and pertinent data from the application. A notice of the affidavit or declaration requirements of section 8(a) of the Act (§ 2.161) will be printed on the certificate.

PUBLICATION OF MARKS REGISTERED UNDER 1905 ACT

AUTHORITY: Secs. 2.153 to 2.156 also issued under sec. 12, 60 Stat. 432; 15 U.S.C. 1062.

§ 2.153 Publication requirements.

A registrant of a mark registered under the provisions of the Acts of 1881 or 1905 may at any time prior to the expiration of the period for which the registration was issued or renewed, upon the payment of the prescribed fee, file an affidavit or declaration in accordance with § 2.20 setting forth those goods stated in the registration on which said mark is in use in commerce, specifying the nature of such commerce, and stating that the registrant claims the benefits of the Trademark Act of 1946.

[31 FR 5262, Apr. 1, 1966]

§ 2.154 Publication in Official Gazette.

A notice of the claim of benefits under the Act of 1946 and a reproduction of the mark will then be published in the *Official Gazette* as soon as practicable. The published mark will retain its original registration number.

§ 2.155 Notice of publication.

A notice of such publication of the mark and of the requirement for the affidavit or declaration specified in section 8(b) of the Act (§ 2.161) will be sent to the registrant.

§ 2.156 Not subject to opposition: subject to cancellation.

The published mark is not subject to opposition on such publication in the *Official Gazette*, but is subject to petitions to cancel as specified in § 2.111 and to cancellation for failure to file the affidavit or declaration specified in § 2.161.

REREGISTRATION OF MARKS REGISTERED UNDER PRIOR ACTS

§ 2.158 Reregistration of marks registered under Acts of 1881, 1905, and 1920.

Trademarks registered under the Act of 1881, the Act of 1905 or the Act of 1920 may be reregistered under the Act of 1946, either on the Principal Register, if eligible, or on the Supplemental Register, but a new complete application for registration must be filed complying with the rules relating thereto, and such application will be subject to examination and other proceedings in the same manner as other applications filed under the Act of 1946. See § 2.26 for use of old drawing.

CANCELLATION FOR FAILURE TO FILE AFFIDAVIT OR DECLARATION DURING SIXTH YEAR

AUTHORITY: Secs. 2.161 to 2.165 also issued under sec. 8, 60 Stat. 431; 15 U.S.C. 1058.

§ 2.161 Cancellation for failure to file affidavit or declaration during sixth year.

Any registration under the provisions of the Act and any registration published under the provisions of section 12(c) of the Act (§ 2.153) shall be cancelled as to any goods or services recited in the registration at the end of six years following the date of registration or the date of such publication, unless within one year next preceding the expiration of such six years the registrant shall file in the Patent and Trademark Office an affidavit or declaration in accordance with § 2.20 setting forth those goods or services recited in the registration on or in connection with which the mark is in use in commerce and attaching a specimen or facsimile showing current use of the mark, or an affidavit or declaration under § 2.20 showing that its nonuse as to any goods or services recited in the registration is due to special circumstances which excuse such nonuse and is not due to any intention to abandon the mark as to those goods or services.

[54 FR 37597, Sept. 11, 1989]

§ **2.162 Requirements for affidavit or declaration during sixth year.**

The affidavit or declaration required by § 2.161 must:

(a) Be executed by the registrant after expiration of the five-year period following the date of registration or of publication under section 12(c) of the Act;

(b) Be filed in the Patent and Trademark Office before the expiration of the sixth year following the date of registration or of publication under section 12(c) of the Act;

(c) Identify the certificate of registration by the registration number and date of registration;

(d) Include the required fee for each class to which the affidavit or declaration pertains in the registration. If no fee, or a fee insufficient to cover at least one class, is filed before the expiration of the sixth year following the date of registration or of publication under Section 12(c) of the Act, the affidavit or declaration will not be refused if the required fee(s) (See § 2.6) are filed in the Patent and Trademark Office within the time limit set forth in the notification of this defect by the Office. If insufficient fees are included to cover all classes in the registration, the particular class or classes to which the affidavit or declaration pertains should be specified.

(e) State that the registered mark is in use in commerce, list the goods or services recited in the registration on or in connection with which the mark is in use in commerce, and specify the nature of such commerce (except under paragraph (f) of this section). The statement must be accompanied by a specimen or facsimile, for each class of goods or services, showing current use of the mark. If the specimen or facsimile is found to be deficient, a substitute specimen or facsimile may be submitted and considered even though filed after the sixth year has expired, provided it is supported by an affidavit or declaration pursuant to § 2.20 verifying that the specimen or facsimile was in use in commerce prior to the expiration of the sixth year;

(f) If the registered mark is not in use in commerce on or in connection with the goods or services recited in the registration, recite facts to show that nonuse as to those goods or services is due to special circumstances which excuse such nonuse and is not due to any intention to abandon the mark as to those goods or services. If the facts recited are found insufficient, further evidence or explanation may be submitted and considered even though filed after the sixth year has expired; and

(g) Contain the statement of use in commerce or statement as to nonuse and appropriate specimen or facsimile, as required in paragraphs (e) and (f) of this section, for each class to which the affidavit or declaration pertains in this registration.

(Secs. 8 and 9, Pub. L. 97-247 (96 Stat. 320); 35 U.S.C. 6; 15 U.S.C. 1113, 1123)

[41 FR 761, Jan. 5, 1976, as amended at 47 FR 41282, Sept. 17, 1982; 48 FR 3977, Jan. 28, 1983; 54 FR 37597, Sept. 11, 1989]

§ **2.163 Notice to registrant.**

If no affidavit or declaration is filed within a reasonable time prior to expiration of the sixth year, the registrant may be notified that the registration will be cancelled by the Commissioner at the end of such sixth year unless the owner files in the Patent and Trademark Office the affidavit or declaration of use or excusable nonuse required by section 8. Failure to notify the registrant does not, however, relieve the registrant of the responsibility of filing the affidavit or declaration within the period required by statute.

§ 2.164 Acknowledgment of receipt of affidavit or declaration.

The registrant will be notified by the Examiner of Trademarks of the receipt of the affidavit or declaration and, if satisfactory, of its acceptance.

§ 2.165 Reconsideration of affidavit or declaration.

(a)(1) If the affidavit or declaration filed pursuant to § 2.162 is insufficient or defective, the affidavit or declaration will be refused and the registrant will be notified of the reason. Reconsideration of the refusal may be requested within six months from the date of the mailing of the action. The request for reconsideration must state the grounds for the request. A supplemental or substitute affidavit or declaration required by section 8 of the Act of 1946 cannot be considered unless it is filed before the expiration of six years from the date of the registration or from the date of publication under section 12(c) of the Act. The certificate of mailing procedure provided by § 1.8 does not apply to affidavits or declarations or to supplemental or substitute affidavits or declarations filed under section 8 (a) or (b) of the Act, but the certificate of mailing by "Express Mail" procedure provided by § 1.10 does apply thereto.

(2) A request for reconsideration shall be a condition precedent to a petition to the Commissioner to review the refusal of the affidavit or declaration unless the first action refusing the affidavit or declaration directs the registrant to petition the Commissioner for relief, in which event the petition must be filed within six months from the date of mailing of the action.

(b) If the refusal of the affidavit or declaration is adhered to, the registrant may petition the Commissioner to review the action under § 2.146(a)(2). The petition to the Commissioner requesting review of the action adhering to the refusal of the affidavit or declaration must be filed within six months from the date of mailing of the action which denied reconsideration.

(c) The decision of the Commissioner on the petition will constitute the final action of the Patent and Trademark Office. If there is no petition to the Commissoner, the Commissioner will notify the registrant of the refusal of the affidavit or declaration after the expiration of six years from the date of registration or from the date of publication under section 12(c) of the Act of 1946, and such notice will constitute the final action of the Office.

(d) A petition to the Commissioner for review of the action shall be a condition precedent to an appeal to or action for review by any court.

[48 FR 23143, May 23, 1983]

§ 2.166 Time of cancellation.

If no affidavit or declaration is filed within the sixth year following registration or publication under section 12(c) of the Act, the registration will be cancelled forthwith by the Commissioner. If the affidavit or declaration is filed but is refused, cancellation of the registration will be withheld pending further proceedings.

AFFIDAVIT OR DECLARATION UNDER SECTION 15

§ 2.167 Affidavit or declaration under section 15.

The affidavit or declaration in accordance with § 2.20 provided by section 15 of the Act for acquiring incontestability for a mark registered on the Principal Register or a mark registered under the Act of 1881 or 1905 and published under section 12(c) of the Act (§ 2.153) must:

(a) Be signed by the registrant;

(b) Identify the certificate of registration by the certificate number and date of registration;

(c) Recite the goods or services stated in the registration on or in connection with which the mark has been in continuous use in commerce for a period of five years subsequent to the date of registration or date of publication under section 12(c) of the Act, and is still in use in commerce, specifying the nature of such commerce;

(d) Specify that there has been no final decision adverse to registrant's claim of ownership of such mark for such goods or services, or to registrant's right to register the same or to keep the same on the register;

(e) Specify that there is no proceeding involving said rights pending in the Patent and Trademark Office or in a court and not finally disposed of;

(f) Be filed within one year after the expiration of any five-year period of continuous use following registration or publication under section 12(c).

The registrant will be notified of the receipt of the affidavit or declaration.

(g) Include the required fee for each class to which the affidavit or declaration pertains in the registration. If no fee, or a fee insufficient to cover at least one class, is filed at an appropriate time, the affidavit or declaration will not be refused if the required fee(s) (See § 2.6) are filed in the Patent and Trademark Office within the time limit set forth in the notification of this defect by the Office. If insufficient fees are included to cover all classes in the registration, the particular class or classes to which the affidavit or declaration pertains should be specified.

(Sec. 15, 60 Stat. 433; 15 U.S.C. 1065; 35 U.S.C. 6; 15 U.S.C. 1113, 1123)

[30 FR 13193, Oct. 16, 1965, as amended at 47 FR 41282, Sept. 17, 1982]

§ 2.168 Combined with other affidavits or declarations.

(a) The affidavit or declaration filed under section 15 of the Act may also be used as the affidavit or declaration required by section 8, provided it also complies with the requirements and is filed within the time limit specified in §§ 2.161 and 2.162.

(b) In appropriate circumstances the affidavit or declaration filed under section 15 of the Act may be combined with the affidavit or declaration required for renewal of a registration (see § 2.183).

CORRECTION, DISCLAIMER, SURRENDER, ETC.

§ 2.171 New certificate on change of ownership.

In case of change of ownership of a registered mark, upon request of the assignee, a new certificate of registration may be issued in the name of the assignee for the unexpired part of the original period. The assignment must be recorded in the Patent and Trademark Office, and the request for the new certificate must be signed by the assignee and accompanied by the required fee. The original certificate of registration, if available, must also be submitted.

(Sec. 7, 60 Stat. 430 as amended; 15 U.S.C. 1057)

[31 FR 5262, Apr. 1, 1966]

§ 2.172 Surrender for cancellation.

Upon application by the registrant, the Commissioner may permit any registration to be surrendered for cancellation. Application for such action must be signed by the registrant and must be accompanied by the original certificate of registration, if not lost or destroyed. When there is more than one class in a registration, one or more entire class but less than the total number of classes may be surrendered as to the specified class or classes. Deletion of less than all of the goods or services in a single class constitutes amendment of registration as to that class (see § 2.173).

(Sec. 7, 60 Stat. 430 as amended; 15 U.S.C. 1057)

[41 FR 761, Jan. 5, 1976]

§ 2.173 Amendment and disclaimer in part.

(a) Upon application by the registrant, the Commissioner may permit any registration to be amended or any registered mark to be disclaimed in part. Application for such action must specify the amendment or disclaimer and be signed by the registrant and verified or include a declaration in accordance with § 2.20, and must be accompanied by the required fee. If the amendment involves a change in the mark, new specimens showing the mark as used in connection with the goods or services, and a new drawing of the amended mark must be submitted. The certificate of registration or, if said certificate is lost or destroyed, a certified copy thereof, must also be submitted in order that the Commissioner may make appropriate entry thereon and in the records of the Office. The registration when so amended must still contain registrable matter and the mark as amended must be registrable as a whole, and such amendment or disclaimer must not involve such changes in the registration as to alter materially the character of the mark.

(b) No amendment in the identification of goods or services in a registration will be permitted except to restrict the identification or otherwise to change it in ways that would not require republication of the mark. No amendment seeking the elimination of a disclaimer will be permitted.

(c) A printed copy of the amendment or disclaimer shall be attached to each printed copy of the registration.

(Sec. 7, 60 Stat. 430, as amended; 15 U.S.C. 1057)

[30 FR 13193, Oct. 16, 1965, as amended at 31 FR 5262, Apr. 1, 1966; 48 FR 23143, May 23, 1983]

§ 2.174   Correction of Office mistake.

Whenever a material mistake in a registration, incurred through the fault of the Patent and Trademark Office, is clearly disclosed by the records of the Office, a certificate stating the fact and nature of such mistake, signed by the Commissioner or by an employee designated by the Commissioner and sealed with the seal of the Patent and Trademark Office, shall be issued without charge and recorded, and a printed copy thereof shall be attached to each printed copy of the registration certificate. Such corrected certificate shall thereafter have the same effect as if the same had been originally issued in such corrected form, or in the discretion of the Commissioner a new certificate of registration may be issued without charge. The certificate of registration or, if said certificate is lost or destroyed, a certified copy thereof, must be submitted in order that the Commissioner may make appropriate entry thereon.

(Sec. 7, 60 Stat. 430, as amended; 15 U.S.C. 1057)

§ 2.175   Correction of mistake by registrant.

(a) Whenever a mistake has been made in a registration and a showing has been made that such mistake occurred in good faith through the fault of the applicant, the Commissioner may issue a certificate of correction, or in his discretion, a new certificate upon the payment of the required fee, provided that the correction does not involve such changes in the registration as to require republication of the mark.

(b) Application for such action must specify the mistake for which correction is sought and the manner in which it arose, show that it occurred in good faith, be signed by the applicant and verified or include a declaration in accordance with § 2.20, and be accompanied by the required fee. The certificate of registration or, if said certificate is lost or destroyed, a certified copy thereof, must also be submitted in order that the Commissioner may make appropriate entry thereon.

(c) A printed copy of the certificate of correction shall be attached to each printed copy of the registration.

(Sec. 7, 60 Stat. 430, as amended; 15 U.S.C. 1057)

[30 FR 13193, Oct. 16, 1965, as amended at 31 FR 5262, Apr. 1, 1966]

§ 2.176   Consideration of above matters.

The matters in §§ 2.171 to 2.175 will be considered in the first instance by the Examiner of Trademarks. If the action of the Examiner of Trademarks is adverse, registrant may request the Commissioner to review the action under § 2.146. If response to an adverse action of the Examiner is not made by the registrant within six months, the matter will be considered abandoned.

TERM AND RENEWAL

AUTHORITY: Secs. 2.181 to 2.184 also issued under sec. 9, 60 Stat. 431; 15 U.S.C. 1059.

§ 2.181   Term of original registrations and renewals.

(a)(1) Registrations issued or renewed under the Act, prior to November 16, 1989, whether on the Principal Register or on the Supplemental Register, remain in force for twenty years from their date of issue or expiration, and may be renewed for periods of ten years from the expiring period unless previously cancelled or surrendered.

(2) Registrations issued or renewed under the Act on or after November 16, 1989, whether on the Principal Register or on the Supplemental Register, remain in force for ten years from their date of issue or expiration, and may be renewed for periods of ten years from the expiring period unless previously cancelled or surrendered.

(b) Registrations issued under the Acts of 1905 and 1881 remain in force for their unexpired terms and may be renewed in the same manner as registrations under the Act of 1946.

(c) Registrations issued under the Act of 1920 cannot be renewed unless renewal is required to support foreign registrations and in such case may be renewed on the Supplemental Register in the same manner as registrations under the Act of 1946.

[30 FR 13193, Oct. 16, 1965, as amended at 54 FR 37597, Sept. 11, 1989]

§ 2.182 **Period within which application for renewal must be filed.**

An application for renewal may be filed by the registrant at any time within six months before the expiration of the period for which the certificate of registration was issued or renewed, or it may be filed within three months after such expiration on payment of the additional fee required.

§ 2.183 **Requirements of application for renewal.**

(a) The application for renewal must include a statement which is verified or which includes a declaration in accordance with § 2.20 by the registrant setting forth the goods or services recited in each class for which renewal is sought in the registration on or in connection with which the mark is still in use in commerce, specifying the nature of such commerce (except under paragraph (c) of this section). This statement must be executed not more than six months before the expiration of the registration and must:

(1) Be accompanied by a specimen or facsimile specimen for each class for which renewal is sought in the registration showing current use of the mark.

(2) Include the required fee for each class for which renewal is sought in the registration, and an additional fee for each class in the case of a delayed application for renewal. If the application for renewal includes insufficient fees to cover all classes in the registration, the particular class or classes for which renewal is sought should be specified.

(b) The declaration or verified statement, specimen or facsimile specimen and the fee for each class for which renewal is sought in the registration must be filed within the period prescribed for applying for renewal. If defective or insufficient, they cannot be completed after the period for applying for renewal has passed; if completed after the initial six month period has expired but before the expiration of the three month delay period, the application can be considered only as a delayed application for renewal.

(c) If the mark is not in use in commerce at the time of filing of the declaration or verified statement as to any class for which renewal is sought, facts must be recited to show that nonuse is due to special circumstances which excuse such nonuse and is not due to any intention to abandon the mark. There must be a recitation of facts as to nonuse for each class for which renewal is sought or it must be clear that the facts recited apply to each class sought to be renewed. If the facts recited require amplification, or explanation, in order to show excusable nonuse, further evidence may be submitted and considered even though filed after the period for applying for renewal has passed.

(d) If the applicant is not domiciled in the United States, the application for renewal must include the designation of some person resident in the United States on whom may be served notices or process in proceedings affecting the mark.

(e) If the mark is registered under the Act of 1920, the application for renewal must include a showing which is verified or which includes a declaration in accordance with § 2.20 that renewal is required to support foreign registrations.

[30 FR 13193, Oct. 16, 1965, as amended at 31 FR 5262, Apr. 1, 1966; 41 FR 761, Jan. 5, 1976]

§ 2.184 Refusal of renewal.

(a) If the application for renewal is incomplete or defective, the renewal will be refused. The application may be completed or amended in response to a refusal, subject to the provisions of § 2.183. If a response to a refusal of renewal is not filed within six months from the date of mailing of the action, the application for renewal will be considered abandoned. A request to reconsider a refusal of renewal shall be a condition precedent to a petition to the Commissioner to review the refusal of renewal.

(b) If the refusal of renewal is adhered to, the registrant may petition the Commissioner to review the action under § 2.146(a)(2). The petition to the Commissioner requesting review of the action adhering to the refusal of the renewal must be filed within six months from the date of mailing of the action which adhered to the refusal. If a timely petition to the Commissioner is not filed, the application for renewal will be considered abandoned.

(c) The decision of the Commissioner on the petition will constitute the final action of the Patent and Trademark Office.

(d) A petition to the Commissioner for review of the action shall be a condition precedent to an appeal to or action for review by any court.

[48 FR 23143, May 23, 1983]

ASSIGNMENT OF MARKS

§ 2.185 Requirements for assignments.

(a) Assignments under section 10 of the act of registered marks, or marks for which an application for registration has been filed, will be recorded in the Patent and Trademark Office. Other instruments which may relate to such marks may be recorded in the discretion of the Commissioner. No assignment will be recorded, except as may be ordered by the Commissioner, unless it has been executed and unless:

(1) The certificate of registration is identified in the assignment by the certificate number (the date of registration should also be given), or, the application for registration shall have been first filed in the Patent and Trademark Office and the application is identified in the assignment by serial number (the date of filing should also be given);

(2) It is in the English language or, if not in the English language, accompanied by a translation signed by the translator;

(3) The fee for recording is received; and

(4) A designation of a domestic representative is made in case the assignee is not domiciled in the United States. The designation must be separate from the assignment and there must be a separate designation for each registration or application assigned in one instrument.

(b) The address of the assignee should be recited in the assignment, otherwise it must be given in a separate paper.

(c) The date of record of the assignment is the date of the receipt of the assignment at the Patent and Trademark Office in proper form and accompanied by the full fee for recording.

(Sec. 3, 79 Stat. 260, sec. 10, 60 Stat. 431; 15 U.S.C. 113, 1060)

[30 FR 13193, Oct. 16, 1965, as amended at 41 FR 762, Jan. 5, 1976]

§ 2.186 Action may be taken by assignee of record.

Any action with respect to an assigned application or registration which may or must be taken by an applicant or registrant may be taken by the assignee provided that the assignment has been recorded or that proof of the assignment has been submitted.

[54 FR 34901, Aug. 22, 1989]

§ 2.187 Certificate of registration may issue to assignee.

The certificate of registration may be issued to the assignee of the applicant, or in a new name of applicant, provided that the party makes a written request in the application record, by the time the application is being prepared for issuance of the certificate of registration, and an appropriate document is of record in the Assignment Search Room of the Patent and Trademark Office. If the assignment or name change document is not of record in the Assignment Search Room, then the written request must state that the document has been filed for recordation. The address of the assignee must be made of record in the application file and in the recorded document.

[54 FR 37598, Sept. 11, 1989]

AMENDMENT OF RULES

§ 2.189 Amendments to rules.

(a) All amendments to this part will be published in the *Official Gazette* and in the FEDERAL REGISTER.

(b) Whenever required by law, and in other cases whenever practicable, notice of proposed amendments to these rules will be published in the FEDERAL REGISTER and in the *Official Gazette*. If not published with the notice, copies of the text will be furnished to any person requesting the same. All comments, suggestions, and briefs received within a time specified in the notice will be considered before adoption of the proposed amendments which may be modified in the light thereof. Oral hearings may be held at the discretion of the Commissioner.

Appendixes

International schedule of classes of goods and services

Goods

1 Chemicals products used in industry, science, photography, agriculture, horticulture, forestry; artificial and synthetic resins; plastics in the form of powders, liquids or pastes, for industrial use; manures (natural and artificial); fire extinguishing compositions; tempering substances and chemical preparations for soldering; chemical substances for preserving foodstuffs; tanning substances; adhesive substances used in industry.

2 Paints, varnishes, lacquers; preservatives against rust and against deterioration of wood, colouring matters, dyestuffs; mordants; natural resins; metals in foil and powder form for painters and decorators.

3 Bleaching preparations and other substances for laundry use; cleaning, polishing, scouring and abrasive preparations; soaps; perfumery, essential oils, cosmetics, hair lotions; dentifrices.

4 Industrial oils and greases (other than oils and fats and essential oils); lubricants; dust laying and absorbing compositions; fuels (including motor spirit) and illuminants; candles, tapers, night lights and wicks.

5 Pharmaceutical, veterinary, and sanitary substances; infants' and invalids' foods; plasters, material for bandaging; material for stopping teeth, dental wax, disinfectants; preparations for killing weeds and destroying vermin.

6 Unwrought and partly wrought common metals and their alloys; anchors, anvils, bells, rolled and cast building materials; rails and other metallic materials for railway tracks; chains (except driving chains for vehicles); cables and wires (nonelectric); locksmiths' work; metallic pipes and tubes; safes and cash boxes; steel balls; horseshoes; nails and screws; other goods in nonprecious metal not included in other classes; ores.

7 Machines and machine tools; motors (except for land vehicles); machine couplings and belting (except for land vehicles); large size agricultural implements; incubators.

8 Hand tools and instruments; cutlery, forks, and spoons; side arms.

9 Scientific, nautical, surveying and electrical apparatus and instruments (including wireless), photographic, cinematographic, optical, weighing, measuring, signalling, checking (supervision), life-saving and teaching apparatus and instruments; coin or counterfreed apparatus; talking machines; cash registers; calculating machines; fire extinguishing apparatus.

10 Surgical, medical, dental, and veterinary instruments and apparatus (including artificial limbs, eyes and teeth).

11 Installations for lighting, heating, steam generating, cooking, refrigerating, drying, ventilating, water supply, and sanitary purposes.

12 Vehicles; apparatus for locomotion by land, air or water.

13 Firearms; ammunition and projectiles; explosive substances; fireworks.

14 Precious metals and their alloys and goods in precious metals or coated therewith (except cutlery, forks and spoons); jewelry, precious stones, horological and other chronometric instruments.

15 Musical instruments (other than talking machines and wireless apparatus).

16 Paper and paper articles, cardboard and cardboard articles; printed matter, newspaper and periodicals, books; bookbinding material; photographs; stationery, adhesive materials (stationery); artists' materials; paint brushes; typewriters and office requisites (other than furniture); instructional and teaching material (other than apparatus); playing cards; printers' type and cliches (sterotype).

17 Gutta percha, india rubber, balata and substitutes, articles made from these substances and not included in other classes; plastics in the form of sheets, blocks and rods, being for use in manufacture; materials for packing, stopping and insulating; asbestos, mica and their products; hose pipes (nonmetallic).

18 Leather and imitations of leather, and articles made from these materials and not included in other classes, skins, hides, trunks and travelling bags, umbrellas, parasols and walking sticks, whips, harness and saddlery.

19 Building materials, natural and artificial stone, cement, lime, mortar, plaster and gravel; pipes of earthenware or cement, roadmaking materials, asphalt, pitch and bitumen, portable buildings, stone monuments; chimney pots.

20 Furniture, mirrors, picture frames; articles (not included in other classes) of wood, cork, reeds, cane, wicker, horn, bone, ivory, whalebone, shell, amber, mother-of-pearl, meerschaum, celluloid, substitutes for all these materials, or of plastics.

21 Small domestic utensils and containers (not of precious metals, or coated therewith); combs and sponges; brushes (other than paint brushes); brushmaking materials; instruments and material for cleaning purposes, steel wool; unworked or semi-worked glass (excluding glass used in building); glassware, porcelain and earthenware, not included in other classes.

22 Ropes, string, nets, tents, awnings, tarpaulins, sails, sacks, padding and stuffing materials (hair, kapok, feathers, seaweed, etc.); raw fibrous textile materials.

23 Yarns, threads.

24 Tissues (piece goods); bed and table covers; textile articles not included in other classes.

25 Clothing, including boots, shoes and slippers.

26 Lace and embroidery, ribands and braid; buttons, press buttons, hooks and eyes, pins and needles; artificial flowers.

27 Carpets, rugs, mats and matting; linoleums and other materials for covering existing floors; wall hangings (nontextile).

28 Games and playthings; gymnastic and sporting articles (except clothing); ornaments and decorations for Christmas trees.

29 Meats, fish, poultry and game; meat extracts; preserved, dried and cooked fruits and vegetables; jellies, jams; eggs, milk and other dairy products; edible oils and fats; preserves, pickles.

30 Coffee, tea, cocoa, sugar, rice, tapioca, sage, coffee substitutes; flour, and preparations made from cereals; bread, biscuits, cakes, pastry and confectionary, ices; honey, treacle; yeast, baking powder; salt, mustard, pepper, vinegar, sauces, spices; ice.

31 Agricultural, horticultural and forestry products and grains not included in other classes; living animals; fresh fruits and vegetables; seeds; live plants and flowers; foodstuffs for animals; malt.

32 Beer, ale and porter; mineral and aerated waters and other non-alcoholic drinks; syrups and other preparations for making beverages.

33 Wines, spirits and liqueurs.

34 Tobacco, raw or manufactured; smokers' articles; matches.

Services

35 Advertising and business.

36 Insurance and financial.

37 Construction and repair.

38 Communication.

39 Transportation and storage.

40 Material treatment.

41 Education and entertainment.

42 Miscellaneous.

FEDERAL TRADEMARK SERVICES CO.
3 Christina Centre
201 N. Walnut Street
Wilmington, DE 19801
1-800-542-2677

September 7, 1989

Industrial Cleaning Services, Inc.
123 Main Street
Anytown, Ohio 99999

RE: MAGIC CLEANER

Dear Sir/Madam:

Enclosed please find your trademark search report conducted for the mark "Magic Cleaner".

Pursuant to your request this mark was searched in class 3.

The attached report has been reviewed and detailed information regarding any pertinent marks is included. Our search produced the following results:

-There were 23 related identicals found when searching for two elements of your mark in any class, with one exact match and two possible conflicts. We have included FullText information for each.
-There were three related identicals found when searching your mark as one word in your selected class, with one exact match and one possible conflict. FullText information is provided for each.
-There were seven related identicals found when searching your mark as one word in other classes, with one exact match. However, as these registrations do not occur in your class of interest, we have not included FullText information.

Further searching produced the following:

-There were 154 related identicals found in a five letter prefix search, with no exact matches.
-There were 71 related identicals found in a five letter suffix search, with no exact matches.
-There were no related identicals found in a vowel substitution search.
-There were no related identicals found in an anagram search.
-There were 26 related identicals found in an additional three letter prefix search, with no exact matches.
-There were 61 related identicals found in an additional three letter suffix search, with no exact matches.
-There were no related identicals found in an additional search on "Magic" only.
-There were 339 related identicals found in an additional search on "Clean" only, with no exact matches.

"Champions of Small Business"

Page 2

    Federal Trademark Services Co. has taken all reasonable steps to insure the completeness and accuracy of this report; however due to the highly subjective nature of trademark searching, we cannot otherwise guarantee these results.

    Please feel free to contact me directly with any questions you may have.

Sincerely,
FEDERAL TRADEMARK SERVICES CO.

Jennifer Smith

Jennifer Smith

enc.

FEDERAL TRADEMARK SERVICES CO.   725 Market St., Wilmington, DE 19801

Client Name: Enterprise Publishing
                  725 Market Street
                  Wilmington, DE 19801

Trademark Searched: MAGIC CLEANER

Our File Number: 235

Request Received: 9/7/88

Goods/Service: Class: 3
                    Goods: All purpose cleanser

Type of Search: Comprehensive Search

Enclosures: (X)   Blue - Patent and Trademark Office Search
              (X)   Green - State Search
              (X)   Yellow - Hit List
              (   )   Other -

TRADEMARK SEARCHED: MAGIC CLEANER

HITLIST

The computer generates a "HITLIST" which includes any identical
mark (related identical or exact match) and, when applicable,
marks that have the same prefix or suffix, marks with one letter
of difference, marks containing phonetic equivalents, translations,
alternative or corrupted spellings, and marks which contain the root
of the mark being searched.

The HITLIST is the internal worksheet. It is reviewed and the most
pertinent references are selected. FULLTEXT information about
these references are found in the enclosed PTO report (see Blue
information sheets) and/or the enclosed State report (see Green
information sheets).

HOW TO READ THE HITLIST

Following is the information which appears on the HITLIST:
Column 1:   Registration or application number. Federal registration
numbers are preceded by the letter R, while state registrations
are proceeded by the two-letter state abbreviation. The letters
SN appearing before a registration number indicate that registration
is either inactive or pending.

Column 2:   International Class is expressed in three digits (006,
025, etc.). Please note that goods or services that are considered
"unclassifiable" appear in Class 000 or 400.

Column 3:   A sequential numbering of hits.

Column 4:   A code identifying the type of mark retrieved:
             P = Pending PTO application
             A = Active PTO registration
             I = Inactive mark (abandoned/cancelled/expired)
             S = State registration

Column 5:   The retrieved mark or HIGH FREQUENCY WORD.
             There may appear an * prior to the word/phrase listed
             in this column. The asterick indicates the goods or
             services described in your search also appear in some
             form in the goods/service description as registered with
             the mark so identified.

WHAT IS A HIGH FREQUENCY WORD?
High Frequency Word refers to a word appearing frequently in the
computer either alone or as part of a trademark.

In the HITLIST, High Frequency is indicated by the letters HF
with an asterik and the approximate number of times the word appears
in the class.
                      Example: *HF 122 Plus
This means that "Plus" is registered in some form approximately 122
times in this class.

TRADEMARK SEARCHED: MAGIC CLEANER

PATENT AND TRADEMARK OFFICE SEARCH REPORT

Our Patent and Trademark Office Search report covers trademarks that
are registered and/or pending with the U.S. Patent and Trademark Office.
Our database includes all active registrations and applications up to
the date designated at the top of the HITLIST. It includes registrations
that were registered or renewed since January 1, 1960 and have become
inactive, and all pending applications abandoned since April 1, 1983.

PERTINENT REFERENCES are attached (Active references first, then
inactive). References were selected from the enclosed HITLIST as
being pertinent to the mark searched. (See Yellow Sheet for an
explanation of the HITLIST).

For each REFERENCE our report includes at least the following FULLTEXT
information when applicable.

> *Mark
> *Goods/Service
> *Classes (International & U.S.)
> *First use/commerce dates
> *Registrant/applicant's name and address
> *Section 8/15 affidavits
> *Renewal status
> *Disclaimers
> *Official Gazette Publication reference and page
> *Description
> *Translations
> *Priority claim(s)
> *Related U.S. and foreign registration(s)

If a FULLTEXT is stamped "Less Pertinent Reference" it means that on
final review we considered this reference less pertinent to the mark
and/or goods or services searched.

> Federal Trademark Services Co. has taken all
> reasonable steps to insure the completeness and
> accuracy of this report; however due to the
> highly subjective nature of trademark searching,
> we cannot otherwise guarantee these results.
> Please note this report in no way constitutes
> a legal opinion.

PATENT AND TRADEMARK OFFICE SEARCH REPORT

FOR

MAGIC CLEANER

Pertinent references are attached (active registrations and applications first, then inactive). Please review the previous page for a description of this Patent and Trademark Office Search Report.

Considering the large number of pertinent marks printed on the enclosed HITLIST (see Yellow sheet for discussion), we restricted our FULLTEXT printouts to those which are, in our opinion, the most relevant.

```
Line #25, Registration #R0797588    MAGIC CLEANER
Line #26, Registration #R1453240    MAGICLEAN
Line #15, Registration #SN544256    MAGIC CLEAN
```

If you have any questions or wish FULLTEXT information for any mark on the enclosed HITLIST which is not indicated above, please write or call us at (1-800-533-2665).

If you select marks from the HITLIST, please consider the pertinency of the class(es) and remember that marks preceded by the letter ''I'' on the HITLIST are inactive (cancelled, abandoned or expired).

```
Your Mark          : magic cleaner

Mark retrieved     : MAGICLEANER
                     ( no design )
Registration nr.   : 0797588 DATED 1965/10/12
Serial number      : 72140287 FILED 1962/03/20
Published in OG    :  dated 1963/09/17
Reference is       : A RENEWED REGISTRATION  DATED 1985/09/17
                     ON THE PRINCIPAL REGISTER
                     WITH A SECTION -8- AFFIDAVIT

Goods / Services   : CLEANING FLUID FOR RUGS AND UPHOLSTERY USE:AUG 7 1933,
                     COMM:AUG 7 1933
                     US CL:52.
                     INT CL:3.

Owner              : STANLEY F. PLATEK, DOING BUSINESS AS MAGICCLEANER CO.
                     64 JONES ST. NEWARK 3, N.J.


Canc. Trademark    : MAGICLIEN
Canc. Serial Nr.   : 72347759
Canc. Owner        : LIEN CHEMICAL COMPANY
Canc. Outcome      : DISMISSED WITH PREJUDICE JAN. 25,1972
Canc. Number       : 9686 FILED SEP. 10,1970

Intf. Serial Nr.   : 129554
Intf. Trademark    : MAGICLEEN
Intf. Owner        : GENERAL HOTEL SUPPLY COMPANY
Intf. Number       : 6149


        ************************************************
```

```
Your Reference     : 235
Full Text for      : R1463240
Mark retrieved     : MAGICLEAN
                     ( no design )
Registration nr.   : 1463240 DATED 1987/11/03
Serial number      : 73652198 FILED 1987/03/30
Published in OG    :  on page 0025 dated 1987/08/11
Reference is       : A REGISTRATION
                     ON THE PRINCIPAL REGISTER

Goods / Services   : FLOOR CLEANING COMPOSITION USE:20 JAN 1987 COMM:20 JAN
                     1987
                     US CL:52.
                     INT CL:3.

Owner              : HUNTINGTON LABORATORIES, INC. (INDIANA CORPORATION)
                     46750 968 E. TIPTON HUNTINGTON INDIANA
```

Your Mark   : magic cleaner

Mark retrieved   : MAGIC CLEAN
                       (no design)
Serial number   : 73544256 FILED 1985/06/21
Published in OG   : dated   / /
Reference is   : AN ABANDONED APPLICATION
                       ON THE PRINCIPAL REGISTER

Goods / Services   : ALL PURPOSE CLEANER USE:26 APR 1985 COMM:26 APR 1985
                       US CL:52.
                       INT CL:3.

Owner   : CELLO CORP. (MISSOURI CORPORATION) 210780366 1354 OLD
                         POST ROAD HARVE DE GRACE MARYLAND

PAUSE AFTER IDENTICALS REQUESTED.

TRADEMARK SEARCHED: MAGIC CLEANER

STATE SEARCH REPORT

Our State Registration Search Report covers over 300,000 active
trademarks registered in all fifty states and Puerto Rico. It
includes those state registrations which have become inactive as
of January 1, 1984.

This report includes references that have been selected from the
HITLIST as being pertinent to the mark searched (see yellow sheet
for an explanation of the HITLIST). FULLTEXT information accompanies
each pertinent mark.

FULLTEXT information for each pertinent reference includes, when
applicable, at least the following information:

> *Mark
> *Goods/Service
> *Classes (International or U.S.)
> *First use date
> *Registrant's name & address
> *Registration Number(s)
> *Registration date(s)
> *Renewal status
> *Disclaimer

Federal Trademark Services Co. has taken all
reasonable steps to insure the completeness and
accuracy of this report; however, due to the
highly subjective nature of trademark searching,
we cannot otherwise guarantee these results. Please
note that this report in no way constitutes a legal
opinion.

STATE SEARCH REPORT

FOR

MAGIC CLEANER

Pertinent references are attached. Please read the information detailed below and see previous page for a description of this State Search Report.

Our search did/~~did not~~ reveal pertinent State References.

Line #2, Registration #IL019576   MAGIC CLEAN
Line #17, Registration #CA886202   MAGIC CLEANER

If you have any questions or wish FULLTEXT information for any mark on the enclosed HITLIST which is not indicated above, please write or call us at (1-800-533-2665).

If you select marks from the HITLIST, please consider the pertinency of the class(es) and remember that marks preceded by the letter ''I'' on the HITLIST are inactive (cancelled, abandoned or expired).

```
Your Mark         : magic cleaner

Mark retrieved    : MAGIC CLEAN
Serial number     : 13019576
Reference is       : A REGISTRATION IN ILLINOIS

Goods / Services  : MULTI-PURPOSE SOAP FOR VEHICLES, HEAVY EQUIPMENT AND
                    FLOORS AND WALLS
                    US CL:52.
                    INT CL:3.

Owner             : MANKOFF EQUIPMENT, INC. *** P. O. BOX 1033F WHEELING,
                    IL 60090
Miscellaneous      : STATE REF: BOOK BBB PAGE 426
Expiration date    : 1993/10/21
Registration nr.  : 0053831



        **********************************************
```

SAMPLE TRADEMARK SEARCH REPORT   13

Your Mark   : magic cleaner

Mark retrieved   : MAGIC CLEANER
Serial number   : 05886202
Reference is   : A REGISTRATION IN CALIF

Goods / Services : MULTIPLE-PURPOSE WIPER FIRST USE IN STATE: 11/02/1987,
                   FIRST USE ANYWHERE: 01/01/1987
                   US CL:50.
                   INT CL:20.

Owner   : E. M. PIERPOINT, INC. *** 23762 FOLEY STREET, SUITE 2,
                   HAYWARD CA 94545
Expiration date : 1998/01/14
Registration nr. : T086558

        ****

Sample Trademark Search Report   159

PAGE   1

PTO search includes : O.G. information through AUGUST   09,   1988
                    : applications filed up to JULY   21,   1988

Search Number   : 16624   date : 09/07/88 time : 09:14:27
Your Mark   : magic cleaner
Reference   : 235
Searched As   : MAGIC CLEANER
Selected Class(es): 03
Related Class(es) : 00
Scan of Goods   : CLEANSER
Matches Only / All: A

   COMPREHENSIVE SEARCH (PTO & STATES)
     --- TWO ELEMENTS IN ANY CLASS ---
     ---   23 HITS FOUND ---   ---   0 HIGH FREQUENCIES FOUND ---

    NUMBER   CLS   LINE   ST   TRADEMARKS FOUND
  C0024050 042   1   S   MAGIC CARPET CLEANING
  IL019576 003   2   S   MAGIC CLEAN
  IL840477 037   3   S   MAGIC KLEAN CHIMNEY SWEEPS (& DESIGN)
  MA851798 037   4   S   DOMESTIC GENIE-WE CLEAN LIKE MAGIC
  NV150772 003   5   S   MAGIC CARPET CLEANER
  PA005691 035   6   S   MAGIC MIST CARPET CLEANING
  R0613651 020   7   A   HEAVY DUTY MAGIC LENS CLEANING STATION
  R0732851 003   8   I   CLEANERS WITH THE MAGIC TOUCH
  R0728738 005   9   I   CLEANERS WITH THE MAGIC TOUCH
  R0765275 003   10   A   PINK IN COLOR-MAGIC IN CLEANING
  R0785962 007   11   A   MAGIC CLEAN
  R1009283 003   12   A   MAGIC MIST MM CARPET CLEANING
  R1009283 005   13   A   MAGIC MIST MM CARPET CLEANING
  R1009283 007   14   A   MAGIC MIST MM CARPET CLEANING
  SN544256 003   15   I   MAGIC CLEAN
  CA713542 035   16   S   MAGIC WAND CARPET CLEANING (& DESIGN OF A WIZARD WITH
                             HAT, BEARD, HOLDING WAND)
  CA886202 020   17   S   MAGIC CLEANER
  ID151502 037   18   S   MAGIC VALLEY CLEANING SERVICE
  ID151502 042   19   S   MAGIC VALLEY CLEANING SERVICE
  IA851417 035   20   S   MAGIC EYE GLASS CLEANER
  SN678018 003   21   P   MAGIC MAID CLEANING SERVICE
  SN678018 037   22   P   MAGIC MAID CLEANING SERVICE
  SN696517 037   23   P   "ON-SITE" A TOUCH OF MAGIC IN HOME DRY CLEANING DRAPERY
                             SERVICE

```
PAGE  2
Your Mark          : magic cleaner

     --- IDENTICALS IN SELECTED (and related) CLASS(ES) ---
     ---         3 HITS FOUND ---        ---        0 HIGH FREQUENCIES FOUND ---

  NUMBER   CLS  LINE  ST   TRADEMARKS FOUND
R0694361 003    24   I   MAGIC LEAF
R0797588 003    25   A   MAGICLEANER
R1463240 003    26   A   MAGICLEAN

     ---- IDENTICALS IN OTHER CLASS(ES) ---
     ---         7 HITS FOUND ---        ---        0 HIGH FREQUENCIES FOUND ---

  NUMBER   CLS  LINE  ST   TRADEMARKS FOUND
CA312653 001    27   S   MAGICLEAN
HI412011 009    28   S   MAGIC LEASH
MN170101 037    29   S   MAGICLEANERS
R0789048 021    30   A   MAGICLEAN
R0842441 009    31   A   MAGICLEAD
R0887168 011    32   A   MAGICLEAN
NY115622 011    33   S   MAGICLEARER


PAUSE AFTER IDENTICALS REQUESTED.
```

```
PAGE  3
Your Mark          : magic cleaner

--- R E S U M E   O F   H I T L I S T ---
    ---NAGIK... 5 LETTER PREFIX IN SELECTED (and related) CLASS(ES)
    ---      154 HITS FOUND ---       ---      395 HIGH FREQUENCIES FOUND ---


  NUMBER   CLS  LINE  ST   TRADEMARKS FOUND
  R0510244 003    34  A    MAGIC
  R0615956 003    35  A    MAGIC
  R0741715 003    36  A    MAGIC
  R0743120 003    37  A    MAGIC
  R0778850 003    38  I    MAGIC
  R0816299 003    39  A    MAGIC
  R0843481 003    40  A    MAGIK KLING
  R0954190 003    41  A    MAGIC
  R1065118 003    42  A    MAGIC
  R1089516 003    43  A    MAGIC
  R1110746 003    44  I    MAGIC
  R1374467 003    45  A    MAGIC
  AL001412 003    46  S    MAGIC SHEEN
  NC006203 003    47  S    MAGIC SHEEN
  NC007049 003    48  S    MAGIC SHEEN
  R0741029 003    49  A    CREME MAGICA
  R0749517 003    50  I    LOVELAND MAGICA
  OH840006 003    51  S    MAGIC ALOE
  SN360923 003    52  I    MAGIC ALOE
  R1248080 003    53  A    MAGICAN
  R1018265 003    54  I    MAGI CARE
  R1078718 003    55  I    MAGICARE
  R0653540 003    56  A    MAGI-CARPET
  R0437728 003    57  A    MAGIC BLUE
  R1392863 003    58  A    MAGIC BOO BOO CREAM
  R0691044 003    59  I    MAGIC DURA-BASE
  R0796988 003    60  I    MAGIC DWARF
  R0923976 003    61  A    MAGIC FLITE
  SN351114 003    62  I    MAGIC FLUF
  R0838046 003    63  A    MAGIC FOAM
  R0780710 003    64  I    MAGIC FORM
  R0924818 003    65  A    MAGIC-FORM
  R1020299 003    66  I    MAGIC GLO
  R0804035 003    67  I    MAGIC GLOW
  IN220082 003    68  S    MAGIC GREEN
  R0969302 003    69  I    MAGIC GRO
  R1055365 003    70  I    MAGIC JADE
  R0687356 003    71  A    MAGIC, JR
  NV150781 003    72  S    MAGICKLEEN
  R0875342 003    73  A    MAGI-KLEEN
  R0592307 003    74  A    MAGIC LENS TISSUE POLISH YOUR LENSES EASIER, BRIGHTER,
                           FASTER, MORE LASTING IT PAYS TO SEE BETTER
  R0932982 003    75  I    MAGICLIEN
  R1035618 003    76  A    MAGIC LIFT
```

PAGE 4
Your Mark   : magic cleaner

R0855266	003	77	I	MAGIC MAID
R0599182	003	78	A	MAGIC MAKE-UP COLOR
R0802847	003	79	I	MAGIC MAC
R0781515	003	80	I	MAGIC-MAN
R0924817	003	81	A	MAGIC-MAN
R1214584	003	82	A	MAGIC MAN AND DESIGN
R1093532	003	83	A	MAGIC NET
R0834886	003	84	A	MAGIC MIST
R0928421	003	85	I	MAGIC MIST
R1029808	003	86	A	TOCCO MAGICO
R1036522	003	87	A	COLOR-TON TOCCO-MAGICO
R1278536	003	88	A	COLOR TIEN TOCCO MAGICO AND DESIGN
R1293683	003	89	A	CURLIN-KUR TOCCO MAGICO AND DESIGN
SN368134	003	90	I	PALVIN-BAD TOCCO MAGICO
R1282007	003	91	A	FISSKUR TOCCO MAGICO (STYLIZED)
SN383234	003	92	I	BRILLO MAGICO
R1310683	003	93	A	PALVIN-BID TOCCO MAGICO (STYLIZED)
R0973591	003	94	A	MAGIC COAT
SN297601	003	95	I	MAGIC OF MUD
R0552132	003	96	A	MAGICOLOR
R0562216	003	97	A	MAGICOLOR
R0755674	003	98	I	MAGIC COLOR
R0835609	003	99	I	MAGICOMB
R0807534	003	100	A	MAGIC-PAD
R1058143	003	101	I	MAGIC PERM
R0770081	003	102	I	MAGIC PLUS
R0816734	003	103	A	DR. ODOR'S MAGIC POWER
CA804489	003	104	S	MAGIC RE-YOUTH NITE CREAM
R1045683	003	105	A	BLACK MAGIC RR
R0784149	003	106	A	MAGIC ROSE
R0689243	003	107	A	MAGIC ROUGE
R0699958	003	108	A	MAGIC TAN
R1149550	003	109	I	MAGIC TIPS AND DESIGN
R0520980	003	110	A	MAGIC TOUCH
R0811852	003	111	I	MAGIC TOUCH
SN433659	003	112	P	MAGIC TOUCH
CA853249	003	113	S	MAGIQUE
NJ262371	003	114	S	MAGIQUE
SN468806	003	115	I	"MAGIQUE"
R1392860	003	116	A	MAGIQUE
TX840853	003	117	S	MAGIC CURL
R0780454	003	118	I	MAGIC-CURL
SN468301	003	119	I	MAGIC CURL
SN583226	003	120	P	MAGIC WASH
R0753457	003	121	I	MAGIC WAND
R0896624	003	122	A	MAGIC WAND
R1154423	003	123	I	MAGIC WAND
R1382933	003	124	A	MAGIC WAND
R1382934	003	125	A	MAGIC WAND

```
PAGE  5
Your Mark          : magic cleaner

   R0811104 003      126  A   MAGIC WATER
   TX033445 003      127  S   MAGIC WAVE
   R1372037 003      128  A   MAGIC WAVE
   R1255023 003      129  A   MAGIC WAX
   FL912177 003      130  S   MAGIC
   SN663413 003      131  P   MAGIC
   SN663414 003      132  P   MAGIC
   CA312713 003      133  S   MAGIC SHEEN
   CA807003 003      134  S   MAGIC SHEEN
   GA160201 003      135. S   MAGIC SHEEN (& DESIGN)
   TN880910 003      136  S   MAGIC SHEEN
   R1429780 003      137  A   MAGIC BEAT
   SN635969 003      138  I   MAGIC BLIND
   FL912206 003      139  S   MAGIC GENIE
   MO372571 003      140  S   MAGIC GENIE
   WV843167 003      141  S   MAGIC GLOVE
   CA883839 003      142  S   MAGIC GROOM
   SN696450 003      143  P   MAGIC GROOM
   CA312161 003      144  S   LUNOIR BLACK MOON MAGIC GWEN (WITH CROWN & WINGS
                                DESIGN)
   CA851092 003      145  S   LUNOIR BLACK MOON MAGIC GWEN (+ DESIGN)
   R1486635 003      146  A   MAGIC LEMON
   SN723857 003      147  P   MAGIC MATCH
   PR018618 003      148  S   MAGICO
   SN651969 003      149  P   MAGICOAT
   R1464175 003      150  A   MAGICONDITIONER
   HF006320 003      151      MAGIC            *HF      321 NAGIK           ********
   KS015039 050      473  S   MAGIK-START FIRECAKES
   TN212011 400      474  S   MAGIC SHEEN
   R0911034 050      475  I   MAGIC BOARD
   R0804027 050      476  I   MAGIC FIT
   TN850697 050      477  S   MAGIC FLAME
   FL919132 050      478  S   MAGIC FLOAT-ON
   AZ190901 050      479  S   MAGICLOR
   HI212402 000      480  S   MAGIC MINI SHELLS
   R0746745 050      481  I   MAGICORK
   FL919120 050      482  S   MAGIC TILT
   KS015038 050      483  I   MAGIC WATER BY AQUA MAGIC (& DESIGN)
   MO372593 050      484  I   MAGIC WATER BY AQUA MAGIC
   NE121081 050      485  I   MAGIC WATER BY AQUA MAGIC (AND DESIGN)
   CA842869 000      486  I   MAGIC SHEEN
   CA840329 000      487  S   MAGICAL MUSIC EXPRESS (+ DESIGN)
   TN852367 050      488  S   A MAGICAL GARDEN
   UT025022 000      489  S   MAGIC BRUSH CHIMNEY SWEEPS INC.
   WV843168 000      490  S   MAGIC GOLD
   CA841136 000      491  S   MAGICGRAMS
   TX850542 000      492  S   CARL POOL B-R 61 PLUS MAGIC GREEN
   TX850543 000      493  S   CARL POOL MAGIC GROW
   CA840897 000      494  S   MAGIC-MIST
```

PAGE 6
Your Mark   : magic cleaner

```
IN881164 000     495   I   MAGIC MONEY HOUR - RADIO CONTEST ENTERTAINMENT
DE880393 000     496   I   MAGIC-PAK
DE880411 000     497   I   GORDON'S MAGIC-PAK
IL882285 000     498   I   MAGIC-PAK
IN881165 000     499   I   MAGIC-PAK - USED IN CONNECTION WITH SNACK FOOD
NV840128 000     500   S   MAGIC-PAK
UT025674 000     501   S   MAGIC PORTA-JOGGER
TX840171 000     502   S   MAGIC TIME MACHINE
WV843172 000     503   S   MAGIC TOUCH
WV843173 000     504   S   MAGIC TOUCH
IA120632 050     505   I   MAGIC WATER BY AQUA MAGIC (AND SILVER WATER DROPS ON
                               BLUE LABEL WITH SILVER BORDER)
SD120261 050     506   I   MAGICWATER BY AQUA MAGIC
UT025508 000     507   S   MAGIC WATER (ON BLUE BACKGROUND WITH CHROME LETTERING)
HF006317 000     508       MAGIC          *HF      74 NAGIK          ********
```

```
       ---...EANER 5 LETTER SUFFIX IN SELECTED (and related) CLASS(ES)
       ---        71 HITS FOUND ---       ---        112 HIGH FREQUENCIES FOUND ---
```

```
  NUMBER   CLS   LINE  ST   TRADEMARKS FOUND
R0896127 003     583   A   LIP BEAMER
NYR19024 003     584   S   LUSTRE GLEAMER
IN171473 003     585   S   TUCHMAN CLEANERS (APPEARING IN DISTINCTIVE LETTERING ON
                               A PALETTE DESIGN)
PA850671 003     586   S   CODER'S CLEANERS
UT024418 003     587   S   ROBIN HOOD SUPER POWER CLEANERS
R0175886 003     588   I   MAGNUS CLEANERS
R1000033 003     589   A   "D" CLEANER
R0300730 003     590   A   A.F.CLEANER
R0922519 003     591   I   PLATEMARIN TANKCLEANER
R0966712 003     592   A   USN CLEANER
R0877528 003     593   I   BEAUTIFUL DREAMER
R1281192 003     594   A   DAISY DREAMER
R1098499 003     595   I   STREAMERS
R1170827 003     596   I   CAPTAIN STEAMER AND DESIGN
IN122122 003     597   S   SUN GLO CARPET CLEANERS (SUN BURST WITH SMILE-IN
                               CENTER)
SN704292 003     598   F   AQUA KLEANER
WI853466 003     599   S   VOLCAN WATERLESS HANDCLEANERS
IN110472 003     600   S   FASTEAMER
HF001926 003     601       CLEANER          *HF      112 KLEANER          ********
R0902331 050     714   I   EYE BEAMER
FL917864 050     715   S   CLEANER PLUS PINE
LA017258 050     716   S   HARAHAN CLEANERS
NE121731 050     717   I   STEAMAOTION CARPET CLEANERS
R1117951 200     718   I   CC CARPET CLEANERS INSTITUTE OF CALIFORNIA
R1009056 200     719   A   GUILD OF PROFESSIONAL DRYCLEANERS GPDC
LA012394 050     720   I   CAJUN RICE'R STEAMER
LA012457 050     721   I   CAJUN RICER STEAMER
```

PAGE   7
Your Mark   : magic cleaner

```
LA851347 050      722  S   CAJUN RICE'R STEAMER
CA840063 000      723  S   MIRACLE CLEANER
CA840077 000      724  S   CCC SUPER CLEANER (+ DESIGN)
CA841937 000      725  S   FINALLY...A BLIND CLEANER THAT REALLY WORKS!
CA842298 000      726  S   MINI-MAX CLEANER
CA857485 000      727  S   STAR RUG CLEANERS
CA857491 000      728  S   MASTER DRY CLEANER (& COAT HANGER DESIGN)
CA885643 000      729  I   RED HANGER KLEANERS
C0031516 050      730  S   PROFESSIONAL CARPET & UPHOLSTERY CLEANERS ASSOCIAT
FL904578 000      731  S   PRIDE FRENCH CLEANERS
FL906669 050      732  S   ABC CARPET CLEANERS
FL907690 000      733  S   SCOTCH CLEANERS & LAUNDRY
IL882020 000      734  I   CRESCENT EVANS LAUNDRY CLEANERS (& DESIGN)
IA120171 050      735  I   STEAMACTION CARPET CLEANERS STEAMACTION
LA003403 000      736  S   DELUXE LAUNDRY-CLEANERS-STORAGE
LA009223 000      737  S   VIEUX CARRE CLEANERS
LA707099 000      738  S   FRANK-LIN DISCOUNT CLEANERS
MO850006 000      739  S   SCOTCH DELUXE CLEANERS
MO850014 000      740  S   SCOTCH DELUXE CLEANERS
OR881279 000      741  S   STARK'S VACUUM CLEANER SALES & SERVICE (W/DESIGN)
SC001130 050      742  S   BEAUTY DRAPE DRAPERY CLEANERS
TN851897 000      743  I   CLASSIQUE CLEANERS
TX840735 000      744  S   SCRUB-IT HAND CLEANER
TX840736 000      745  S   HPC-88 GENERAL PURPOSE CLEANER
TX852042 000      746  S   MR. K'S CLEANERS
UT025642 000      747  S   SUPERIOR ROOTER MAN COMING OUT OF CLEANER
UT026849 000      748  S   BLOCK CLEANER
UT026963 000      749  S   BEST-O-PINE PINE OIL DEODORANT CLEANER
UT026964 000      750  S   GOLDEN LEMON DISINFECTANT-CLEANER
UT026973 000      751  S   GOLDEN - SHEEN MULTI - SURFACE CLEANER, POLISHER,
                           PROTECTOR (ETC)
UT026980 000      752  S   UNIQUE ALL-PURPOSE CLEANER
UT026986 000      753  S   SPARKLE PINK LOTION CLEANER
UT026987 000      754  S   RESTORIT CARPET CLEANER
UT026989 000      755  S   HERCULES CLEANER-DEGREASER
UT880070 000      756  S   COLONIAL 1 HOUR CLEANERS -CLEANERS THAT CARE -BRITISH
                           MAN HO
WV841720 000      757  S   EXCLUSIVE WHOLESALE CLEANERS
WV843393 000      758  S   MIRACLE-CLEANER
WV843863 000      759  S   ORANGE CLEANERS
WV845189 000      760  S   SUPERIOR DRY CLEANERS
WV845766 000      761  S   UNITED DRY CLEANERS, INC. CASH AND CARRY
WI852550 000      762  S   CLARK'S CLEANERS
CA841842 000      763  S   STREAMERS OF CALIFORNIA
OR881158 000      764  I   OCEANEER
CA842299 000      765  S   MINI-MAX STEAMER
```

PAGE 8
Your Mark   : magic cleaner

        ---   --- VOWEL SUBSTITUTION IN SELECTED CLASS(ES) ---
        ---   O HITS FOUND ---   ---   O HIGH FREQUENCIES FOUND ---

        ---   --- ANAGRAMS IN SELECTED CLASS(ES) ---
        ---   O HITS FOUND ---   ---   O HIGH FREQUENCIES FOUND ---

     ---NAG...   ADDITIONAL PREFIX SEARCH IN SELECTED CLASS(ES)
     ---   26 HITS FOUND ---   ---   O HIGH FREQUENCIES FOUND ---

NUMBER	CLS	LINE	ST	TRADEMARKS FOUND
PRO22134	003	766	S	MAGIE
R0589574	003	767	A	MAGIE DE LANCOME PARIS FRANCE
R0797578	003	768	I	MAGGY ROUFF
R0816301	003	769	I	MAGI-TEX
R1043913	003	770	A	BLACK MAGI
R1154383	003	771	A	MAGIE NOIRE AND DESIGN
R1303369	003	772	A	MAGGIE C.
R0930945	003	773	I	MAGIC HOURS
R1128125	003	774	A	MAGIC HOURS
R1082159	003	775	I	*MAGIMAX
SN382521	003	776	I	CHE MAGGIO
R1339904	003	777	A	MAGIC EYE SEAL
R0910462	003	778	I	MAGISKIN NEOTIS
R0875767	003	779	A	MAGISTRALE
HI461961	003	780	S	ULTRA TONE MAGIC SALVE
R0628843	003	781	A	MAGIC SILK
R0729549	003	782	A	MAGIC SCRUB BOAT
R1293695	003	783	A	*MAGIC SCRUB
R0823072	003	784	A	MAGIC STAR
R0823085	003	785	A	MAGIC STAR
R0730552	003	786	I	MAGIC STICK
R0916014	003	787	A	MAGIC SUDS
SN698727	003	788	P	*FRANKINCENSE MYRRH AND GOLD - THE GIFT OF THE MAGI
SN740966	003	789	P	MOHOLY-NAGY
FL912511	003	790	S	MAGIA
SN703757	003	791	P	ANITA CASSANDRA MAGIA PERFUME

     ---...NER   ADDITIONAL SUFFIX SEARCH IN SELECTED CLASS(ES)
     ---   61 HITS FOUND ---   ---   O HIGH FREQUENCIES FOUND ---

NUMBER	CLS	LINE	ST	TRADEMARKS FOUND
R0258620	003	792	A	ARM & HAMMER
R0502261	003	793	A	ARM & HAMMER
R0501904	003	794	A	ARM & HAMMER AND DESIGN
R0501905	003	795	A	ARM & HAMMER
R0502070	003	796	A	ARM & HAMMER
R0675121	003	797	A	ARM & HAMMER SAL SODA CONCENTRATED

PAGE 9
Your Mark   : magic cleaner

```
R0689663 003    798  A   ARM & HAMMER SAL SODA CONCENTRATED WASHING SODA
R0818095 003    799  A   AMER-REZ
R0826637 003    800  I   AMER-SHEEN
R0930654 003    801  A   ARM & HAMMER
R1021831 003    802  A   ARM &HAMMER
R0197281 003    803  A   BANNER
R0793063 003    804  A   BANNER
R1104599 003    805  A   AGAMER
R0830744 003    806  A   WINDJAMMER
R0830752 003    807  A   WINDJAMMER
R0773815 003    808  I   BUCCANEER
R0935778 003    809  A   BUCCANEER
R0932976 003    810  A   BUCCANEER
R1245722 003    811  A   CREME DE LA MER
R1339888 003    812  A   LA MER
R0850340 003    813  A   GOLDEN MANNER
R0973036 003    814  A   FOAMER 303
SN411912 003    815  I   HAIR TREATMENT PROGRAMMER
R0543368 003    816  A   CRAMER OF GARDNER KANSAS
R0819691 003    817  A   CRAMER OF GARDNER, KANSAS
R1117975 003    818  I   CRAMER
R0945026 003    819  A   GOSSAMER
R0952849 003    820  A   GLOSSAMER
CA243273 003    821  S   KID'S OWN TANGLE TAMER IN FUN FRAGRANCES
CA524001 003    822  S   WILD MANE TAMER
FL918756 003    823  S   EMBRYON LINE-TAMER
FL922705 003    824  S   SUN TAMER & DESIGN
IL840668 003    825  S   THE MANE TAMERS (& DESIGN)
PR022481 003    826  S   LINE TAMER
R0894315 003    827  A   *OL'TANNER
R0932438 003    828  A   OLD-TANNER
R1039065 003    829  I   LINE-TAMER
R1122634 003    830  I   SUN TAMER
R1132955 003    831  I   OL'TANNER
R1162378 003    832  I   TENSION TAMER
R1223067 003    833  A   BROW TAMER
R1248794 003    834  A   THE MANE TAMER AND DESIGN
SN366722 003    835  I   WILD MANE TAMER
R1365136 003    836  A   LINE-TAMER
R0791148 003    837  I   SUNTAMER
R0709444 003    838  I   PANTALOON DAILY MAINTAINER
R0863662 003    839  A   MAGIC MIRROR MAINTAINER
SN457657 003    840  I   MAINTAINER
R0774263 003    841  I   MAINLINER
CA313861 003    842  S   MARINER'S BRAND (WITH SAILBOAT, POWERBOAT, AND HELM
                         DESIGN)
R0894316 003    843  A   MARINER'S
SN687186 003    844  P   ARM & HAMMER DENTAL CARE
SN687187 003    845  P   ARM & HAMMER DENTAL CARE
```

PAGE 10
Your Mark   : magic cleaner

```
TN882099 003      846  S  LAMER (STY)
SN706549 003      847  P  LA MERE POULARD
R1458933 003      848  A  LIP SLAMMER
SN701521 003      849  P  CRAMER COLOR
NV880240 003      850  S  GOSSAMER
R1439747 003      851  A  SUNTAMER
TX029293 003      852  S  FLOOR MAINTAINER
```

```
    ---NAGIK   IN SELECTED CLASS(ES) & CLASS '00' ---
    ---    0 HITS FOUND ---      ---     0 HIGH FREQUENCIES FOUND ---


    ---KLEAN   IN SELECTED CLASS(ES) & CLASS '00' ---
    ---   339 HITS FOUND ---     ---     488 HIGH FREQUENCIES FOUND ---
```

```
  NUMBER   CLS  LINE  ST  TRADEMARKS FOUND
R0147762 003      853  I  GREASE-OFF "IT CLEANS EVERYTHING."
AZ150952 003      854  S  (PRODUCT NAME) KRC-II, (RAINBOW) DEVICE ENCLOSING BLACK
                          OILDROP HOLDING MOP IN HAND, WITH SLOGAN) IT CLEANS UP
                          YOUR ACT (AT THE TOP OF ILLUSTRATION.)
MN121832 003      855  S  CLEAN +
R0276001 003      856  A  KOWAXO CLEANS-WAXES
R0661199 003      857  A  BON AMI JET SPRAY PUSH-BUTTON CLEANER JET BON AMI
                          CLEANS
R0750311 003      858  I  CLEAN
R0754372 003      859  I  BON AMI JET SPRAY CLEANS & POLISHES WINDOWS MIRRORS
                          CHROME ENAMEL
R0780040 003      860  A  CLEANS LIKE A WHITE TORNADO!
R0805743 003      861  I  CLEANS LIKE 60
R0828024 003      862  I  THAT POWER CLEANS WITH DETERGENT
R0845660 003      863  A  SIMONIZ LIQUID KLEENER SHINES AS IT CLEANS IN ONE QUICK
                          EASY OPERATION
R0872807 003      864  I  CLEANS RIGHT DOWN TO THE GERMS
R0907294 003      865  A  THE ROLL OF THE BOAT CLEANS THE BILGE!
R1031931 003      866  I  "IT CLEANS" LP-43
R1148575 003      867  I  LIGHTNING CLEANS IN A FLASH AND DESIGN
SN363551 003      868  I  TRICHLOROETHYLENE-DRY-CLEANE
R1358724 003      869  A  CLEAN +
SN394537 003      870  I  GLASS PLUS...CLEANS GLASS, PLUS A WHOLE LOT MORE!
SN406914 003      871  I  CLEANS-IT
R1327825 003      872  A  KLEANZ-EASY
R1424440 003      873  A  CLEANS CLEAR-SHINES CLEAR-PROTECTS CLEAR
SN513744 003      874  I  KLEAN
SN549470 003      875  P  KLEAN 'N SHINE
R0502446 003      876  A  KLEAN SHYNE
SC002032 003      877  S  CLEAN AS A WHISTLE
R0857190 003      878  A  CLEAN AS A WHISTLE
R1101120 003      879  A  CLEAN-A-DIAMOND AT
R0679014 003      880  A  CLEANAGEN
```

PAGE   11
Your Mark   : magic cleaner

```
SN482880 003     881   I    CLEAN NAIL
R0517774 003     882   A    CLEANALL
R0691411 003     883   I    CLEANALL
R1386497 003     884   A    CLEAN-ALL
R0642734 003     885   A    CLEAN AND CLEAR
R0861105 003     886   I    CLEAN AND SPARKLE
R0841760 003     887   A    'CLEAN AND CLEAR'
R0841779 003     888   A    CLEAN AND BRIGHT
R0974446 003     889   I    CLEAN AND BEAUTIFUL
R1055865 003     890   A    CLEAN AND CURL
R1067052 003     891   I    CLEAN AND SIMPLE
SN450598 003     892   I    CLEAN HANDS
R0408488 003     893   I    CLEANAMEL
R0971539 003     894   A    CLEAN MATE CM
R0731277 003     895   I    A LITHO-KLEAN B
R0989742 003     896   A    CLEAN BREAK
R1285712 003     897   A    CLEANBRIGHT AND DESIGN
IN172182 003     898   S    KLEAN BURN AQUA FUELS
IN172192 003     899   S    KLEAN BURN
PR025110 003     900   S    CLEANDISH
R1097141 003     901   A    CLEANDITIONER
PR023681 003     902   S    KLEAN DOG
R1099157 003     903   I    CLEAN & DRY
R1428049 003     904   A    CLEAN-N-DRI
R1019121 003     905   A    CLEAN DROPS
R1012744 003     906   I    CLEAN EARTH FACE
R1019138 003     907   I    CLEAN EARTH SKIN
R0858449 003     908   I    KLEAN HED
R0526459 003     909   A    CLEANEGG
R0805760 003     910   I    CLEANERINO
R1023573 003     911   A    ALVA VACUUM CLEANERCENTER
SN451088 003     912   I    THE DAILY CLEANETTE
R0742150 003     913   A    CLEAN FILM
R1347097 003     914   A    CLEAN FREE
R0914287 003     915   A    CLEAN & FRESH
R0865480 003     916   I    GOOD CLEAN FUN
R0865491 003     917   I    GOOD CLEAN FUN
R1031928 003     918   A    CLEAN & GLIDE
R0749897 003     919   I    CLEAN GLOW
R0852037 003     920   I    CLEAN GRAY
R1125115 003     921   I    KLEANING MAN
R0736152 003     922   A    CLEANICIDE
R1191019 003     923   I    CLEANITE
R1353561 003     924   A    CLEANITE
R1148610 003     925   I    CLEAN CARE
R1246159 003     926   A    CLEANCARE
R1234227 003     927   A    CLEAN CARGO
R0870276 003     928   I    CLEAN KILL
TX013142 003     929   I    CLEAN & KIND
```

PAGE 12
Your Mark   : magic cleaner

```
R1070839 003    930  A  CLEAN & KIND
WI440552 003    931  S  PRO KLEAN KIT
HI450631 003    932  S  CLEAN CLEAN
CT006315 003    933  S  CLEAN' CLEAR
SN424485 003    934  I  CLEAN & CLEAR
R1085218 003    935  I  CLEANCO
R0817523 003    936  A  CLEANCONTROL
MN704025 003    937  S  CLEAN-COTE
LA013305 003    938  S  CLEANCRAFT PRODUCTS
R0894328 003    939  A  KLEAN-KRETE
R0998834 003    940  I  COVER GIRL SKIN CLEAN CREAM
R0437844 003    941  A  *CLEAN QUICK
R1146998 003    942  A  CLEAN-CUT
R1022433 003    943  A  CLEAN LIFE
R1010255 003    944  I  GREATEST CARGO OF CLEANLINESS SUPER UPKEEP
FL925237 003    945  S  CLEANLUX CON PIREY Y FUERZA BLANCA
R0737653 003    946  A  PRE-KLEANO
R0792408 003    947  I  CLEAN O PLATE
R0697292 003    948  A  CLEAN OFF
FL930326 003    949  S  CLEANOIL
R0819331 003    950  A  CLEANOLA
R0237412 003    951  A  CLEAN-O-LITE
R0307840 003    952  A  CLEAN-O-MIST
R0705341 003    953  I  CLEAN-O-RAMA
R0995520 003    954  A  KLEAN PAWS
PR022145 003    955  S  KLEAN PINE
SN474867 003    956  I  CLEAN-PLEX
R0935875 003    957  A  CLEAN POWER
CA140422 003    958  I  CLEAN & RICH
R1071714 003    959  I  CLEAN & RICH
PR020307 003    960  I  BRECK CLEAN RINSE
R1026012 003    961  A  BRECK CLEAN RINSE
R1051645 003    962  I  NEW IMAGE CLEAN RINSE
R1275696 003    963  A  NEW IMAGE CLEAN RINSE
MN121841 003    964  S  CLEAN-RITE
R1129100 003    965  A  CLEAN-RITE
R1295454 003    966  A  CLEAN ROOM
MN241731 003    967  S  SOFT-KLEANSE
PR025755 003    968  S  CLEAN SEE (DESIGN)
R0979566 003    969  I  CHANGE & CLEANSE
R1075317 003    970  A  CLEANSE-PHREE
R1394581 003    971  A  OPTI-CLEANSE
R1226409 003    972  A  CLEAN-SAFE
R1275688 003    973  A  CLEAN N SAFE
AZ840150 003    974  S  O TO 80 KLITONE DIO-AMAZE COMPLETE BODY CLEANSER
CA855292 003    975  S  DERMA CLEANSER
DE110185 003    976  S  ROMAN CLEANSER
FL851956 003    977  S  SONIC CLEANSER
MT151582 003    978  S  OLD DUTCH CLEANSER-SEISMOTITE-SPICK AND SPAN-CHASES
```

PAGE 13
Your Mark   : magic cleaner

```
                          DIRT
NC009161 003     979  S  ROMAN CLEANSER
WV843760 003     980  S  OLD DUTCH CLEANSER-SEISMOTITE-SPICK AND SPAN-CHASES
                          DIRT
R0050697 003     981  A  OLD DUTCH CLEANSER CHASES DIRT MAKES EVERYTHING "SPICK
                          AND SPAN"
R0102650 003     982  A  CLOROX LIQUID BLEACH CLEANSER GERMICIDE
R0217453 003     983  A  *SANIDENT DENTAL PLATE CLEANSER
R0249398 003     984  A  ANNETTE'S PERFECT CLEANSER
R0408233 003     985  I  *CAMEO CORPORATION CLEANSER
R0405009 003     986  I  *KIRKMAN CLEANSER
R0406272 003     987  I  *OTT-O-CLEANSER
R0426826 003     988  A  KEN-CLEANSER
R0511098 003     989  A  ELIZABETH ARDEN MILKY LIQUID CLEANSER
R0754373 003     990  I  *BON AMI CLEANSER WITH MIRACLE GERMICIDE NO CHLORINE
R0766137 003     991  A  N-L CREME CLEANSER
R0828337 003     992  I  SUPER CLEANSER
R0854838 003     993  A  SWIRL MOUTH CLEANSER
R0914409 003     994  A  VACU-CLEANSER
R0995404 003     995  I  COVER GIRL SKIN PORE CLEANSER
R1103268 003     996  A  *GERMA-CARE THE CARE SYSTEM LOTION SKIN CLEANSER
R1103269 003     997  A  *WASH THE CARE SYSTEM LANDLIZED SKIN CLEANSER
R1304556 003     998  A  *CLOCKWISE FOAMING CLEANSER AND DESIGN
R1361306 003     999  A  AMERICA'S CLEAN CLEANSER
R1404549 003    1000  A  CHRISTIAN CLEANSER
R0380705 003    1001  I  BRILLO CLEANSER AND DESIGN
R0991589 003    1002  I  CLEAN SET
R1278564 003    1003  A  KLEANZILLA
R0876716 003    1004  I  CLEAN SILK
R0987048 003    1005  I  CLEAN SILK
CA314421 003    1006  S  MAXIMUM CLEANSING WASH (WORD CLEANSING DISCL.)
HI430981 003    1007  S  WAIKIKI CITRUS CLEANSING LOTION
R1099962 003    1008  I  REAL BEAUTY CLEANSING WHITE
SN390479 003    1009  I  NATURAL BEAUTY CLEANSING BAR
SN419748 003    1010  I  RESPONDS TO THE SPECIAL CLEANSING NEEDS
TX013147 003    1011  S  CLEANZYT (& DESIGN)
R0702419 003    1012  I  SURE KLEAN ZIT
R1143056 003    1013  A  CLEAN SCRUB
R1055378 003    1014  A  CLEAN SLATE
R0904080 003    1015  A  CLEAN'N'SOAK
R0879306 003    1016  I  CLEAN SOFT
R0879310 003    1017  I  CLEAN SOFT
R1024440 003    1018  I  CLEAN & SOFT & LAVENDER
R1092060 003    1019  I  CLEAN 'N SOFT
R1275698 003    1020  A  KLEAN & SOFT
R1382927 003    1021  A  CLEAN 'N SOFT
R1108343 003    1022  A  CLEAN SOUND
R1041593 003    1023  A  CLEAN START
HI450271 003    1024  S  CLEAN 'N SURE
```

PAGE 14
Your Mark   : magic cleaner

```
HI450272 003    1025  S   CLEAN 'N SURE
R0739159 003    1026  I   CLEAN SWEEP
R0891840 003    1027  A   CLEAN-TABS
R1259040 003    1028  A   A CLEAN STARTS WITH A CLEAN TANK AND DESIGN
R0989140 003    1029  I   CLEANTECH
R1055864 003    1030  I   CLEAN TEAM
CA140462 003    1031  S   CLEAN-TIME
CA808436 003    1032  S   CLEAN-TIME
R0810874 003    1033  A   CLEAN-TINT
R1392864 003    1034  A   CLEAN'N TOSS
R0755682 003    1035  A  *CLEAN TOUCH
R1244088 003    1036  A   CLEANTRONICS AND DESIGN
R1000031 003    1037  I   CLEAN UP A MILLION
R1280383 003    1038  A  *CLEAN UP CREW
R1278545 003    1039  A   BALSAM FIBRE CLEANUP AND DESIGN
SN394650 003    1040  I   CLEAN-UP
R1370787 003    1041  A   CLEAN-UPS
SN512324 003    1042  I   CLEANUPS
R1256523 003    1043  A   CLEAN VAC
R0873606 003    1044  A   CLEAN WATER PRODUCTS
CA140433 003    1045  S   CLEAN 'N WAX (WITH SAME WORDS IN MULTIPLE ON SCREENED
                              BACKGROUND)
CA865556 003    1046  S   DIABLO GLASS CLEANE (AND) SPARKY (+ DESIGN)
CA865567 003    1047  S   DIABLO PLASTIC CLEANE SPARKY (+ DESIGN)
IA142461 003    1048  S   PINE-SOL-CLEANS, DISINFECTS, DEODORIZES KOCAL,
                              (WHITENER, BRIGHTENER AND DESIGN)
SC880194 003    1049  S   PERMA GLO (AND) CLEANS, POLISHES, AND PROTECTS (+
                              DESIGN)
R1417109 003    1050  A   OK ORAL KARE CLEANS TEETH & MOUTH WHEN YOU CAN'T BRUSH
R1476375 003    1051  A   CLEANS OIL
SN716275 003    1052  P   CLEAN-SHOT
WI212161 003    1053  S   CLEAN-ALL
R1498233 003    1054  A   CLEAN AND BRIGHT
R1471887 003    1055  A   KLEAN-AR
R1479249 003    1056  A   CLEANAWAY, INC.
SN676866 003    1057  P   BEARY KLEAN BEAR
NY852285 003    1058  S   CLEAN-N-DRI
CA863618 003    1059  S   CLEANEAR (& DESIGN)
SN710162 003    1060  P   CLEAN & FRESH
CA140423 003    1061  S   CLEAN GLOSS (& DESIGN OF A GROUP OF ELF-LIKE WORKERS
                              WORDS CLEAN GLOSS DISCL.)
R1488978 003    1062  A   CLEAN GREEN
IL852763 003    1063  S   KLEANIT (& DESIGN)
R1496431 003    1064  A   KLEAN KIDS
SN708585 003    1065  P   CLEAN COLOR
FL913435 003    1066  S   KLEAN LIFE
SN676245 003    1067  P   CLEAN 'N LITE
SN715687 003    1068  P   CLEANOLEUM
R1464140 003    1069  A   CLEAN PAK
```

```
PAGE  15
Your Mark        : magic cleaner

AZ132041 003    1070    S    DE CARLO'S KLEAN-RITE
MO322261 003    1071    S    CLEAN RITE AIKEN CHEMICAL MERCHANDISE
WA132022 003    1072    S    CLEAN-RITE
PA880936 003    1073    S    TOTAL CLEANSE
WA851030 003    1074    S    NUTRA CLEANSE
WA851757 003    1075    S    NUTRA CLEANSE
SN695544 003    1076    P    CLEANSE CLEAN
SN728212 003    1077    P    LANDE' TOTAL CLEANSE
WI212202 003    1078    S    CLEANSAFE
SN692392 003    1079    P    CLEAN 'N SAFE
WI212201 003    1080    S    CLEAN SEAT
AR001278 003    1081    S    ROMAN CLEANSER BLEACH
AR001310 003    1082    S    ROMAN CLEANSER BLEACH
LA702106 003    1083    S    ROMAN CLEANSER BLEACH
MA017270 003    1084    S    ROMAN CLEANSER BLEACH
MI151772 003    1085    S    ROMAN CLEANSER BLEACH
TN241772 003    1086    S    ROMAN CLEANSER
SN708359 003    1087    P    *NEUTROGENA EXTRA MILD ACNE-SKIN CLEANSER
SN727301 003    1088    P    PURE PERFORMER VITAMIN CLEANSER
SN724917 003    1089    P    CLEANSING SERIES
SN728333 003    1090    P    PERSONAL CLEANSING MADE COMFORTABLE
R1491804 003    1091    A    CLEAN START
R1486634 003    1092    A    CLEAN STICK
R1485839 003    1093    A    CLEAN SWEEP
R1481310 003    1094    A    CLEANSWEEP
R1488042 003    1095    A    *CLEANTABS
CA864800 003    1096    S    CLEAN-TIME
NJ340601 003    1097    S    RAPID CLEANUM
SN690633 003    1098    P    CLEANVIEW WINDSHIELD CLEANING KIT
CA882514 003    1099    S    CLEAN WIPE
HF001916 003    1100         CLEAN         *HF     391 KLEAN      ********
HF001935 003    1492         CLEANN        *HF       O KLEAN      ********
HF005619 003    1493         KLEAN         *HF      33 KLEAN      ********
HF001931 003    1527         CLEANING      *HF      64 KLEANING   ********
CO019544 050    1592    S    K-KLEAN
CO020409 050    1593    S    FIBER-CLEAN AND DESIGN
CO020410 050    1594    S    FIBER-CLEAN OF COLORADO
FL917863 050    1595    S    CLEAN & DEODORIZE
FL920204 050    1596    S    FILL 'N CLEAN
FL920700 050    1597    S    SERI CLEAN
GA840485 400    1598    S    KEEP IT CLEAN (& DESIGN)
GA840562 400    1599    S    CLEAN AS A HOUND'S TOOTH (& DESIGN)
LA708133 050    1600    S    TECHNI-CLEAN
SC002031 050    1601    S    CLEAN AS A WHISTLE
SD110052 050    1602    S    ACRO QUALITY CLEAN SERVICES
UT024562 050    1603    S    CLEAN JET - HIGH PRESSURE CLEANING SYSTEMS
R0884285 050    1604    I    STEP & CLEAN
R0903662 00A    1605    A    TEFLON-S DU PONT APPROVED FINISH SELF LUBRICATING, NO
                             STICK, EASY CLEAN NO RUST
```

PAGE   16
Your Mark   : magic cleaner

CT840035 400	1606	S	CINDERELLA CLEANING SERVICE (AND DESIGN)
GA171921 050	1607	S	RAINBOW INTERNATIONAL CARPET DYEING & CLEANING CO. (& DESIGN)
GA840270 400	1608	S	THE CLEANING WOMAN (& DESIGN)
KS021002 050	1609	S	RAINBOW INTERNATIONAL CARPET DYEING & CLEANING CO. (& DESIGN)
KY140801 050	1610	S	SMILES - THE TEETH CLEANING COMPANY (& DESIGN OF A TOOTHBRUSH)
R0699588 00B	1611	I	BEAUTITONE CLEANING
R1350093 200	1612	A	MEMBER A S C R ASSOCIATION OF SPECIALISTS IN CLEANING AND RESTORATION
R0951555 200	1613	I	CAPTAIN CLEANUP
AR850574 050	1614	S	KENDO CLEAN CARE
CA424632 000	1615	S	SCUM CLEAN
CA840044 000	1616	S	POWER CLEAN
CA840119 000	1617	S	COFFEE CLEAN
CA841448 000	1618	S	DEAN CLEAN (+ DESIGN)
CA842081 000	1619	S	CLEAN IT BRIGHT
CA842886 000	1620	I	KIT-N-KLEAN
CA843011 000	1621	S	GREEN KITTY KLEAN
CA857401 000	1622	I	WE WANT TO CLEAN YOUR WINDOWS
CO028380 050	1623	S	MIRACLE CLEAN
FL912207 000	1624	S	AMER-CLEAN
FL913435 050	1625	S	KLEAN LIFE
GA851407 050	1626	S	SO KLEAN (& DESIGN)
ID150502 000	1627	S	IT PAYS TO KEEP CLEAN
IN111492 000	1628	S	MOBILE-CLEAN
IN120112 000	1629	S	BUDGET CLEAN
KS840139 000	1630	S	LEAN CLEAN COPY MACHINES
LA008113 000	1631	S	PRE-CLEAN
LA716327 000	1632	S	ULTRA-CLEAN SERVICES
LA717109 000	1633	S	CLEAN AIR, INC.
NV880055 000	1634	S	SAF-T- CLEAN, INC.
NJ850369 000	1635	S	ECONO-CLEAN
NJ850486 000	1636	S	ECONO - CLEAN'S THE NAME FOR EVER SEWER & DRAIN
NM161282 400	1637	S	HELP DUSTY ROADRUNNER KEEP NEW MEXICO CLEAN AND BEAUTIFUL(A/K/A)DUSTY ROADRUNNER
OK121003 000	1638	S	CLEAN-RITE
OR880459 000	1639	I	GREEN KITTY KLEAN
OR881080 000	1640	I	CLEAN
RI111512 000	1641	S	CLEAN N TREAT
TN130601 000	1642	S	CLEAN-RITE
UT025143 000	1643	S	CLEAN SAFE
UT025289 000	1644	S	ACOUSTI-CLEAN
UT026815 000	1645	S	THE CLEAN GUY'S, WE'LL TAKE YOUR DIRT AND LOVE IT ...
UT880403 000	1646	S	ULTRA-CLEAN - OVAL (AND DESIGN)
WV841067 000	1647	S	CLEAN TOWEL SERVICE
WV842217 000	1648	S	GREAT SEAL E-Z CLEAN
WV842531 000	1649	S	HOOVER MODEL 541 (AND) IT BEATS-AS IT SWEEPS-AS IT

PAGE   17
Your Mark   : magic cleaner

```
                              CLEANS
    IL881161 000    1650   I   THE CLEANERY
    KS015050 050    1651   S   MAJESTIC WATER CONDITIONERS THE CLEANEST SOFTEST WATER
                              ON EARTH
    AZ851348 400    1652   S   THE CLEANING SOLUTION
    CA867842 000    1653   I   CLEANING CREW
    FL904313 000    1654   S   JALCAR INDUSTRIES CLEANING INDUSTRY THRU CHEMISTRY
    FL908302 000    1655   S   ULTRASONIC CLEANING
    IN111483 000    1656   S   BUSY BEE SELF-SERVICE LAUNDRY AND DRY CLEANING
    KY880156 050    1657   S   RAINBOW INTERNATIONAL CARPET DYEING & CLEANING CO (&
                              DESIGN)
    LA003385 000    1658   S   DEEP SPIN CARPET CLEANING SYSTEM
    LA006011 000    1659   S   KEAN'S ONE HOUR CLEANING
    LA008225 000    1660   S   RAINBOW INTERNATIONAL CARPET DYEING & CLEANING CO. (AND
                              LOGO CONSISTING OF A DESIGN OF THE GLOBE WITH CAPITAL
                              CENTERED IN THE NORTHERN HEMISPHERE OF THE EARTH WITH A
                              RAINBOW AROUND THE GLOBE)
    ME002433 000    1661   S   DOWNEAST SWEEPS THE BEST CHIMNEY CLEANING AVAILABLE
                              (WITH LOGO OF SWEEP WITH BRUSH IN CHIMNEY)
    MD003094 000    1662   S   AMERICAN CLEANING SERVICES
    MD003253 000    1663   S   AARDVARK STEAM CLEANING (& DESIGN)
    OR881153 000    1664   I   IRON MIKE'S SAVE A BUNDLE CLEANING PLACE
    UT026782 000    1665   S   HEAVEN SCENT, A NEW IMAGE IN CARPET CLEANING
    UT026932 000    1666   S   CERTIFIED CARPET & FURNITURE CLEANING COMPANY
    UT880162 000    1667   S   HEAVEN'S BEST A NEW IMAGE IN CARPET CLEANING (ANGEL
                              WITH CAR+)
    UT880293 000    1668   S   PUSH BUTTON HOUSE CLEANING
    WI840143 400    1669   S   WISCONSIN PIPE CLEANING COMPANY
    WI840452 400    1670   S   THE DUST BUSTERS CLEANING SERVICE
    UT025494 000    1671   S   CLEANLINE BRAND
    UT026850 000    1672   S   SANA CLEANSE
    WV842361 000    1673   S   HEAL.THE.SICK.RAISE.THE.DEAD+CLEANSE.TH
                              E.LEPERS.CAST.OUT.DEOMONS (& DESIGN)
    DE880305 000    1674   I   ROMAN CLEANSER
    GA172691 050    1675   S   ROMAN CLEANSER
    UT024139 000    1676   S   CAMELOT CONTACT LENS CONDITIONER & CLEANSER
    WV840797 000    1677   S   CAMEO CLEANSER]
    WV844547 000    1678   S   ROMAN CLEANSER
    WV844548 000    1679   S   ROMAN CLEANSER WHITENS CLOTHES SAFELY
```

------------ E N D   O F   S E A R C H ------------   time : 09:42:30

SAMPLE LETTER TO AN INFRINGER

```
Infringer Bakery
100 Main Street
Anytown, USA
```

Gentlemen:

I am the President of Rounder Bakeries, Inc., the owner of the trademark ROUNDERS, United States Trademark Registration Number 0,000,000 (copy enclosed), which has been granted to the trademark for use with our circular doughnut.

It has come to our attention that you have been using the word ''ROUNDERS'' in connection with your bakery products. For example, last week's issue of the Anytown Shopper's News carried an advertisement for your bakery in which you offered ''rounders'' for sale.

This letter is written to advise you that you have infringed upon our trademark. Unless you agree in writing within ten days to stop using our mark, and also agree not to use it again, we shall be forced to bring legal action against you. Such action shall seek damages for any profits you may have made by virtue of sales of circular doughnuts, and any other product which you improperly termed ''rounders'' and shall charge you with falsely describing the source of your product.

Sincerely,

Joseph E. Rounder

Joseph E. Rounder
President,
Rounder Bakeries

Communications with the PTO

The application and all other communications should be addressed: The Commissioner of Patents and Trademarks, Washington, DC 20231. It is preferred that the applicant indicate his or her telephone number on the application form. Once a serial number is assigned, the applicant should refer to this number in all telephone and written communications.

Glossary

Class Refers to a system of classification set up by the Patent and Trademark Office. This system helps determine in which group of goods and/or services your application belongs. This is important because trademark conflicts are determined not only by the similarity of the marks but also by the proximity of class of the goods and services.

PTO The United States Patent and Trademark Office.

Principal Register The primary register of the PTO. Approval for this register indicates that the applicant has a unique mark that currently distinguishes his or her goods or services from those of another. Registration on the Principal Register provides the maximum benefits and protection to the applicant (see Chapter 3).

Servicemark A word, symbol, design or combined word and design, a slogan or even a distinctive sound used to identify and distinguish the *services* of one person from those of another. Ownership of a servicemark may be indicated by the use of the symbol ^{SM}, even if no federal servicemark application is pending.

Supplemental Register The secondary register of the PTO. Approval for this register has more limited benefits than those of the Principal Register (see Chapter 3). The Supplemental Register is used when a proposed mark has the *potential* to distinguish an applicant's goods or services but does not yet do so. Other restrictive criteria for the Principal Register may result in an application being accepted for filing on the Supplemental Register.

Trademark A word, symbol, design or combined word and design, a slogan or even a distinctive sound used to identify and distinguish the *goods* of one person from those of another. Ownership of a trademark may be indicated by the use of the symbol ™, even if no federal trademark application is pending.

Trademark search A method of accessing trademark data that will allow an applicant to discern whether or not his or her desired mark is currently registered to another individual or business. An extensive search can be expensive and time-consuming if pursued by an individual or through a patent and trademark attorney. It is recommended that the services of a trademark search company be used for the most extensive search available at a reasonable fee (see Appendix B).

Index

Legal action. *See* Lawsuits

McDonald's Corporation, 13
Mark, defined, 80. *See also*
    Servicemark;
    Trademark
Mistakes, by registrant or
    Trademark Office, 138
Mobile Corporation, 13

Name, as asset, 3, 7
Notice of Allowance, 43,
    105–6
Numbers, as trademarks,
    13–14

*Official Gazette of the Patent
    and Trademark Office,*
    69
    conflicting marks,
        publication of, 103
Opposition to registration,
    65, 110–12

Partnerships, and trademark
    registrations, 22, 25
Patent and Trademark Office
    (PTO), 11
    application process. *See*
        Federal registration
    conduct of proceedings,
        rules and regulations
        for, 76
    correction of office
        mistakes, 138
    PTO Form 1478, 43, 45–50
    PTO Form 1579, 43, 51–52
    PTO Form 1580, 43, 53–54
    PTO Form 1581, 43, 55–56
    registers of, 11, 13, 14
    registration denial,
        grounds for, 14–15
    registration process,
        31–33
Pending trademark
    application index, 198
Person, defined, 79
Principal Register, 11, 14,
    17, 59, 60, 61–62, 70,
    72
    Code of Federal
        Regulations and, 94
    defined, 79

foreign registration and,
    78
Portrait use, and
    registration denial, 15
Publication and post
    publication, 102–5, 134
Public domain, famous
    names in, 7–8, 38
Purchaser without notice, 64

Recovery for violation of
    rights; profits;
    damages; fees, 75
Registered mark, defined, 80
Registrant, defined, 79
Registration. *See* Federal
    registration
Related company, defined, 79
Renewal, of trademark
    registration, 3, 7, 64,
    138–40
Reputation, 3

Search, importance of, 31,
    32–33
    after registration, 39
Servicemark
    application for, 93–94.
        See also Federal
        registration
    assignment of, 140–41
    categories of, 12–14
    defined, 3, 11, 79
    grounds for denying
        registration of, 14–15
    specimens or facsimiles
        of, 97
Services, classification of, 71
Slogans, as trademarks, 14
Sound, and trademark
    protection, 25–26
Specimens, and registration
    application, 25–26
Statement of Use, 25, 106–7
Statutory procedures, 37
Suggestive words, as
    trademarks, 12
Supplemental Register, 11,
    13, 15, 17, 59, 69, 70
    Code of Federal
        Regulations and, 94
    defined, 79
    foreign registration and,
        78
    interference and, 108

publication of marks and,
    103
Surnames, 11, 15

3M, 13
Trademark
    application forms, 43–56
    application procedures.
        See Federal
        registration
    assignment of, 140–41
    categories of, 12–14
    change of ownership, new
        certificate on, 137
    defined, 3, 11, 79
    displaying, 70–71
    grounds for denying
        registration of, 14–15
    incorporation and, 7
    mark search, importance
        of, 31, 32–33
    protection of, 37–39
    publication of, 102–5, 134
    registration benefits,
        15–17
    renewal of, 3, 7, 64,
        138–40
    term of, 138–39
Trademark Act of 1946. *See*
    Lanham Act
Trademark Examining
    Attorney, 31
Trademark Official Gazette,
    31, 69
Trademark Trial and Appeal
    Board, 31, 69
    concurrent use and, 109
Trade name, defined, 79
Trade secrets, 74

Underwriters Laboratories,
    14
Unfair competition, 16
Union labels, 14
Violation of rights, recovery
    for, 75

Wordmarks, 12–13
Written application, 90–92
Xerox Corporation, 38–39

About the Author

Ted Nicholas is a multifaceted business personality. In addition to being a well-known author and respected speaker, Mr. Nicholas remains an active participant in his own entrepreneurial ventures. Without capital, he started his first business at age 21. Since then, he has started 22 companies of his own.

Mr. Nicholas has written 13 books on business and finance since his writing career began in 1972. The best known is *How To Form Your Own Corporation Without a Lawyer for under $75*. His previous business enterprises include Peterson's House of Fudge, a candy and ice cream manufacturing business conducted through 30 retail stores, as well as other businesses in franchising, real estate, machinery and food.

When the author was only 29, he was selected by a group of business leaders as one of the most outstanding businessmen in the nation and was invited to the White House to meet the President.

Although Mr. Nicholas has founded many successful enterprises, he also has experienced two major setbacks and many minor ones. He considers business setbacks necessary to success and the only true way to learn anything in life, a lesson that goes all the way back to childhood. That's why he teaches other entrepreneurs how to "fail forward."

Mr. Nicholas has appeared on numerous television and radio shows and conducts business seminars in Florida and Switzerland. Presently, he owns and operates four corporations of his own and acts as marketing consultant and copywriter to small as well as large businesses.

If you have any questions, thoughts or comments, Mr. Nicholas loves to hear from his readers! You are welcome to call, write or fax him at the following address:

Nicholas Direct, Inc.
19918 Gulf Boulevard, #7
Indian Shores, FL 34635
Phone: 813-596-4966
Fax: 813-596-6900